Crucial Decade

—AND AFTER

AMERICA, 1945-1960

THE
Crucial Decade
—AND AFTER

AMERICA, 1945-1960

BY

ERIC F. GOLDMAN

FIND ~~main~~ THESIS OF BOOK

Vintage Books

A DIVISION OF *Random House*

NEW YORK

VINTAGE BOOKS

are published by Alfred A. Knopf, Inc.

and Random House, Inc.

This is an enlarged edition of *The Crucial Decade: America,
1945–1955,* originally published by Alfred A. Knopf, Inc.,
August 1956.

Preface
to the Vintage Edition

THIS BOOK was first published in a hardback edition under the title *The Crucial Decade: America, 1945-1955*. In that form it told the history of the United States from the end of World War II in the summer of 1945 to the Geneva Summit Conference in the summer of 1955. This new, Vintage edition includes two fresh chapters and an epilogue which continue the history from 1955 to 1960.

The decade covered by the original volume, 1945-55, was certainly a crazy-quilt era. That taut Thursday when Franklin Roosevelt died, the first sickening fall of an atomic bomb, the heartfelt roar when Jackie Robinson trotted out in a Dodgers uniform, the meat you couldn't buy and the apartment you couldn't rent, high prices and boom times and higher prices and still more boom, a brilliant young man named Alger Hiss, President Harry Truman now fumbling, now making the bold decision to go into Korea, Arnold Toynbee and Mickey Spillane, Ezio Pinza singing "Some Enchanted Evening" and the bloody wastes of the Changjin Reservoir, "We like IKE," "We LIKE IKE," "WE LIKE IKE," pyramid games, the poodle bob, chlorophyll toothpaste, chlorophyll chewing gum, chlorophyll dog food, Senator Joseph McCarthy intoning "Point of order, point of order, Mr. Chairman," President Dwight Eisenhower worrying millions and reassuring still more millions by his folksy middle-roadism—these and a thousand other memories flood back from the frightening, heartening, whirligig years after the end of World War II.

Despite all the swirl of events, it seemed to me while working on *The Crucial Decade*, the years from 1945 to 1955 did have their own genuine unity and their own definable meaning. Beneath everything, two critically important questions were pressing to be answered. One of the questions concerned affairs inside the United States: would America continue, through extensions of the welfare state and of welfare capitalism and through a variety of other techniques, the economic and social revolution which had marked the previous decades? The other question concerned foreign affairs: would the United States keep moving along the path marked out in the early Truman years, a path suggested by the words "containment" and "coexistence" and one which represented a sharp departure from deep-seated American traditions? What seemed to me crucial about the Crucial Decade was that during the years 1945-55 the people of the United States faced these questions, worried and wrangled over the answers, almost spoke a double no, then finally answered both with a decisive affirmative.

In preparing this new Vintage edition of the book, I mulled over, from the perspective of the passage of additional years, whether I still believed 1945 to 1955 was a definable epoch in American history and whether the decade was, more than any other recent one, a "crucial" decade. My conclusion on both points was a clear-cut yes. As a matter of fact, it seemed to me that events since 1955 have made even more plain that during the previous decade the American people, in their haphazard way, arrived at fundamental decisions and that our history now and for the foreseeable future amounts to the working out of those decisions. Consequently, in this extended form of *The Crucial Decade*, the contents and the interpretation of the original book remain the same and the history of the years after 1955 simply builds on the preceding chapters.

The Crucial Decade—And After is, quite consciously, interpretative history, but it is decidedly not the kind of interpretative history which attempts to serve as a tract for the times. The volume is based on no special theories about man or about history; it contains no ringing plea to save America. As a matter of fact, implicit throughout is the assumption that America will be saved—whatever precisely that may mean —not by men with banners but by those who are able to escape the banners long enough to think. *The Crucial Decade—And After* is history in the most direct sense of the word. It is a narrative, written with a careful regard for facts, an attempt to escape partisanship or other bias, an effort to place events in the long perspective, and the assumption that the history of man is the story of men. Insofar as I was able, I have had people take over these pages, the leaders who changed the nation by winning votes and the movers who worked their revolutions oblivious of politics, the bitter and the wise, the indignant and the smug, the faceless millions who proceeded to show a thousand faces ranging from utter inanity to utter good sense.

Naturally, in writing of events so recent and so controversial, I have been especially concerned about the danger of factual inaccuracy. Beyond the usual scholarly checks, I tried to ward off error through a direct appeal to the participants in the story. Wherever it seemed to me feasible or sensible, I sent a copy of the appropriate manuscript pages to the man or woman I had written about and asked for a check on my facts, and I did this without regard to whether the person was a waiter or a world statesman and without regard to whether I had written about him favorably or unfavorably. The comments and corrections that came back were not always the kind that would pass muster in a university seminar. Memories have a way of slipping; they also have a way of being convenient. Yet many genuine errors were caught and I would like to thank very warmly the people who gave time and energy to help keep this history straight. They and others to whom I am indebted are listed in the "Note on the Sources and Acknowledgments" which appears at the end of the book.

EFG

Princeton, N. J.
July 16, 1960

Contents

THE
Crucial Decade
—AND AFTER

AMERICA, 1945-1960

I

Mood Maybe

A U.S. radio monitor in a little frame house in Oregon caught the first hint. The Japanese were interested in peace, the Domei broadcast said, provided that the prerogatives of the Emperor would not be "prejudiced." Then came two days of diplomacy, a few hours of false armistice, more waiting through an interminable weekend. Finally, on Tuesday, August 14, 1945, reporters were summoned to the Oval Room of the White House. President Truman glanced at the clock to make sure he was holding to the agreement of simultaneous announcement in Washington, London, and Moscow. At exactly 7 p.m. he began reading: Late that afternoon a message had been received from the Japanese Government which "I deem . . . full acceptance of . . . unconditional surrender."

Across America the traditional signs of victory flared and shrieked. In Los Angeles, yelling paraders commandeered trolley cars, played leapfrog in the middle of Hollywood Boulevard, hung Hirohito from scores of lampposts. Salt Lake City thousands snake-danced in a pouring rain and a St. Louis crowd, suddenly hushing its whistles and tossing aside the confetti, persuaded a minister to hold services at 2 a.m. New York City, hardly unaccustomed to furor, amazed itself. With the first flash of V-J, up went the windows and down came the torn telephone books, the hats, bottles, bolts of silk, books, wastebaskets, and shoes, more than five thousand tons of jubilant litter. Whole families made their way to Times Square until two million people were milling about, breaking into snatches of the conga, hugging and kissing anybody in sight, greeting each twinkle of V-J news on the *Times* electric sign with a cheer that roared from the East River to the Hudson. The hoopla swirled on into the dawn, died down, broke out again the next afternoon, finally subsided only with another midnight.

Americans had quite a celebration and yet, in a way, the celebration never really rang true. People were so gay, so determinedly gay. The nation was a carnival but the festivities, as a reporter wrote from Chicago, "didn't seem like so much. It was such a peculiar peace. . . . And everybody talked of 'the end of the war,' not of 'victory.'" The President himself spoke with a mixed tone. When the crowds around the White House chanted "We want Harry," he appeared beaming with Bess on his arm and proclaimed this "a great day." His face quickly sobered as he added warnings of an "emergency" ahead—a crisis "as great . . . as Dec. 7, 1941." At V-J, 1945, the United States was entering the newest of its eras in a curious, unprecedented jumble of moods.

Peace had not come to the nation with the soothing coo of a dove. Instead it came in swift hammer blows of news, smashing old sure stand-bys. Four months before the Japanese surrender, cerebral hemorrhage struck down Franklin Roosevelt, a second father to millions of Americans during their worst depression and their worst war. Another three months and the British were sweeping out of office Winston Churchill, doughty symbol of steadiness to much of Western Civilization. Eleven days later, just before V-J, President Truman announced: "An American airplane [has] dropped one bomb on Hiroshima. . . . It is an atomic bomb. It is a harnessing of the basic power of the universe."

Over all the victory celebrations, the fact of the atomic bomb hung like some eerie haze from another world. Americans tried to make jokes. The Japanese were suffering from <u>atomic ache,</u> people giggled to each other. Or when God made Atom, he sure created a handful for Eve. Americans were sententious. The bomb meant the end of civilization and atomic energy was certain to usher in a golden age of peace and plenty. Americans argued furiously. John Foster Dulles intimated that atomic bombs and "Christian statesmanship" were hardly compatible and scores of leaders answered hotly that a truly Christian nation ended wars as quickly as possible. Some-- how neither the arguments nor the jokes nor the sententiousness meant much. People fumbled along, trying to comprehend the incomprehensible, to fit a sense of terrifying newness into their accustomed ways of thinking. And in almost every American mind, there was one corner that could respond to the words reported from a European prison cell. "A mighty accomplishment," the captured Nazi leader Hermann Göring said. "I don't want anything to do with it."

The sense of a scarifying future was accompanied by memories of the last postwar, jabbing, mocking memories. In the America of V-J, the story went around how Franklin Roosevelt had kept a picture of Woodrow Wilson hanging in the meeting room of the War Cabinet, frequently glancing toward it when he discussed the coming years, and everybody got the point of the tale. Woodrow Wilson also had led the United States to victory in a world war. Then came the hard times of 1920-1, less than a decade of prosperity, the brutal depression of the 1930's, and the furies of World War II.

For one large section of the American people, memories were particularly disturbing. Cotton-pickers, professors, and secretaries, auto workers, writers, and the man who collected the garbage, they had given their minds and their hearts to the credo represented by Franklin Roosevelt. The cotton-pickers and the secretaries might speak of the "New Deal"; the professors and the writers were inclined to talk of "liberalism." Whatever the term, the groups joined in a zest for legislation in favor of lower-income groups, for questioning and nose-thumbing, for chopping away at the crust of social castes. Now that World War II was over, the liberals also shared an apprehension provoked by history. The least educated among them were acutely aware that the previous generation's "New Deal," the reformism of Theodore Roosevelt and Woodrow Wilson, had passed through World War I and come out Warren G. Harding.

Worriedly, yearningly, the liberal leaders were talking of sixty million jobs, the figure that Franklin Roosevelt had used in his vista of the postwar. Sixty million jobs, the argument ran, were a symbol of the full employment and social advances which could be; they were also a measuring-rod that would warn of oncoming disaster. And this time, a thousand New Deal commentators added, failure to solve America's domestic problems would mean something worse than hard times. As the end of World War II neared, *Harper's Magazine*, certainly a restrained liberal journal, was running an article which argued that "the veterans are not going to accept unemployment with the bewildered docility which was characteristic of most of the jobless in the last depression. . . . What action will result from that attitude . . . ? Nobody knows, of course. But we have some hints, and they are hints which should make any American start worrying. One of them is the report of a historian who watched fascism rise in Italy and Germany after the last war."

In the eyes of many educated New Dealers, the national scene already included dangerously large areas of rightism. During the month of V-J, Bernard De Voto, a favorite of liberal readers, pointed to the dismissal of Homer Rainey from the presidency of the University of Texas. The situation was complex, De Voto wrote. But basically Rainey was dismissed because of his New Dealish opinions and his insistence on academic freedom for subordinates. The case resulted from a rapidly spreading doctrine of "ruthless industry and finance," which equated both free inquiry and New Dealism with Communism.

This kind of argument, De Voto went on, "is a powerful sentiment, and one easily polarized by a rabble-rouser or an honest deluded man. The communists [so the argument runs] were responsible for the New Deal and they intend to inflict a labor dictatorship on us. . . . They want to destroy initiative and profit, business and freedom, the individual and the United States. . . . Get rid of the communist professors—who are all homosexuals and New Dealers anyway—and everything will be all right once more. We will be back in the days before . . . the New Deal conspiracy was hatched, before labor unions had to be dealt with, . . . before socialists and bureaucrats in Washington could tell us . . . what we had to do and whom we had to hire and how much we had to pay him, before the foundations of our society were undermined by atheism and bolshevism."

De Voto was ready for a grim prediction. Free universities are "the central mechanism of democracy." Yet "as the waves of reaction gather strength in the years immediately ahead of the United States, this same attack will be made repeatedly, in many colleges, always by the same kind of men representing the same interests and forces, employing the same or equivalent means."

The anti-New Dealers, the people who more and more were coming to be called "conservatives," had their portentous reading too. Late in the war, the University of Chicago Press published *The Road to Serfdom*, by an Austrian-born economist, Friedrich A. von Hayek. The Press knew well the usual fate of

scholarly treatises; it printed only two thousand copies. But Hayek had set his scholarship within a general
proposition that caught perfectly the mood of much
of American conservatism. Nazism, he contended,
had not grown up in opposition to New Deal-type
liberalism; such liberalism and Nazism came from
the same roots. All Western Civilization had been relying increasingly on ideas of national economic planning, and the ideas, whether called liberalism, Nazism,
socialism, or Communism, led inevitably to totalitarian
serfdom. Hayek's volume was scarcely in the bookstores before the University of Chicago Press discovered that it had published not only a scholarly mon-
ograph but a manifesto for American conservatism.
Hailed by anti-New Deal publications, purchased in
quantity by a number of American corporations, *The
Road to Serfdom* promptly made its way to the best-
seller list and stayed on month after month into the
V-J period. The severely intellectual Hayek, dumfounded at the sales of the volume and half-protesting
that he did not want to be a spokesman for any political group, found himself lecturing up and down the
country to rapt anti-New Deal audiences.

The defeat of Winston Churchill by the British
Labour Party shortly before V-J stoked the fears of
American conservatives. Here was repudiation of a
beloved national hero for a bluntly socialist regime;
here was precisely the swing toward economic controls against which Hayek was warning. People in
conservative commuter communities read the election
headline with "shock," to use the term of the *New
Canaan* (Conn.) *Advertiser*. The Labour victory,
Business Week added, brought worried reconsidera-
tion of the general strength of "New Deal" forces in
and outside Britain. The most optimistic conservative
survey could not fail to note one great fact. At V-J,
the long-time trend toward controls over economic
life had gone so far that no government in Western
Civilization except Washington gave even lip service

to free enterprise—and in the White House sat Franklin Roosevelt's chosen heir.

Some American conservatives were avid for an all-out effort to get rid of the New Deal and turn America back toward unregulated capitalism. Others acquiesced in what the New Deal had done but insisted upon drawing a stern line, beyond this not one step further. Both conservative groups often talked a formula that was decades old but now had a fresh significance and a new name, "welfare capitalism." Industry itself, the formula ran, should protect the welfare of its employees to such an extent that social legislation, and perhaps unions, would lose their appeal. Whatever the emphasis, conservatives joined with liberals in considering the postwar a battleground on which domestic issues of far-ranging significance would be fought out, with results that could mean heaven or hell.

At V-J, the field of foreign policy brought its own sense of great possibilities for good or evil. Throughout the war, most liberals had been little bothered by the alliance with the Soviet Union. After all, they argued, the Soviet stood for anti-fascism, for collective security against aggression, and for the betterment of the underprivileged. With patience, Russia could be brought more and more to the ways of democratic nations; besides, if the United States did not co-operate with the Soviet, how could it win the war? Many liberals went beyond these sidewise justifications to the argument that the Soviet alliance was a positive good. It meant a peace that would endure because it would be built on unity between the powers that counted, the United States and Russia; it foreshadowed a postwar in which, through the pressure of both New Dealism and Communism, social reform would become a prime concern of world leadership.

During World War II, only a minority among the conservatives sharply differed with the liberal attitude toward the Soviet alliance. Stalin's public statements and actions seemed devoid of double-dealing; the Russians were obviously saving American lives by smashing Nazi divisions; the fierce Soviet holding operation at Stalingrad and then the hammer blows back across Russia had a heroic quality about them which won general American admiration. Public-opinion polls indicated that most business executives were thoroughly optimistic about Russia's postwar intentions. The powerful anti-New Deal Luce publications were explaining away the Russian secret police as "a national police similar to the FBI," with the job of "tracking down traitors," while the high-Republican Main Line filled the hall with cheers when the Philadelphia Orchestra introduced the new Russian anthem, "Hymn to the Soviet Union." The Yalta Conference of February, 1945, seemed a triumph of Allied unity for purposes on which all groups in the United States could agree, and the Yalta communiqué was greeted by almost unanimous praise in the United States.

Yet beneath the conservative acceptance of the Soviet alliance ran irritations and misgivings. The man who had long considered the New Deal dangerous radicalism hardly took real pleasure in joining hands with out-and-out Bolsheviks. He was the more edgy because the camaraderie was being promoted by Franklin Roosevelt. He could not help but feel that a peace built on a Communist–New Deal understanding would move everything away from the kind of pattern he considered sensible and decent. This underlying disturbance of the conservatives over the Soviet relationship was especially marked in the Midwestern Republican faction led by Senator Robert A. Taft. "It's all very well to win a war with socialist New Dealers and Bolsheviks having a love feast," Senator Kenneth Wherry of Nebraska expressed the attitude, "but what follows then?"

As the war drew to a close and the day approached

when Russian divisions would no longer be needed, the conservative restiveness mounted. It was further increased by headlines which began breaking soon after the Yalta communiqué of February, 1945. The news was revealed of a secret Yalta agreement, easily deemed favorable to the Soviet. The Russians made moves in flagrant violation of the Yalta provisions for free elections in the liberated countries of eastern Europe. Stalin seemed to speak contempt for the whole idea of world peace by announcing that he would send merely an underling of his Foreign Office to the San Francisco conference for setting up the United Nations —a decision that was reversed, it was widely assumed, only by strong pressure from President Truman.

At the time of the Japanese surrender, most liberals were still optimistic about American-Russian relations; if they doubted, it was largely because Franklin Roosevelt had been removed from the negotiating table. But many an anti-New Dealer was beginning to wonder aloud if the whole Roosevelt policy had not been a tragic blunder. Some conservatives, particularly the Taftian Republicans, were projecting into the V-J air doubts whether peace itself could long endure between the United States and the Bolsheviks.

Russians or no Russians, Hayek *vs.* the New Dealers, atom bomb or not, World War II was over, and all America joined in a sense of coming home. At V-J, the first groups of veterans were already fidgeting in trains and buses, straining for some half-remembered clump of billboards, a bed of petunias, a funny-shaped building that meant they were almost there. Defense workers were pulling out of the Quonsets in Los Angeles and Detroit and Hartford, heading back to Alabama, Oklahoma, and the hills of Maryland. Men and women who had taken the same commuter train, prepared dinner in the same kitchen, punched the same time clock for twenty years, were coming home too. At last they could fill their gasoline tanks, use a second chunk of butter, watch the long lazy curl of a fishing line flicker in the sunlight, or get royally tight, without feeling that they were cheating some GI in the flak over Berlin or on the bloody ash of Iwo Jima.

It was good to be home; for millions, it was better still to be in what home had become. The America of V-J was prosperous, more prosperous than the country had been in all its three centuries of zest for good living. The boom rolled out in great fat waves, into every corner of the nation and up and down the social ladder. Factory hands, brushing the V-J confetti out of their hair, laid plans for a suburban cottage. Farmers' children were driving to college classes in glossy convertibles. California border police, checking the baggage of Okies returning east, came across wads of hundred-dollar bills.

For many an American, the new era brought an added exhilaration. It offered not only increased income but a break-through in status, a chance at schooling and occupations and ways of living that previously had been barricaded from them. All through the New Deal period and the war years, the powerful thrusts of minorities had been ramming more and more holes in the walls of discrimination. By V-J, Jews seeking admission to professional schools had a ten-to-fifteen-per-cent better chance than the applicant of 1929. First-generation Catholics of eastern or southern European backgrounds reported far less difficulty in purchasing homes in upper-middle-class neighborhoods. During the four swift years of the war, Negroes for the first time knew the white-collar kudos of working as salesgirls in the swank department stores of the North, and Negro representatives on labor grievance committees were becoming accustomed to speaking up as freely as their white colleagues.

If the upsweep was plainest among the minority groups, it touched the whole bottom of American society with a tonic sense of new possibilities. The GI

Bill of Rights became law in 1944 and with the first
release of veterans during the war, the legislation began working its revolution. Men who had entered the
army as employees returned to borrow money from
the government and set up their own businesses. Hundreds of thousands who had thought of the university
as a preserve of the rich found themselves headed toward an A.B.—in many cases, toward the highest of
professional degrees.

In or outside veteran ranks, lower-status groups had
lifted their sights. "Times have changed," Maurice
O'Connell, of the CIO, notified a Los Angeles Chamber of Commerce meeting shortly after the Japanese
surrender. "People have become accustomed to new
conditions, new wage scales, new ways of being
treated." Even the fabled Rosie the Riveter was a different woman. "Rosie the Riveter," O'Connell announced, "isn't going back to emptying slop jars."

Nobody, it seemed, was going back to emptying the
slop jars. Ads for unskilled labor on farms or in fac-
tories produced a resounding lack of response; maids
came only at Tiffany prices and then, as likely as not,
with a Tiffany manner. "People were probably never
choosier . . . ," an Indianapolis reporter described
the nation-wide trend. "Job dreams are golden,
bright golden."

The sense of wonderful possibilities ahead kept
breaking into every part of living. In the year when
man mastered the atom, a good many people did not
smile at the feature-page stories which predicted that
the average American would soon work twenty-five
hours a week, return to a dinner cooked by the flick
of a single button, educate his children through the
finest authorities televised into a sun-heated living-
room, and take his vacation a continent away. In a
period when medical research had just produced the
yellow magic of penicillin only to have it promptly
topped by streptomycin, it did not seem utopian to

talk of conquering tuberculosis, infantile paralysis, even cancer. As for the bread-and-butter of living, the U.S. Director of War Mobilization and Reconversion, Fred Vinson, was saying: "The American people are in the pleasant predicament of having to learn to live 50 percent better than they have ever lived before." From somewhere deep in the national psychology came the surest affirmation of tomorrow. Throughout the depression days of the 1930's, well into the war period, millions of couples had made the decision against children or ventured only as far as a single son or daughter. Now a rampant birthrate was turning community life into one vast gurgle.

In St. Louis, an Inquiring Reporter stopped a young mother and asked about her personal expectations for the postwar. "Oh, things are going along just wonderfully," she bubbled. "Harry has a grand job, there's the new baby—"

Then she frowned. "Do you think it's really all going to last?"

A zest in today, wondrous hopes for tomorrow— but always, in the America of V-J, there were shadows. A nation accustomed to the categorical yes and no, to war or peace and prosperity or depression, found itself in the nagging realm of maybe. The liberals worried over the conservatives and the conservatives watched the liberals with an uneasiness akin to dread. Conservatives, liberals, and the half of the nation which was not really either asked: Would events follow the same pattern as during the last postwar? Was unprecedented boom to bring unprecedented delights only to turn into unprecedented bust? Was peace just a prelude to another war?

The questions broke into conversations as persistently, as much up and down the social scale, as the relish in victory and prosperity and a limitless future. Behind these questions was a further one, often too deeply felt to be expressed. If the pattern held, if history repeated itself, wouldn't another war suck everything into doomsday under those billowing atomic mushrooms?

After war uncertainty about future exists, even in the atmosphere of good feeling + good living.

II

Strikes, Russians, and Harry Truman

THE DAY after V-J, the new President started his morning with a bit of office shifting. He replaced a model gun on his desk with a shiny model plow and he delighted in pointing out the change to visitors. "It's the simple feelings that count," he would say. "I like the feeling of having the new little fellow there."

Life had prepared Harry Truman for the simple. Life was Jackson County, Missouri, where you grew up near-sighted and the other boys snickered, you went courting Bess Wallace in the big house and her parents tried to get rid of you, you came back from the war to start the haberdashery with Eddie Jacobson and the store went broke. But you stuck at it. You kept in mind the simple things that any sensible man in Jackson County knew were the really important ones—a hard day's work, loyalty to your family and your friends, holding your eye on the cheerful side of life, remembering that "nobody is as big as he thinks he is or so small as his enemies are sure." And things had happened in Jackson County, good things, just as you were sure in your bones that they would happen anywhere if a man would only hold to the simple rules.

Despite the uppity parents, you married Bess and

got started in politics under the wing of Tom Pendergast. The "damned New York liberals" might keep attacking Pendergast as a corrupt Boss. Did your friend Tom ever ask you to do anything dishonest? And it was quite a life, this being a County Judge, then United States Senator, riding off to the Capital and coming back to Independence with people gathering around and asking, "Harry, what are they up to in Washington?"

"They're up to getting whatever they can get," you would say. Everybody would laugh and there was a night of bourbon and poker with the boys and a long visit with Mother, who would always send you off with "Now, Harry, hew to the good line." You hewed to the good line. You never went near a tainted dime. You were a loyal Democrat, almost always voting for the New Deal laws proposed by the Democratic President. You liked reading Civil War history and you remembered World War I; this time no smart-aleck businessmen were going to make off with huge war profits. So you stood up from your back bench in the Senate and called for a committee to keep a suspicious eye on the whole hurry and grab. Naturally you were chairman and naturally you worked nights watching over every dollar spent and soon all kinds of people had a good word for Harry Truman's Special Committee Investigating the National Defense Program.

You kept holding to the simple rules and good things went right on happening. 1944 and Democratic party leaders were telling Franklin Roosevelt that Henry Wallace simply would not do. Why not someone who had voted New Deal yet was not too much stamped as a New Dealer, a friendly man who had stirred up few enmities but nevertheless had some national standing, a Senator from the Border States which could easily decide the election? When they first told you at the convention that you were to get the Vice-Presidential nomination, you were so upset an attack of nausea came and you urged that the place should go to Jimmy Byrnes. But you got used to the idea and before many hours you felt like the boyhood day when you came home holding a twelve-inch trout behind your back. "Who's getting the Vice-Presidential nod?" delegates asked. You grinned and said: "Me."

The Vice-Presidency was wonderful. Bess no longer had to work as your secretary and she would have friends in all the way from Independence for bridge. More and more organizations were asking Margaret to sing. And everybody was glad to meet Harry Truman now, even the movie stars like Lauren Bacall, who came and sat on the top of the piano while you played the "Missouri Waltz."

The afternoon it happened you were having a drink in Sam Rayburn's office. You turned ashen and your voice stuck in your throat. The next day you said to the reporters: "Boys, if you ever pray, pray for me now. I don't know whether you fellows ever had a load of hay fall on you, but when they told me yesterday what had happened, I felt like the moon, the stars, and all the planets had fallen on me."

The first weeks in the White House were awful. You had never really wanted this. Sure, you were a good man, good as the next one, and there was no reason why you shouldn't be Vice-President. But that didn't mean you should be President of the United States, especially not after Franklin Roosevelt and in times like these. His shadow was always over your shoulder. You had been let in so little on really important affairs that you had to keep summoning Roosevelt intimates, Harry Hopkins, Admiral Leahy, or Jimmy Byrnes, merely to get the basic facts. And every day there was some tremendous decision to make in that lonely room where Abraham Lincoln and Woodrow Wilson and Franklin Roosevelt had sat. You said it privately and you said it publicly: If only I could be back in the Senate.

But the Senate days were gone; you even had to stop slipping over to the Senate cafeteria for lunch because it made such a fuss. Well, you weren't going to flinch and you weren't going to forget the important things. You kept hard at work, up at 5:30 a.m. and tackling a stack of papers after dinner. You didn't high-hat your friends. You drew them around you, old buddies you knew you could trust, like solid John Snyder, who talked horse sense to all the crackpot theorists buzzing around the White House, and your other sidekick from World War I days, Harry Vaughan, always such a comfort with his funny stories and his booming "I'm still with ya, Chief," and Ed Pauley, who had pitched in and raised hundreds of thousands when the Democratic Party needed money so badly. Above all, you were determined to keep smiling—the newspapers noticed that you referred to reasons for hopefulness seven times in one speech. And there you were behind the big desk with the shiny model plow on it, your suit neatly pressed and your bow tie dapper, good father, good Democrat, good fellow, and the man who also happened to have the most awesome job in the world.

In the final months of 1945, all through 1946, one situation clamored for the attention of the White House more insistently than anything else—the problem that everybody was calling "reconversion." Governmental and business plans for shifting the nation's economy back from war to peace had generally assumed the necessity of a lengthy invasion of Japan. Now that atomic bombs had abruptly ended the hostilities, the economic blueprints were dangerously fuzzy and incomplete.

The arguments concerning reconversion centered on the scores of wartime federal controls, particularly the controls over prices and wages. Everybody wanted to get back to "normal" conditions. Everybody was ready with his prediction of dire depression if reconversion should be mishandled. But the nation's most powerful economic blocs violently disagreed over what was normal and how you arrived there.

The slogans of liberal New Dealism and conservative anti-New Dealism filled the air, and each group varied doctrine in a way to suit its own interest. Organized labor, for years a bulwark of New Dealism, was all for reconversion under stern governmental supervision—which it was inclined to define as price controls but no wage controls. Industry, for so long the chief center of anti-New Dealism, wanted to hurry toward free enterprise—which usually ended up in meaning wage controls but no price controls. Agriculture, deeply divided in its attitudes since the late 1930's, spoke in a dozen voices but always with an insistence that the purchasing power of the farmer was to be kept high.

No one questioned that the war had brought inflation and that the postwar was continuing it. Equally plain was the fact that most industrial labor had worked forty-eight hours during the war—eight at overtime—and now the normal work week was back to forty. Could industrial wages be increased to compensate for these developments without raising prices and thus bringing still more inflation? Businessmen's organizations, with an imposing battery of statistics, proved that it was impossible for industry to go on making a reasonable profit if wages were increased without hiking prices. The labor unions, with an equally impressive array of figures, proved that business was making so much that it could amply afford to absorb large wage increases.

In the White House, Harry Truman sat listening to the endless arguments and forebodings and he wished people would "stop singing the blues." Once in a while he fell into the language of the day and talked of crisis. For the most part he would speak to the public as he did when he dedicated a dam at Gilbertsville, Kentucky, two months after V-J: "We are having our little troubles now—a few of them. They are not serious. Just a blowup after a let-down from war."

When the President acted, he moved along a wavering line. In his mind, being a loyal Democrat meant carrying on at least the New Deal's general tendency to use governmental powers in ways favored by the lower-income groups. On the other hand, he was anxious to get along with a Congress that was controlled by a coalition of anti-New Dealers. His most trusted advisers, particularly John Snyder, were decidedly favorable to the attitudes of business, and he could not entirely down his own feeling that there was something un-American about price controls in peacetime. ("Police state methods," he was soon to call them in a press conference.) During late 1945 and 1946, the President was less either a New Dealer or an anti-New Dealer than a man reacting to the strongest pressures of the moment.

The V-J celebrations were hardly over when he began tossing out by the armloads rationing regulations and other controls affecting prices. At the same time he was supporting the proposal for a Council of Economic Advisers with considerable powers over industry, and in the ensuing tug-of-war Congress did pass a watered-down version of the bill. The President told the livestock men that he would "never, never" lift price controls on meat as long as there was a shortage; twenty-one days later, at the height of the shortage, he scrapped all ceilings on meat. He carried on a sporadic battle with Congress to preserve an OPA with real powers over general prices, sometimes applying full White House pressure, sometimes doing more talking than acting and permitting his subordinates to aid the anti-OPA forces. Because of, in spite of, and in a very real sense regardless of Harry Truman, during most of 1946 price controls were more sieve than ceiling.

All the while labor was up in arms against wage controls. Three months after the Japanese surrender, the United Automobile Workers read out the declaration of war. Inflation or no inflation, forty-eight or forty hours' work, the UAW demanded that its members should take home at the end of the week at least as much purchasing power as they received before V-J. Specifically the union called on General Motors to raise wages thirty per cent.

Soon the country's biggest union and its richest corporation were locked in a bitter strike, and walkouts were spreading across the country. Usually the major struggles ended up on the President's desk. Usually the White House arranged a settlement by proposing an 18 to 22 cent-per-hour wage boost with fringe benefits. And usually one strike was ended only to be followed by two more.

On April 1, 1946 John L. Lewis, refusing a White House compromise, led his four hundred thousand soft-coal miners out, and the nation's economy slowed, faltered, wobbled toward a dead stop. Within a month, freight loadings dropped seventy-five per cent and steel plants were beginning to bank their fires. A fury of anti-labor feeling swept the country, bursting into denunciations on the floors of Congress. Virginia's conservative Senator, Harry Byrd, cried: "[Lewis is] drunk with power." Senator Scott Lucas of Illinois, usually a supporter of the unions, added: "If this Government has not the power to outlaw strikes of this character, then this Government has no power of self-preservation."

After forty days of the crippling coal strike, a truce was arranged only to be followed by the threat of a still more paralyzing walkout. The United States had never gone through a total railroad stoppage but in May, 1946, Alvanley Johnston, Grand Chief of the Brotherhood of Locomotive Engineers, and Alexander F. Whitney, President of the Brotherhood of Railway Trainmen, were ready to pull the switch. Just twenty-six minutes before the deadline, Johnston and Whitney accepted a telephone plea from the White

House to delay the strike for five days while the negotiations continued.

The five days rushed by and still the two union leaders refused to accept compromise terms. Beginning at 4 p.m. on May 23, the United States had a preview of a national rail strike. Within forty-eight hours, air and bus terminals were pandemonium, runs were starting on gas stations and food stores, unemployment in fringe industries was mounting, and news stories were pouring in of fortunes in lettuce rotting away at Salinas, in citrus fruit at Redlands, in vegetables on the Rio Grande. From federal officials came the bluntest possible warning that hundreds of thousands in Europe would starve if shipments of grain and meat to eastern ports were delayed as much as two weeks.

Now Harry Truman was anything but smiling. Years later the White House physician, Dr. Wallace Graham, remembered how disturbed the President was. Johnston and Whitney, Truman was clear in his mind, were taking an impossible position. "What decent American would pull a rail strike at a time like this?"

The President summoned the two union chiefs for a final conference. He had never had much use for Johnston, a grumpy bureaucratic type and "a damned Republican," but he and the sprightly Whitney had been friends for years.

Neither union leader would budge. Whitney said: "I've got to go through with it."

The President hunched forward in his chair. "Well then, I'm going to give you the gun."

That night Harry Truman went on the radio with the toughest public language he had used since entering the White House. A new figure, the St. Louis attorney Clark Clifford, was appearing in the White House inner circle, and Clifford, following the President's mood, drafted sentences that rasped through the loudspeakers like angry blows. "The crisis of Pearl

Harbor was the result of action by a foreign enemy," the President told the nation. "The crisis tonight is caused by . . . men within our own country who place their private interests above the welfare of the nation."

Throughout the night Clifford and other Presidential aides worked feverishly in the White House on the special message Truman was to deliver to Congress the next afternoon. In the Hotel Statler another aide, John Steelman, worked just as feverishly to negotiate a settlement of the strike. Shortly before the President left for the Capitol, word came from the Statler that agreement seemed near, but Truman began his speech with no settlement signed.

The President's face was gray and tight as he read his tartly worded message. He was a warm friend of labor, Truman emphasized; he did not want sweeping anti-strike legislation. But the railroads had been taken over by the government in order to keep them running and he would not tolerate a strike against the government of the United States. He felt compelled to ask for the power which would permit him, as Commander-in-Chief, "to draft into the Armed Forces of the United States all workers who are on strike against their government."

While Truman spoke, Clark Clifford sat in the office of Speaker of the House Sam Rayburn, hoping for word from the Hotel Statler. Finally, after what seemed like an interminable wait, John Steelman telephoned. Clifford scribbled off a note and hurried it to Leslie Biffle, Secretary of the Senate. As the President spoke his final emphatic word, Biffle handed him the slip of paper. Truman read the note out loud: "Mr. President, agreement signed, strike settled." A great roar of applause, from Republicans and Democrats alike, swept across Congress.

So the railroad strike was over and the Congressmen cheered, but an unprecedented paralysis had been prevented only by the threat of an unprecedented curtailment of liberties. Pro-labor liberals were not the only Americans who winced at the Presidential demand for the right to draft strikers. Senator Robert A. Taft stood up in the Senate and declared that the Truman proposal "offends not only the Constitution, but every basic principle for which the American Republic was established. Strikes cannot be prohibited without interfering with the basic freedom essential to our form of Government." With the danger of a railroad stoppage over, the Presidential recommendation was quickly pigeonholed. But the whole episode was a peculiarly disturbing moment for thoughtful Americans of a wide variety of views.

For most Americans, thoughtful or not, the strikes were spectacular evidence that economic affairs were badly askew. Ugly splotches of unemployment began to appear with the first cancellations of war contracts. While the battle over price controls went on, prices kept inching up until by the end of 1946 living costs were an estimated thirty-three per cent above the level of Pearl Harbor Day. All the while, the 1946 strikes were piling up a record loss of 107,475,000 man-days of work, hobbling production and pushing prices toward still higher levels.

The inflation jabbed people wherever they turned. Trolleys and subways went up two cents, then a nickel. The ten-cent Sunday newspaper was disappearing in America. For years the insurance company, Bankers Life, had run a magazine ad which began: "You can become financially independent. Mary and I did . . . we're living on a life income of $150 a month." In June, 1946 the ad changed. Now Mary and I were "happy as kids on a life income of $200 a month."

Still more irritating were the things that were hard to buy at any price. A public with billions of dollars stored up in war bonds and savings accounts, avid to replace the worn-out and push on to a higher standard of living, found itself queuing up in long nerve-jangling lines. Women had trouble getting furniture, nylons, a new electric iron; men found clothing, even a razor blade that would shave clean, in short supply; families were forced on to hopeless-appearing waiting lists for a new car.

Everywhere the housing shortage was the subject of irritated conversation. The potent real-estate lobby fought federal subsidies for low-cost housing; the equally powerful unions were leery of assembly-line construction; the swing toward prefabs ran into the difficulty of using enormous quantities of scarce sheet steel. Housing units kept going up, hundreds of thousands of them, but rarely according to schedule and never enough. Many new dwellings promptly started falling apart. They had been thrown together with green lumber, ersatz plumbing, slapdash carpentry, and a general air of who-cares. Everybody knew a story like the one from Mineola, Long Island: the house had cost $9,950 and now its cellar was flooded with sewage.

Food shortages came grinding in on top of the housing debacle. This city lacked sufficient sugar; another was short of coffee. New Englanders grimaced at a scarcity of beans, and Southerners were forced into cooking like damyankees and boiling vegetables without fatback.

In Detroit, a woman walked into a butcher shop. The butcher eyed the stranger, turned to the boss. "Who is she?"

The boss said: "I don't know. Starve the bitch."

As the summer of 1946 closed, the food shortages were reaching their climax in meat famine. First came a meteoric rise in prices.

PRICES SOAR, BUYERS SORE
STEERS JUMP OVER THE MOON

ran the *New York Daily News* headline. Then the steers disappeared behind the moon. While the White House and the livestock men argued over the wisdom of price ceilings on meat, the producers staged their own strike and refused to send the cattle to market. In some communities, meat of any kind was only a savory memory. In many cities, housewives who did not reach the counters early were lucky to pick up a half-pound of bologna or three frankfurters. Even hospitals were frantically telephoning Washington, asking emergency provisions of red meat for their patients' trays.

But there were ways and ways of getting things. Housewives kept an eye on the front street, alerting each other that a supply truck was on its way to the chain store. Tipping became more and more correct—perhaps a half-dollar to the butcher for the back-breaking labor of handing the chops over the counter. The tie-in sale was commonplace; you could get Scotch if you were also ready to load up on wine and rum. Here and there barter came back. A car would get you an apartment; football tickets, good liquor, soap, auto batteries, and sugar were all part of the day's currency.

And there were the under-the-table deals, on a scale far beyond the wartime activity. The black market was most extensive in the new-car field (an estimated seventy-five per cent), and the techniques took on rococo variety. Customers would drop four or five hundred-dollar bills on the desk and quickly look the other way. You could get a new automobile by trading in your old car for a reasonable price—say ten dollars. In other salesrooms, the customer would look toward a wall a hundred feet away and say: "Bet you five hundred dollars I can hit that wall with my hat." In Oklahoma City, a dealer sold you the car and, for four hundred dollars more, a hound dog. The dog, decidedly a postwar model, would then shuffle back to its master.

"Round and round we go," the *Seattle Post-Intelligencer* editorialized in verse rocky enough to be worthy of the occasion. "And where we stop, nobody, not Harry, not the Chamber of Commerce, not the CIO, not even the *Post-Intelligencer* doth know." To millions of Americans, the country did seem caught in a never-ending circle of vexation. The unhealthy economic situation, especially inflation, produced strikes; the strikes cut down production and thus pressed prices upward; they were settled by wage hikes that were quickly made up by further price increases; and so on.

And so on—to where? As 1946 drew to an end, the answers were many and loud and hardly convincing.

The more Americans fretted over home affairs, the more plain a fact of fundamental importance became. For the first time during an American era of peace, it was next to impossible to discuss domestic problems coherently without having the points become entangled in foreign affairs.

To millions this was an intensely irritating fact. They felt, as generations of Americans had felt before them, that concern over international matters was to be confined to unfortunate periods of war. Foreign policy was something you had, like measles, and got over with as quickly as possible. This attitude was especially common among the Midwestern conservatives led by Senator Robert A. Taft. A number of years later, when circumstances had forced the Ohio Senator into the field of world policy, he remarked with shrewd insight into himself and his following: "I am charged with moving in on foreign policy; the truth is that foreign policy has moved in on me."

The Taftites were strengthened by people from all sections of the country who were simply acting from primordial instincts. American troops around the world were organizing "I Wanna Go Home" demonstrations, and their wives, girl friends, sisters, mothers, and the lady next door were mailing Senators a pair of baby boots with a note that read: "I miss my Daddy." Many businessmen, their fortunes and their careers staked on existing economic relationships, were decidedly suspicious of proposals for world-wide monetary agreements or for an increase in the number of reciprocal tariff agreements. Efforts to determine where the new United Nations organization should be located in the United States produced tortured rationalizations from people who worried about what would happen to property and social values if their suburb was invaded by Greeks and Peruvians, not to speak of Russians. Greenwich, Connecticut, which had as high a percentage of UN enthusiasts as any community in the country, staged an anguished referendum on the subject. Five out of every seven people who voted thought it would be better if the splendid organization would do its magnificent work somewhere else.

Yet all of this was not the main stream. As World War II neared an end, the United States Senate witnessed the most meaningful conversion in modern American history. For two decades Arthur H. Vandenberg of Michigan, top-ranking Republican on the powerful Senate Foreign Relations Committee, had been an all-out isolationist. While the Nazi threat mounted, he voted against repeal of the Neutrality Acts and against the Draft Act, the Draft Act Extension, and Lend-Lease. Four weeks after the Germans invaded Poland, he said: "This so-called war is nothing but about 25 people and propaganda." Then, under the pressures of World War II, Vandenberg began to swing. The final turn in his thinking came when he stood in London in 1944 and listened to German robot bombs snarl overhead. "How can there be immunity or isolation," he mused to a friend, "when man can devise weapons like that?" By early 1945, Vandenberg was ready to renounce formally his lifelong belief.

Before a hushed Senate, his strong voice punching home his points, Vandenberg declared: "I hasten to make my own personal viewpoint clear. I have always been frankly one of those who has believed in our own self-reliance. I still believe that we can never again—regardless of collaborations—allow our national defense to deteriorate to anything like a point of impotence. But I do not believe that any nation hereafter can immunize itself by its own exclusive action. . . . I want maximum American cooperation. . . . I want a new dignity and a new authority for international law. I think American self-interest requires it."

As Vandenberg finished his brief address, both sides of the Senate floor broke into an applause more heart-felt than Washington had heard for years. "A speech of unquestioned greatness," "the most important to come from the Senate Chamber in the last 80 years," "a shot heard round the world," rang the praise from journals of many points of view. Senator Taft, who had little desire to advertise splits in the Republican Party, managed to confine his comment to faint derision. But no degree of derision could gainsay the fact that one thirty-nine-minute address had transformed Vandenberg from just another powerful Midwestern Republican into a leader whose stature was commanding in and outside the Midwest and in and outside the Republican Party.

Consciously or unconsciously, Vandenberg had taken the immemorial path of effective leadership in a democracy: he led where people were going anyhow. In the final stages of the war, most Americans were also making their way toward a great decision. They announced it to no cheering galleries. As a matter of fact, they arrived at the judgment so unobtrusively that experienced politicians and journalists were caught off guard—including men like the *New Republic*'s highly knowledgeable "T.R.B.," who wanted very much to believe that the decision was being made.

"Let me begin by candidly admitting a mistake . . . ," T.R.B. wrote. "Every now and then a

wind starts blowing in Washington and suddenly all
the little weathervanes point one way. It is blowing
now, off the grass roots, and it is saying that Hank
Jones, American, is sick of isolationism. . . . Six
months ago it seemed impossible that the House would
pass the Bretton Woods plan [for international monetary agreements]. Yet it did. . . . Six months ago
chances seemed dubious for the reciprocal-trade-
agreements bill. . . . But the wind started and the bill
passed the House, 239 to 153. It blew some more, and
the Senate passed it last week, 54 to 21. Sometimes you
can almost see public opinion working on Congress.
It is doing so now."

When the ratification of the United Nations Charter
came up in the Senate, reporters packed the press gallery, expecting a repetition of the dramatic battle over
the League of Nations. The debate had its moments—
Burton Wheeler's revealing spleen against a world that
was "forcing" him to vote for the Charter, William
Fulbright's lone, bold questioning of national sover-
eignty, the touching appeal for peace by Walter
George, whose son had been killed in the Navy Air
Corps. But on the whole, the debate produced less
clash than many a scuffle over an appropriations bill.
At the end only two Senators voted no, and they were
men long stamped as lame ducks from another political era.

Most of the country viewed the beginnings of the
United Nations with a determined beneficence. So the
delegates had hardly assembled before they were at
each other's throats. So what? A nation snapping and
snarling over nylons and rents, which took pride in the
Bronx cheer and the quick punch in the nose, was
ready to understand. Television was just coming into
use as the UN held its early meetings, and large parts
of America went along with the argument that the
very difficulties of the new organization, so intimately
revealed, showed that diplomacy was being rescued
from back-room deals. And there *was* something enor-

mously comforting about having the delegates in full exposure, posturing, sneezing, arguing their cases in your living-room.

The trouble was that the more Americans ventured into the world, the more disconcerting were the facts that confronted them. War-crimes trials were going on and the picture of other civilizations that emerged was hardly encouraging. In France, Pierre Laval, three times Premier of the country, had no defense whatsoever against charges of total collaboration with a bestial and often senseless brutality. He could only stand smirking while the Judge, the Prosecutor, and all twenty-four jurors disgraced the courtroom by trying to shout down anything he said. In the Japanese trials, men who had led millions only months ago turned all American efforts at seriousness into a grisly *opéra bouffe*. Ex-Premier Hideki Tojo sat picking his nose and trying to flirt with an American secretary. Ex-propagandist Shumei Okawa would open his shirt and rub his scrawny chest, dart from his chair to smack Tojo's gleaming pate, shout in weirdly clever English: "I hate the U.S.; it is democrazy."

From the German trials came evidence that sounded like an echo of the primitive forests. There was Major General of Police Otto Ohlendorf matter-of-factly telling how his Task Force D killed ninety thousand men, women, or children. (Other task forces were said to have killed more, the Major General added, but he suspected they were just boasting.) Or the testimony of Dr. Franz Blaha, a Czech surgeon who had managed to live through Dachau: "It was dangerous to have a soft, fine skin. . . . Soft human skin was prized for leather and bindings." Or the reports from the trials of women workers at the Belsen and Oswiecim concentration camps: of gentle-voiced Juana Borman, whose wolfhound enjoyed tearing prisoners to pieces; of wispy Anna Hampel, who took a liking to a French internee and, being rebuffed, beat him daily with a hose; of Irma Grese, she of the delicate features and the warm smile, who calmly fixed her hair while the prosecution showed movies of a bulldozer pushing a huge pile of rotted corpses into a pit. And what thoughtful American could fail to ponder the fact that many an ordinary German was expressing utter bewilderment that the Allies, having won the war, should conduct rigorously fair trials for enemy prisoners?

Whatever the state of people's minds, there was the equally terrifying condition of their bodies. In Europe and Asia, hunger rode the wake of war like some leering devil of man's stupidity. To war's devastation, nature added floods in China and Indochina, a tidal wave in Madras, drought in Australia, South Africa, Greece, and Mexico. After a survey of twenty-four countries, Herbert Hoover broadcast his report on food conditions and the stark facts gave eloquence even to the well-remembered monotony of his voice. Most heartrending of all were the photographs of children that kept appearing in American newspapers, always the same, always the sagging shoulders, the spidery legs, the Adam's apples sticking out, the dull stare of young faces that had never laughed.

Working as friends with a world in such a condition was a formidable enough task but the relationship, the United States was learning, was not going to overflow with camaraderie. Modern Americans, probably more than any other large nation in history, have yearned to be liked by other peoples, and most Americans, rightly or wrongly, had assumed that at least western Europe and Asia looked to them with affection. Now a new and ominous word—"anti-Americanism"—was emphasized in reports from every continent. Even in England, the most friendly of America's former allies or enemies, people were delighting in an acrid jingle about the Statue of Liberty:

> I wonder is freedom still holding the light—
> Or is she just calling the waiter?

The most widely quoted report came from the

Rev. Renwick C. Kennedy, certainly no alarmist newspaperman but an army chaplain out of small-town Alabama who was home after twenty months in western Europe. "From England to Germany," the Rev. Mr. Kennedy wrote, "they have had enough of us. . . . [The American soldier in Europe has proved] more than a little pathetic. . . . He is not very clear in his own mind about why he fought, nor about what his victory means. As a matter of fact, he is not much interested in such matters. . . . His interests are chiefly three: 1) to find a woman and sleep with her; 2) to buy or steal a bottle of cognac and get stinking drunk; 3) to go home. . . . There he stands in his bulging clothes, fat, overfed, lonely, a bit wistful, seeing little, understanding less—the Conqueror, with a chocolate bar in one pocket and a package of cigarets in the other. . . . The chocolate bar and the cigarets are about all that he, the Conqueror, has to give the conquered."

Americans, naturally enough, bridled at such talk. Yet the reports kept coming and they helped to insinuate into the national mind deeply worrisome questions: Could the United States pull off the new world role it was assuming? Wasn't it especially likely to fail in view of the way the Soviet was acting?

Yes, the Soviet—always the Russians pushed their way into the discussion. Everything about the Soviet Union that bothered the Taftite Republicans at V-J Day was now, in greatly magnified form, troubling a much wider circle. Even for many liberals, Yalta was becoming a goading symbol of American failure in dealing with the Russians. "Oh God, Yalta this and Yalta that!" old Tom Connally, the Democratic foreign-policy leader in the Senate, cried out in weariness at the endless criticism of the Crimean agreements. Soviet threats to eastern Europe were no longer mere threats; the only question left was whether any of the area would remain free. In the UN, the Russian representatives were incessantly vetoing, staging stormy walkouts, presenting their arguments in a shrieking billingsgate. On the most critical issue of all, international control of atomic energy, the Russians conducted themselves in a way which seemed to most Americans categorical proof that the Soviet wanted no genuine international control.

The activities of the American Communist Party itself were taking on a different and sinister meaning. To most Americans the struggles between political parties in the United States had always seemed a kind of family row, bitter perhaps and certainly hard-fought but never raising any question that all groups were loyal to the one flag. In the months after V-J, American Communist leaders began deserting the Party with a jarring set of declarations. The most publicized deserter, Louis Budenz, ex-editor of the *Daily Worker,* quit with a flat statement that Communist parties anywhere were not political parties at all but conspiracies which gave their loyalty first and last to the Soviet Union.

Yet the news from around the world was of continuing gains by Communist parties. In France, Italy, and Czechoslovakia, the Red groups emerged from the war the strongest single political units and their growth was rushing ahead. Aid from the Soviet was helping Red Armies bring one region of China after another under the control of Communists. Even from the Latin countries to the south, which Americans had long considered a region of amenable rumba-dancers, the news was portentous. Communist parties, reliable estimates ran at the end of 1946, would poll a million to a million-and-a-half votes if free elections were held, and their support was mounting with the steadiness of a Cugat beat.

In the middle of it all, a Doukhobor farm girl began testifying in a Canadian court. While working as a cipher clerk in the External Affairs Department, Emma Woikin told her story, she had met Major Sokolov, of the Soviet Embassy. The Major, a "handsome man," and Mrs. Sokolov had been most friendly; repeatedly they invited her to come to their home, where she had "interesting" talks. She "had a feeling of love for Russia," the pathetic young widow said in a tense whisper. "I wanted to help the Soviet but not to hurt Canada." After Emma Woikin came the testimony of thirteen other Canadians who had enjoyed interesting talks with members of the Soviet Embassy, especially about atomic and other defense secrets.

Americans looked homeward; was it going on here too? A Gallup Poll indicated wide support for the proposal to bar all Communists from federal offices in the United States. The House Un-American Activities Committee went to work with increased zeal and members of the Senate Foreign Relations and Appropriations committees sounded alarms. In and outside Washington, another new phrase was rapidly gaining in usage. The Soviet Union, with its brutal imperialism, its sabotaging of the UN, its world-wide spying, was hurrying the nations toward an "East-West" clash.

The phrase caught a special aspect of the situation as it appeared to the American mind. Communism, centered in Russia and spreading most rapidly in eastern Europe and in the Orient, seemed peculiarly eastern. But many of the troubles of the world appeared eastern in a sense not entirely connected with Red armies or parties. Out across the Pacific, along North Africa and the Middle East, colonial peoples were in revolt, sometimes led by Communists and sometimes not but always keeping the eastern regions in a dangerous churning.

What should American policy be? In international affairs as in domestic matters, President Truman kept issuing sunny statements and he kept wavering. After calling for Universal Military Training, he quickly gave in to the popular clamor for demobilization; a military establishment which had included eleven million men on V-J Day was soon down to about one million. The Administration backed large loans for a number of countries in Europe or Asia but permitted food shipments to lag enough so that many a World War II ally was enraged and despairing. It sharpened its notes of protest to the Soviet but built no political, economic, or military arrangements which would give substance to the pieces of paper. Month after month of 1946 the Administration wobbled along and little was clear concerning its foreign policy except that it sincerely backed the UN, hoped for a Soviet-American understanding but was not relying on one, and assumed some responsibility for restoring the war-wrecked economies of Europe and Asia.

As international tensions sharpened in the spring of 1946, Franc L. McCluer, president of tiny Westminster College in Fulton, Missouri, had an idea. It was quite an idea; the awed townsfolk had long since taken to calling their college president "Bullet" McCluer. Westminster had a fund for inviting a speaker of "international importance" each year and Winston Churchill, a man with qualifications, was expected to visit the White House. The Bullet confided his idea to Harry Vaughan, the star football center at Westminster when McCluer was the star debater. Vaughan arranged an appointment with Truman, who endorsed McCluer's letter of invitation with a penned note at the bottom of the paper. Churchill replied that he had some things on his mind he would very much like to say at Fulton.

With the President of the United States sitting on the platform, Churchill reminded his listeners that he had seen World War II coming and "cried aloud to my own fellow-countrymen and to the world. . . . There never was a war in history easier to prevent by timely action. . . . But no one would listen." Now, once again, tyranny was spreading. "From Stettin in the Baltic to Trieste in the Adriatic an iron curtain has descended across the Continent. . . . I do not believe that Soviet Russia desires war. What they desire is the fruits of war and the indefinite expansion of their power and doctrines. . . . From what I have seen of our Russian friends and allies during the war, I am convinced that there is nothing they admire so much as strength, and there is nothing for which they have less respect than for weakness, especially military weakness." Churchill outlined his formula for strength —an ironclad American-British alliance, possibly gathering in the other Western powers in time. The speech sent an unmistakable chill of belligerence into the balmy Fulton air. To the Soviet it said, with the authentic Churchillian cock of the head: Desist or fight.

Churchill, the gallant warrior, was as popular as ever. The crowd jammed into the little college gymnasium roared its applause for the man, but his doctrine brought few cheers in Fulton or anywhere else in the United States. President Truman, who later said that he had sponsored the speech as a trial balloon, was given an unmistakable view of public opinion. The typical Congressman or newspaper added the phrase "iron curtain" to the swiftly growing postwar vocabulary and wondered out loud if Churchill's proposals would not wreck the UN and provoke the Soviet into war.

The old master, who could read national political reactions as other men read a billboard, knew he had not won his real audience. Rumbling off to Richmond to address the Virginia Assembly, Churchill was decidedly testy. "You have not asked to see beforehand what I am going to say," he snapped. "I might easily blurt out a lot of things people know in their hearts are true."

Six months after Bullet McCluer scored his Fulton coup, another American had an idea. Henry Wallace, the Roosevelt intimate and ex-Vice-President who was now a politically potent member of the Truman Cabinet, considered himself the heir of true New Dealism, and to Wallace, true New Dealism meant insistence that the Soviet Union was a peaceful power.

The stiffening attitude of the Truman Administration toward the Russians, Wallace believed, was war-mongering. He was scheduled to address the National Committee of the Arts, Sciences, and Professions in New York City and he determined to use the occasion to rally the forces of "peace"—and perhaps to rally them around Henry Wallace as the Democratic Presidential candidate in 1948.

Wallace wrote out a speech which included passages that amounted to an attack on American policy toward the Soviet. The United States, he charged, had not been trying to meet Russia halfway. If it did, it would find co-operation toward peace. In 1955 Harry Truman stated categorically that he read no part of the speech before it was delivered. In 1956 Henry Wallace stated categorically that he and the President had gone over the manuscript page by page, each with a copy in his hand.

On the afternoon before the speech was to be delivered, the subject came up in a White House press conference. William Mylander, of the Cowles newspapers, had an advance copy in his hand and he quoted from Wallace: " 'When President Truman read these words he said that they represented the policy of his administration.' "

That is correct, the President replied.

"Does that apply just to that paragraph or to the whole speech?" Mylander pressed.

It applies to the whole speech, Truman said.

Later in the press conference Raymond Brandt of the *St. Louis Post-Dispatch* returned to the subject. Did not the Wallace address, Brandt asked, represent a departure from the policy of Secretary of State James Byrnes?

No, the President insisted, the two were right in line.

That evening, Wallace found himself before a crowd that was, at least in part, vociferously pro-Soviet. He adjusted his speech. Once he looked up

from his text and remarked extemporaneously: "I realize that the danger of war is much less from Communism than it is from imperialism." He left out two
points. The first was a reference to "native Communists faithfully following every twist and turn in the
Moscow party line." The second was the sentence:
"The Russians should stop teaching that their form
of Communism must . . . ultimately triumph over
democratic capitalism."

Reaction to the episode was volcanic. Secretary of
State Byrnes, then negotiating with the Russians in
Paris, sent a teletype message to the White House
which stated: "If it is not completely clear in your own
mind that Mr. Wallace should be asked to refrain from
criticizing the foreign policy of the United States
while he is a member of your Cabinet, I must ask you
to accept my resignation immediately." Senator Vandenberg, now the chief symbol of bipartisan foreign
policy, told reporters: "We can only cooperate with
one Secretary of State at a time." The President summoned a special press conference and performed the
inevitable. This time he permitted no questions. He
read off a statement that he had meant only to approve
Wallace's right to express his opinions, not the actual
points that had been made. The next week Wallace
was fired from the Cabinet.

And where did that leave things? Churchill, talking
blunt belligerence toward the Soviet, walked into a
national leeriness; Wallace, calling for faith in the Russians, found himself hustled out of Washington. As
1946 ended, the sagacious *Christian Science Monitor*
ventured a reading of the state of American opinion on
foreign affairs. "Nobody," the paper editorialized,
"seems to be sure what is going to happen. And few
are sure what should be done, no matter what happens."

In New York City, other observers offered their
comment on postwar America. Parfums Weil Paris

Company put out a new perfume called "GriGri." It was designed, the ads explained, "to replace the atom bomb with a dash of the inconsequential."

Americans of late 1945 and 1946, their zest for luxuries pent up by four long years of war, their victory turned into an endless nagging of problems, were hardly averse to the inconsequential. The big football weekend roared back; television sets sold like red meat; women snapped up lamé skirts, sequin-trimmed aprons cartwheel hats with pastel blooms waving in billowing nets. Any night was likely to burst into New Year's Eve. People jammed swish restaurants, lavished millions on dog races that did not even pretend to be honest, wheedled, bribed, and pushed their way to pay $8 to $125 a couple for an evening drinking watered Scotch and having their eardrums clouted by indifferent jazzmen.

"The Year of the Bullbat," "The Year of Frenzy," "The Year of Frustration," journalists were calling 1946, and through all the spreeing there did run an unmistakable sense of displacement, a feverish running away, a bitterness that reveled in the harsh, the mocking, the blatant. The great movie box-office success was Jane Russell in *The Outlaw*, which was announced with the unabashed placard: "The Music Hall gets the big ones. What are the two great reasons for Jane Russell's rise to stardom?" Wider and wider audiences were won by novels of the raw and the amoebic, of men whose calling card was a battered body or women who delivered themselves from temptation by never knowing that you had to be tempted. The new radio sensation was Henry Morgan, master of the melancholy onslaught and "a nice enough fellow," as he would explain, "but all screwed up, like you are."

Hundreds of thousands bought *The Snake Pit*, Mary Jane Ward's novel of a woman's struggle with schizophrenia in a mental hospital. At the sanatorium, the patient went through shock therapy, hydrotherapy, psychoanalytical questionings, paraldehyde dosings, and old-fashioned madhouse discipline.

"I just don't know where it's all going to end," an ex-nurse, now a patient, says.

The head nurse of the ward answers: "I'll tell you. . . . When there's more sick ones than well ones, by golly the sick ones will lock the well ones up."

In every section of the United States, on all levels of society, the ill-tempered, the mean, the vicious in human beings pushed to the fore. These were the months when Justices of the Supreme Court of the United States insulted each other in newspaper headlines and New England poultry farmers whined to their Congressmen about grain being sent overseas to the starving. They were the months, too, when the North disgraced itself by two major race riots, and the South, by six lynchings; West Coast ruffians threw bricks at the windows of Japanese-American veterans; and Dartmouth's President, Ernest Hopkins, blandly explained that of course his college admitted only a quota of Jews. In Atlanta, violence against Negroes and Negro houses was mounting, Jews were being threatened, and observers pointed to a newly chartered organization which, they warned, might prove the base for another nation-wide Ku-Klux Klan. "All the advances which minorities made during the New Deal and the war seem to be in question," the *Cleveland Plain Dealer* added. "And what is the longtime trend? Who knows?"

Who knew—who could be sure of anything in such an atmosphere? All approaches that offered confidence, or at least solace, found ready clienteles. The couches of psychiatrists were kept endlessly warm. Russell Janney, a gagman turned philosopher, scored unprecedented first-novel sales with *The Miracle of the Bells*, which somehow jumbled press agents, a Polish stripteaser, and St. Michael "taking on Kid Lucifer and putting him down for the count" into a demonstration that America would be saved by an "emotion deeper than love—the emotion of Palship." From the Federal Council of Churches of Christ came a declaration of incontestable accuracy, which suggested a major shift in thinking. "For at least half a century Americans have been drifting away from religion," the Council pointed out. "But at the present time all signs—the cheap and the reverent, the serious and the trivial—lead to only one conclusion. Americans are going back to God."

Eugene O'Neill was in New York City for the opening of his new play, *The Iceman Cometh*, and reporters put the matter to him. "Back to religion?" O'Neill mused. "Perhaps. Perhaps that will be the answer for some. At any rate, I realize that I have been putting my faith in values that are gone. . . . There is a feeling around, or I'm mistaken, of fate. Kismet, the negative fate. . . . It's struck me as time goes on, how something funny, even farcical, can suddenly without any apparent reason, break up into something gloomy and tragic. . . . A sort of unfair *non sequitur*, as though events, as though life were being manipulated just to confuse us."

For almost half a century, intellectual America, along with its great playwright, had taken its main sustenance from the exuberantly hopeful liberal tradition. Few were now ready to break with it; fewer still were yet sure why they were so disturbed. Yet the sense of that unfair *non sequitur*, of a soiled and befuddled imperative, went on spreading.

In New York, San Francisco, or Greenville, South Carolina, Americans concerned with words and ideas waited for the postwar outburst of literary talent that would mean excitingly fresh emphases. Hadn't 1919 brought Sherwood Anderson's *Winesburg, Ohio*, Irving Babbitt's *Rousseau and Romanticism*, Joseph Hergesheimer's *Java Head*, Eugene O'Neill's *The Moon of the Caribbees*, not to speak of John Maynard Keynes's *The Economic Consequences of the Peace* which was about to appear? 1945 gave way to 1946,

1946 careened ahead and the outburst did not come. Restively, irritably, American intellectuals turned toward a hangdog self-criticism.

At least there was one outlet for everyone, whether the troubled writer or the housewife waspish over the disappearance of chops. The President of the United States is many things. He is the symbol of the nation, the head of the dominant political party, the man who makes the crucial decisions. He is also the final focus of the national mood, a subject for adulation when things go well and the butt of anger in a period of turmoil and troubles. As 1946 ended, Harry Truman sat in the President's chair a perfect target. Not since another simple man, Andrew Johnson, tried to fill the place of another strong President in another postwar had such a fury of unpopularity lashed the White House.

Truman's determined optimism, his addiction to his Missouri buddies, to platitudes, and to Mother? "Every day is Mother's Day in the White House," people said with a bitter snicker. His handling of John L. Lewis, symbol of the strikes? "The President lets the public freeze while his guts quiver," roared Robert R. Wason, president of the National Association of Manufacturers. His back-and-forth on price controls? "Poor Mr. Truman," the liberal columnist Samuel Grafton sneered, "an object for pity." His fumbling of the Wallace speech? Even the secretaries were saying: "You just sort of forget about Harry until he makes another mistake." People of a dozen points of view passed around a wisecrack. Why had the President been late to today's press conference? He got up this morning a little stiff in the joints and had trouble putting his foot in his mouth.

For fourteen long years, Republicans had been trying to capture the national mood. They cried: "Roosevelt and Ruin," "Dictatorship," "Bankruptcy," "Warmongering," "Bureaucracy," and "Communism." Nothing had worked. Then, as the Congressional elections of November, 1946, came on, the Harry M. Frost Advertising Company of Boston hit upon two words with magic for the day.

"Had enough?" the Republicans asked the country. A nation which had quite enough of inflation and the Russians, of strikes, shortages, and the atom bomb, of everlasting maybe's about peace and prosperity, rose up in a hiss of exasperation and elected the first Republican Congress since the far-distant days of Herbert Hoover.

America discontent, didn't
know what it wanted.
Was era of stumbling.
Truman gave no direction.
Consequently — a mess.
~~Repub.~~ ~~has~~.

III

The Postwar Takes Shape

GRADUALLY THE store shelves began to fill. Within months after the election of 1946, steaks and roasts were no longer drawing crowds. Canned beer was back and so were white sheets, alarm clocks, nylons, and golf balls. The black-marketeers were slithering away. Here and there startled householders opened the door and actually heard a salesman ask them to buy an automobile.

Shortly after the election John L. Lewis marched his coal miners out on strike and this time a government injunction marched them right back again. Labor leaders, no aspirants for defeat, saw to it that strikes quickly dwindled. Raw materials were becoming plentiful; the reconversion of machinery was nearing completion. "Let 'er rip" was the mood of the front offices and production, already approaching prewar levels, spurted ahead.

Prices kept on climbing. Even the kids of the Cape Cod resort towns, who for years had dived to retrieve pennies thrown in the water by vacationers, now refused to budge except for nickels. But the public was learning to roll with the inflation and the free-spending spree of 1946 was quieting into budget-wary living. Expensive Scotch and bonded bourbon piled up in liquor stores. Despite the most honeyed words of *Vogue* and *Mademoiselle*, women did not rush to buy Paris's new padded hips and the long skirt; instead buttons for home sewing were selling briskly. The great vacation migrations slowed and night-club business was off sharply from Manhattan's Latin Quarter to the Hollywood Mocambo. "The geese are out there," the headwaiter of the Latin Quarter sighed, "but they ain't comin' in here and layin' them golden eggs."

Across the river in Brooklyn, telephones in newspaper offices jangled crazily. Was the terrible rumor true, was Manager Leo Durocher really shifting over to the Giants? "Jeez," one choked-up caller took the news, "it's Poil Hobba for the Dodgers." The nation could smile indulgently at the dither, could find the mood for all the old stand-bys of sports and sentiment. Things were less hectic, less feverish. The divorce rate tumbled; the South staged fewer lynching bees; Supreme Court Justices stopped caterwauling at each other in public. And the pro-feminist novelist, Fannie Hurst, who had managed to find a bright dawn for women over many years, could only complain to her audiences: "A sleeping sickness is spreading among the women of the land. . . . They are retrogressing into . . . that thing known as The Home."

As the nation returned to more workaday acting and thinking, a spectacular fact emerged: the America that was settling was not so much settling down as it was settling upward. The high hopes of V-J were, at least in one important respect, beng realized. Whatever the ravages of inflation, the masses of ordinary Americans were living at a higher material standard than their groups had ever known and with a much greater sense of status in the community.

The postwar period was proving to be the beneficiary of at least fifty years of bloodless but drastic change in the United States. During this Half-Century of Revolution, mass-production techniques in industry and the mechanization of agriculture raced ahead.

Powerful political forces pushed toward a welfare state while businessmen countered with welfare capitalism. Two world wars affected the domestic society like giant leveling bulldozers. The results of all these developments, intertwined in a dozen ways, came to a temporary climax in the amazing America of the late 1940's.

Trim workers' suburbs were rising in testimony to the fact that almost half of organized labor was in or quite near the middle-income brackets of the country. All but the unluckiest or least provident of farmers were living decently, often amid so many machines that a nine-to-five workday was possible for both husband and wife; among the eight million farm families of the top-income group, a year's gross return of ten thousand dollars was average. The rampant inflation itself was in part a result of the fact that the country as a whole was living better. The American Meat Institute issued the most revealing figures. Before the war housewives had turned to macaroni, egg-and-cheese mixtures, or some other inexpensive dish for about half the family meals; in 1947 the average American ate meat five out of seven nights a week.

Economics was only part—and perhaps the least important part—of the developing scene. The sense of heightened status which farmers and workingmen were beginning to feel at the end of the war was now coming in large, deeply satisfying draughts. As a young man Leslie Heiser, a farmer of upstate Illinois, had been so mortified by the clothes he had to wear to town that he cursed the fate which gave him his occupation. In 1947 Heiser was talking the changed attitude of much of agricultural America. His annual income well over six thousand dollars, the whole family trim in Chicago-style clothing, each year bringing the sense of upward movement which came with new farm machinery or more electrical appliances for the home, Heiser deferred to no man. "There isn't a job in New York City that's good enough for me," he would say.

Labor too was lifting its head high. As a new era of union-management relations came in, a team of girls locked in a room on the eleventh floor of the General Motors Building in Detroit finished a secret typing job. Six floors below, a little group of men, haggard from seventeen consecutive hours of collective bargaining, called in reporters and handed out the sensational news: the world's largest automobile manufacturer had agreed to what the union liked so much—a formula for hitching wages to living costs. The GM agreement was many things, including a way of keeping the labor front quieted in an inflationary period while protecting corporations from a sudden deflation. But perhaps most importantly, the pact was another and especially striking indication of the role that unions were coming to play in American life. These organizations may have grown primarily as economic weapons but they had become something far beyond that. Regularly taking on the biggest corporations, winning an increasingly large part in management discussions, raising and distributing vast welfare funds, wielding political power that could mean a key role in picking the President of the United States, the unions were bringing to industrial workers a sense of being men who counted.

In the cities or out across the countryside, the GI Bill of Rights, now in full operation, went on its revolutionary way. In 1947 more than four million young men and women were benefiting from the legislation. Thousands did not need the aid; others used it to take rumba lessons at Arthur Murray's, to learn archery, or, in the case of one veteran from Des Moines, to equip himself with a fine set of burglary tools. But for millions the GI Bill of Rights was opportunity written in large, alluring letters. Turning to it for more education, to set up a business of their own or an independent farm, perhaps to purchase a home, they knew the zest of the upsweep in status. "I've talked to hundreds and hundreds of these kids," James Gardner, a Veterans' Administration official in San Francisco, remarked, "and you get the same story over and over again. They like the idea of making more money but they like even more the idea—as they keep putting it—of 'getting to be somebody.'"

Amid it all, a powerful, lithe Negro was turning the base paths of Ebbets Field into a holy war. For Jack Roosevelt Robinson living had always been fierce competition. Growing up in a Pasadena slum, he made his first money by sneaking onto golf courses, retrieving lost balls, and outrunning the cops. Given athletic scholarships to Pasadena Junior College and U.C.L.A., Jackie Robinson drove himself to stardom in so many different sports that West Coast writers were rhapsodizing about the new Jim Thorpe. After World War II, as Robinson was slugging and darting his way up in the Negro baseball leagues, the Brooklyn Dodger general manager Branch Rickey heightened the competition. Half Barnum and half Billy Sunday, Rickey had decided to defy baseball's ancient color line and sign Robinson to a Brooklyn contract. Now the sensitive, quick-tempered young Negro faced the most brutal kind of contest; this time he had to battle by not battling at all.

Rickey drove at the matter hard the first time Robinson came to his office. At the height of the emotional talk, the Brooklyn owner moved behind his big desk. He posed as a clerk in a Southern hotel, insultingly refusing Robinson a room; as a prejudiced sports writer, twisting a story to make the Negro look bad; as a foul-tongued fan jostling him in a hotel lobby or railroad station. Rickey took off his coat and charged out in front of the desk. "Now I'm playing against you in the World Series. . . . I go into you, spikes first. But you don't give ground. You stand there and you jab the ball into my ribs and the umpire yells, 'Out!' I flare—all I see is your face—that black face right on top of me. So I haul off and I punch you right in the cheek."

A white fist barely missed Robinson's sweating face. The head did not budge.

"What do you do?" Rickey roared. "What do you do?"

The heavy lips trembled for an instant and then opened. "Mr. Rickey," Jackie Robinson said in a taut whisper, "I've got two cheeks."

People who should have known were openly skeptical. "Players on the road live close together," one baseball veteran expressed the feeling. "It just won't work." Rickey was saying very little. Instead he was organizing in each city of the National League a how-to-handle-Robinson committee, composed of leading Negro citizens. Jackie Robinson, it was agreed, would stay away from night spots, endorse no products, leave the ball parks by a secret exit to avoid displays of Negro adulation as well as pop bottles, and, at least for a period, turn down social invitations from blacks or whites.

Robinson took his position at first base and more than occasionally players came smashing against him, at times with spikes out; the Negro ground his teeth and said nothing. Hotels in St. Louis and Philadelphia registered the rest of the Dodgers and refused Robinson a room. He turned away without a word and slept at a friend's home. Some members of his own team walked past without saying hello; some members of other teams poured verbal filth from the dugout or yelled insults as he rounded the bases. "I'd get mad," Jackie Robinson said. "But I'd never let them know it."

The 1947 season rushed ahead. The first baseman's dazzling hitting and running were heading him for sure Rookie-of-the-Year honors, teammates began inviting him for a poker session. Baseball Commissioner Albert Chandler cracked down on the rowdies, national popularity polls showed Jackie Robinson running a close second to Bing Crosby. Down the home stretch in September, with the Dodgers and the Cardinals first and second in the National League, the Cardinals' catcher hurtled into the Negro at first base. Next time at bat Jackie Robinson suddenly was Jackie Robinson. He turned to the catcher and let fly with all the furious language of a rhubarb and the Cardinal, in the routine tradition, rhubarbed back. The stands hushed, then broke into a vast murmur of approval. A newspaperman said to a friend: "By God, there's a black boy squawking just like everybody else and nothing happening. I don't mean to be silly but somehow I think this is one for the history books."

The history books will have to record that Jackie Robinson's triumph, so widely publicized and admired, enormously furthered acceptance for the Negro in many fields of American life. They will also have to record a still more important fact. This revolutionist in a baseball suit was the flashing symbol of an era in the national life when, for all minority groups, for all lower-status Americans, the social and economic walls were coming tumbling down.

In Washington, Congressmen would pause for an occasional pat on the back to Jackie Robinson, an apostrophe to the American Way of Life. Then the chambers hurried back to the main business at hand. The Congress elected in the Republican sweep of 1946, the Eightieth Congress, was led by men with a mission. They had come roaring into the Capital filled with spleen and plannings.

Behind them was a nation-wide rancor. It spurted out from all regions of the country and from a dozen different groups, each with its own special resentment. Democratic Georgia Crackers hated "what the Niggers are getting away with"; Republican businessmen in any community had their furies at the labor unions; New Dealish secretaries, plumbers, and hairdressers in New York, Toledo, or Seattle sputtered every time they saw the size of the withholding tax on their pay checks. But the most powerful thrust of discontent came from one readily identifiable group, the men and women who had come to be called conservatives and who now emphatically did not want to conserve the existing America.

These malcontents were as much a product of the Half-Century of Revolution as the situations which annoyed them so much. All during the years since the 1890's, the emerging society had been making enemies. Many of these foes were members of the high-income strata, who saw the period as one long aggravating process of redistributing their wealth. Foreign and domestic affairs alike seemed to mean increasingly the same thing—spending great sums of money which came disproportionately from their pockets.

Yet the grievance was not wholly economic; men from middle and low economic groups joined wealthy Americans in an impatience with things that had little to do with finances. The Half-Century of Revolution, particularly the jolting changes since 1933, had been a trial to all those whose temperaments yearned for stability. One change was proving particularly upsetting. Once upon a time, white, Protestant, relatively old-stock Americans had been the arbiters of the national life. Small-town storekeepers or big-city bankers, they were "nice people," the "Best People," expecting and receiving a certain deference. Now the established classes were having to make room for groups from the bottom and they were feeling uncomfortable, jostled, almost displaced in an America which they had assumed belonged peculiarly to them. "What kind of a country is it," John Hurst, an old-family small businessman of Champaign, Illinois, cried out the feeling at a druggists' convention, "I ask you, what kind of a country is it that fusses over anybody who makes a big noise and ignores Robert A. Taft?"

Robert A. Taft—here, to an extraordinary extent, was the symbol and the spokesman, the glory and the hope of the malcontents. The Taft family had stood for reputability, for solid, ultra-respectable achievement, ever since grandfather Alphonso doggedly walked from a Vermont farm to New Haven, became the first of twenty-one Tafts to graduate from Yale, quit working in a New York law office because he found his colleagues too grasping ("money is the all in all"), and settled into Cincinnati's most esteemed legal and political circles. Alphonso's son gave the family tradition a firm nudge forward. William Howard Taft was quite a man of achievement; he was also a President of the United States who stood, with all the strength his amiable and decorous self would permit, against the whole social-reform movement of his day. Almost as a matter of course, the President's son, Robert Taft, was number one in his class at Yale University and Harvard Law School, an extraordinarily able attorney giving most of his time to trust funds and impeccable real estate, a United States Senator who took over the leadership of the battle which established America was waging in the 1930's against the New Deal.

The most striking personal qualities of Senator Taft were precisely the ones which this traditional America liked to believe belonged especially to its way of life. His habits were as unpretentious as his baggy serge suits; Taft's idea of a good time was a family picnic where everybody sat around munching drugstore candy bars and playing hearts. He permitted his brilliant mind no heretical adventures, keeping it tightly reined by the logic of the ledger-book. Despite his mounting yearnings to follow his father into the White House, he remained honest, outspoken, almost unbelievably ready to make plain exactly what Robert Taft thought on any public issue. "I look at that man," Mrs. Edith Busbey, an Idaho Taftite phrased what the Senator could mean to his supporters, "and I see everything which my father taught me to hold good."

Taft's greatest political liability before the general public only increased his hold on his special following. The man was a study in discomfiture, a deep-seated, persistent lack of rapport with his America. Taft would go campaigning at fairs or city rallies, where the local titans, crowding and backslapping him, made sure that everybody knew they were as good as any Taft, by God, and the Senator's smile would come out as radiant as a very small and very lopsided persimmon. Republican politicians might shudder. The Senator's devotees, squirming with him amid the incessant leveling of the new era, cherished him the more for the things he could not tolerate.

Taft's doctrine had its compromises; the yearnings for the White House did not leave his policies entirely unaffected. Yet basically Taftism amounted to a call for counter-revolution against the Half-Century of Revolution. The Senator reacted to almost any foreign-affairs situation by trying to limit American commitments; the issue was at home and it was urgent. For too long, as Taft saw things, the emphasis had been on economic and social opportunities. The stress should be returned to the "traditional American heart of things, liberty"—the greatest practicable freedom of the individual in both his economic and his governmental relationships.

The usually flat voice would take on a high-pitched urgency as Taft said: "We have got to break with the corrupting idea that we can legislate prosperity, legislate equality, legislate opportunity. All of these good things came in the past from free Americans freely working out their destiny. . . . That is the only way they can continue to come in any genuine sense." Once the credo was expressed more simply. At the height of the furor over meat prices, reporters asked the Senator for his solution and he replied: "Eat less." It was the purest Taftiana—in its magnificent tactlessness and its bedrock assumption that a real American solved his own problems.

Taft was unquestionably the powerhouse of the new Eightieth Congress and he and most of the other leaders took the Republican victory as a mandate to remake

America along anti-New Deal lines. Committee after committee went under the chairmanship of veterans of the struggle against Rooseveltism. In a kind of caricature of the trend, the chairmanship of the powerful House Appropriations Committee passed to cantankerous John Taber, who in the long-past days of 1940 had roared so loud fighting a New Deal bill that he restored the hearing in the deaf ear of Congressman Leonard Schuetz ("I had spent thousands of dollars on that ear," Schuetz said in grateful wonderment). Now, John Taber stormed, he was going to apply a "meat-axe to government frills."

When the actual record of the Congress began to emerge in 1947, it proved an assault on the legislation and the tendencies of the Half-Century of Revolution. The practical political basis of the session was a deal between Southern Democrats and right-wing Republicans, which meant the end of any hopes for civil-rights legislation. The two most important laws passed were the Taft-Hartley Act, which weakened the power of unions, and a new income tax formula that reduced the disproportion of taxes on high incomes. (The bill cut the levies three per cent for families with incomes of $2,400 or less; eight per cent for those in the $10,000 bracket; fifteen per cent for the $20,000 a year class; and forty-eight to sixty-five per cent for the group over $100,000.) The structure of government aid to farmers was attacked by cuts in funds for soil conservation and for crop storage. The Congress refused demands for federal help in the form of more public housing, strong price controls, extended social security, or aid-to-education. Both what was done and what was not done in the field of immigration legislation reflected distaste for immigrants of southern and eastern European origins. Over the whole session hung the air of wrathful counter-revolution. "T.R.B.," the New Deal columnist of the *New Republic*, was as accurate as he was melancholy when he wrote: "This Congress brought back an atmosphere you had forgot-

ten or never thought possible. . . . Victories fought
and won years ago were suddenly in doubt. Everything
was debatable again."

"It would be ironical," Taft remarked early in the
session, "if this Congress which really has its heart set
on straightening out domestic affairs would end up in
being besieged by foreign problems." The world of
1947 had a way of being ironical. The Eightieth Congress had hardly assembled when news from abroad
was hammering at the door of every Congressman.

Since the end of World War II, the anti-Communist
government of Greece had been under attack from
Red guerillas and had survived only because the British gave it sizable economic and military support. In
February, 1947 the British, hard-pressed financially
and embroiled in troubles throughout the Empire,
notified the American government that they would no
longer be able to serve as the prop in Greece. With
this support removed, Greece almost certainly would
gravitate into the Soviet orbit, the independence of
Turkey would be undermined, and the whole eastern
Mediterranean might slide behind the Iron Curtain.
Secretary of State George Marshall, reaching into his
military past, found the phrase that expressed the
Washington reaction. This was "like the Battle of the
Bulge," the Secretary declared, a sudden thrust of danger that carried within it potential disaster for the
whole defense of the democracies.

Shortly after the bad news from London, Secretary
Marshall flew to a Big Four conference in Moscow
which was supposed to arrange peace treaties for Germany and Austria. For forty-four sessions the meetings ground on, all utterly sterile except in giving the
West an unmistakable indication of what the Soviet
meant by diplomacy. One especially poignant moment was caught on the front pages of the American
newspapers. George Marshall, trying desperately to
break through the Russian twistings of language, read

off a little lecture on what Americans meant by democracy, in central Europe or anywhere else.

"We believe," the Secretary said, "that human beings have certain inalienable rights—that is, rights
which may not be given or taken away. They include
the right of every individual to develop his mind and
his soul in the ways of his own choice. . . . To us a
society is not democratic if men who respect the
rights of their fellow-men are not free to express their
own beliefs and convictions without fear that they
may be snatched away from their home or family.
. . . [A democratic society must] assure such rights
to every individual and effectively prevent any government or group, however powerful or however
numerous, from taking such rights away from or imposing any such fears on any individuals, however
weak or however few."

Foreign Minister Molotov stirred impatiently. "A
number of valuable remarks," he said and then hurried
into another tirade against "war-mongering capitalist
piracy."

In rapid succession the Soviet Union threw loud-
clanging *nyets* into the machinery of the United Nations. One day the Soviet was rejecting more plans for
the international control of atomic energy. Another
two weeks and it was using its tenth veto—this time to
shield Communist Albania from an investigation of the
charge that she planted mines which damaged British
destroyers. A few days more and the Soviet boycotted
the opening session of the UN Trusteeship Council
with cries of "barbarous American imperialism." Nothing, not even a sense of the ridiculous, restrained the
malevolent self-righteousness of the Russians. Do you
know, the Soviet delegate to the UN Commission on
Human Rights asked indignantly, that Alabama has a
law which permits a man to beat his wife provided that
the stick is not more than two inches in circumfer-
ence?

The White House was in a fury of activity. Legislation was being rushed to cope with the Greek-Turkish crisis and Congressional leaders were soon summoned to smooth the way for quick passage of the bill. Secretary Marshall took the lead in explaining the situation. With his mind on the poverty that was so powerful an ally of the Communists in Greece, the Secretary emphasized the need for economic relief. The Republican leaders stirred irritably. Did this Administration really expect the Congress of Robert Taft to play WPA to the Greeks?

Undersecretary of State Dean Acheson, sensing the trouble, turned to President Truman and asked if he might add some remarks. Acheson said little about economic distress. Instead he moved over to the big wall map with pointer in hand and described in detail just what strategic consequences would follow the fall of Greece to Red armies. The Republican leaders began relaxing and one of the most important of them, Senator Arthur Vandenberg, went away with a cooperative word of advice. As Vandenberg left, he remarked to Truman: "Mr. President, if that's what you want, there's only one way to get it. That is to make a personal appearance before Congress and scare hell out of the country."

On March 12, 1947, Truman went before Congress with a message which would have scared hell out of any nation. He had a good deal to say about the American desire for peace. But basically the speech was a blunt warning that Communist actions were directly and gravely threatening American security. Specifically, the President proposed that Congress should bolster the hard-pressed Greek and Turkish governments by appropriating $400,000,000 in military and economic help and by authorizing the sending of American military and civilian personnel to supervise the use of the aid. He was fully aware, Truman said, of the broad implications involved in such actions. But the time had come when America had to take a stand. "I believe that it must be the policy of the United

States," the President declared in words that immediately became known as the Truman Doctrine, "to support free peoples who are resisting attempted subjugation by armed minorities or by outside pressures."

The Congressional and public debate of the Presidential proposals, wordy as it was, soon made plain that the country was quite ready to authorize the funds and the personnel which Truman had recommended. As the national determination to take action against Soviet imperialism became clear, Bernard Baruch began preparations for a speech he was to make in South Carolina and Baruch turned for assistance to an old friend, the veteran newspaperman Herbert Bayard Swope. About a year before, Swope, working on another address for Baruch, had used the phrase "Cold War" to describe American-Soviet relations but a number of mutual friends thought the term too strong and Baruch removed it. Now Swope wrote into his draft of the South Carolina speech the sentence: "Let us not be deceived—today we are in the midst of a cold war." This time the phrase did not seem too strong and Baruch spoke it in Columbia, South Carolina on April 16, 1947. Walter Lippmann spread it through his widely syndicated column and the public, recognizing "Cold War" as an accurate expression of the situation that had developed, immediately made the term a commonplace of the American language.

Just before Baruch's speech, American bookstores received their first shipment of an abridgment of the massive *Study of History* by the London University professor, Arnold Toynbee. Even in shortened form the work was hardly the usual popular reading; the 589 pages, part history, part philosophy, and part poetry, wound a labyrinthine way through the rise and fall of twenty-six civilizations. Yet the book quickly made its way to best-seller lists and stayed on week after week. Soon the slim, pale professor, with the long grave face and the uncompromising language, was the rage of the American lecture circuit, and Toynbee-ism in some vague and simplified form was reaching amazingly far into the semi-literate public. No matter what Toynbee had meant to say, his brooding discussion of the rise and fall of civilizations bore directly upon a feeling that had been growing in the United States ever since the first postwar difficulties with Communism and was now hardening into a conviction. By the spring of 1947, a good many Americans, whether talking the language of the universities or the corner taverns, were ready to state that the United States faced not simply the threat of war with another country but some kind of vast and fundamental conflict between ways of acting and thinking, the kind of clash, as Professor Toynbee said, which time and again had sent whole civilizations crashing down.

So it was to be war, at least Cold War, certainly a portentous struggle. So it was not to be depression, at least not tomorrow, but social and economic upsurge and inflation and the headaches that inflation brought and the Taftite assault on many of the laws and attitudes associated with the upsurge. The postwar America emerging in the spring of 1947, so zestfully careering, so replete with evidence that the careering would take you fast and far, so formidably threatened, was like nothing so much as some great gaily colored balloon bounding along just above craggy wastes. The people of the United States, more and more aware of their situation, were to react in quite different ways. Their first major national response was to be so rational, so hard-headed, that they utterly dumfounded themselves.

Americans on upswing. Grew sensible in living. Castes broken. Foreign policy important:

IV

Containment, Foreign and Domestic

THE REPORTERS who covered the White House during the spring of 1947 almost all agreed on one thing. Bert Andrews of the *New York Herald Tribune* put it succinctly: "Harry Truman is becoming President of the United States."

The man in the White House was getting used to the big lonely room where Lincoln and Wilson and Franklin Roosevelt had sat. The year and a half in office had given Truman a chance to catch up on the background of affairs, easing his feeling that he was overwhelmed. ("I don't know how I ever got out of that mudhole," he said as he recalled how he had been forced to rely on Roosevelt holdovers for the most basic facts on this or that situation.) In its own way, the Republican victory in the Congressional elections of 1946 helped to put Truman on his feet. During the first period after Roosevelt's death, he had not been able to down the feeling that he was something of an executor for the deceased President's Administrations. The elections of 1946, however Republican the returns, started things afresh. Now Truman felt freer to be himself, to act on his own in his own ways.

A new air was permeating the White House. The President's incessant cheerfulness of the early days was

becoming mixed with a sober recognition of the difficulties facing the United States. The lines of authority
tightened. "The boys are learning," Presidential Secretary Charles Ross observed, "that Harry Truman is
no pushover." John Snyder still talked blowzy platitudes to the President and Harry Vaughan's brassy
laugh was as audible as ever around the White House,
but Truman was also recognizing the need for a different type of adviser. Particularly noticeable was the
growing role of Clark Clifford, who had first come to
public attention because of his part in drafting the
Presidential message which marked the end of the
1946 railroad strike.

When Clark Clifford was growing up in St. Louis,
all the nice ladies would say: "My, what a beautiful
youngster." Half the coeds at Washington University
had their eyes on this six feet two inches of graceful
muscularity, topped by waves of taffy-colored hair
and a smile that dimmed the toothpaste ads. Like many
handsome men, Clifford could be annoyed by the
fuss over his appearance but he was never so annoyed
that he failed to realize how his striking good looks,
coupled with a friendly manner and a clear, agile mind,
gave him a head start toward success. From college
days, Clifford was driving hard. At Washington University he was the biggest of the Big Men on Campus.
Entering the Missouri bar, he commanded an income
of thirty thousand dollars a year as a trial lawyer before
he was out of his thirties. Volunteering for the Navy
during World War II, Clifford rose, or rather rocketed,
from a lieutenant j.g. to a captain in twenty-one
months.

By now success was a habit. When a friendship with
a Truman crony, Jake Vardaman, led to Clifford's appointment as a White House naval aide, the bright
young man wore his new importance as easily as he
wore his faultless clothing. Truman liked the confidence of his young associate. He was no less pleased
by Clifford's Missouri colloquialisms, his hardheaded

thinking and his way with words, above all by his habit of talking to the boss with no intimation that Harry Truman was a smudged carbon copy of Franklin Roosevelt. By the spring of 1947 Clark Clifford, just turned forty, was Special Counsel to the President of the United States, serving as a combination speech-writer, political strategist, and general co-ordinator of White House affairs and doing it all with the bland assurance that the Truman Administration, like Clark Clifford, would be quite a success.

Two or three times a week the President and Clifford ate together in the basement lunchroom of the White House. Six or eight times a day Clifford walked the twenty paces which were all that separated his office from Truman's door. Always the counselor pushed vigorously for positive, broad-gauged policies in domestic and foreign affairs. 1947 had already brought action aplenty. That formidable government injunction had been thrown at John L. Lewis; the Greek-Turkish proposals were being rushed through Congress. But none of these moves bespoke a genuine policy. None offered a comprehensive, practicable guide for future steps on either the domestic or the foreign front.

Clifford's own special interest was in domestic affairs, and here his urgings were especially confident. A nephew and admirer of Clark McAdams, the crusading liberal editor of the *St. Louis Post-Dispatch*, Clifford had grown up with a marked tendency toward the kind of policies represented by the New Deal. A close student of political affairs, he was convinced that the long lines of development indicated victories for the party which identified itself with the hopes and the worries of ordinary men and women. As Clifford looked out at the America of the late 1940's, with its vast social upsweep, he was more sure than ever that success for the Truman Administration and continuation of the Half-Century of Revolution were inextricably entwined.

Clifford wanted no emotional New Dealism, no sweeping new programs; such things were foreign to this unideological moderate, as he believed they were foreign to the mood of the country. Clifford sought, as it were, to codify the New Deal. He wanted to protect what it had done by fending off the Eightieth Congress, to improve on its accomplishments by tying together loose ends here and there, to bring it up to date by applying its general approach to certain key problems which had arisen since the war.

Such doctrine sat well with Harry Truman. The President, whatever his allergy to intellectualish New Dealers, had long leaned in the direction of wanting to use the government to help the lower economic groups. An unreconstructable Democrat, he was inclined to believe that anything a Republican Congress did was pernicious. A politician to the bone, he had an instinctive sense of the millions of votes that lay down in the rows of little white houses where men worried about keeping up the payments on the car or getting the daughter a formal.

On through 1947, then during 1948, President Truman, prodded and aided by Clifford, was working out his own variety of liberalism in domestic affairs. Under the circumstances of the Eightieth Congress, it was expressed most conspicuously in negatives. Sixty-two times Truman wielded the Presidential veto and for his most important attempt at blockage, the rejection of Taft-Hartley, he accepted language written by Clifford which was more vigorous than the country had heard since the bellicose vetoing days of Grover Cleveland.

Meanwhile the President spelled out the proposals which represented his program for positive adjustments and updatings of the New Deal: for farmers, a series of minor changes in existing legislation which were intended to make more beneficial the federal aid to agriculture; for labor, a raise in the minimum wage from forty to seventy-five cents; for the foreign-born, an amendment to immigration policy which would remove any stigma from citizens of southern and eastern European birth; for the general public of medium or low incomes, favorable modifications in the social security program, the re-enactment of strict price controls, and a tax bill that would have helped the rich the least by cutting everyone's income tax the same forty dollars. Of all the lower-status groups, the Negroes had received the fewest New Deal laws specifically designed to help them and they were now pressuring the hardest for federal aid. Down to Congress went a strong Truman message urging the heart of the Negro legislative demands—an anti-lynching bill, the elimination of the poll tax, and a permanent Fair Employment Practices Commission.

In foreign affairs, the sheer force of events was helping to push the Administration toward a genuine policy. Even before President Truman received the formal Congressional authorization of aid for Greece and Turkey, the first ships were being loaded with food and bullets for the Mediterranean. Greece and Turkey held. But the foreign crisis only went on mounting. In Asia, almost nothing was improving from the American point of view. In western Europe, conditions were deteriorating so rapidly that an unending stream of Congressmen and government officials were crossing the Atlantic and coming back crying disaster.

The spring of 1947 found Britain and most of the Continent teetering near economic collapse. From Paris to Naples and on up to Oslo, tens of thousands of the undernourished were speaking with a racking cough. Tuberculosis, on the rise in western Europe for the first time in a century, was turning into the region's number-one killer. "What is Europe now?" Winston Churchill declared on May 14, 1947. "It is a rubble-heap, a charnal house, a breeding-ground of pestilence and hate." Bitterness, hunger, and disease could only mean more Communist strength and it

was clear that France and Italy were gravely threatened.

The Truman Doctrine itself added to the difficulty
of the American position. Edward Barrett, the overseas information specialist, has described how "the Truman Doctrine, well-meant but drafted without enough
awareness of foreign reactions, backfired in many parts
of the world. Since the then Greek Government had a
reputation for corruption and oppression, America
seemed to many to be underwriting the forces of reaction. Since . . . the President had said American officials would supervise the use of U.S. dollars in
Greece, he seemed to underscore the theme that America was hell-bent on economic imperialism. More important still, it indicated to some that America had
embarked on a program of using troubled small
nations as pawns in a gigantic contest with the
U.S.S.R."

In the State Department lights burned late seven
nights a week. President Truman, who more than
once publicly called Secretary of State George Marshall "the greatest living American," was leaning
heavily on the gnarled, fatherly Marshall for guidance
in foreign affairs. The Secretary, no novice at brain-
picking, was reaching out for information and ideas.
William L. Clayton, who for years had headed the
largest firm of cotton brokers in the world and who
now was Undersecretary of State for Economic Affairs, was providing a seasoned assessment of the economic state of Europe. The luminous mind of Undersecretary of State Dean Acheson was putting Administration thinking together into a general approach.
Speaking in Cleveland, Mississippi, on May 7, Acheson
expressed the developing pattern. "Since world demand exceeds our ability to supply, we are going to
have to concentrate our emergency assistance in
areas where it will be most effective in building
world political and economic stability, in promoting
human freedom and democratic institutions, in fos-

tering liberal trading policies, and in strengthening the
authority of the United Nations. This is merely common sense and sound practice."

Meanwhile Secretary Marshall was turning for additional aid to a board which he himself had set up.
The War Department had long contained a Strategy
and Policy Section, concerned not with day-by-day
affairs but with long-range planning. As Secretary of
State, Marshall ordered the establishment of a State
Department "Policy Planning Staff," to be composed
of specialists whose function would be to formulate
foreign policy projected from ten to twenty-five
years into the future. The meeting place of the PPS,
a spacious room next to the Secretary's office, was
deliberately given an atmosphere of unhurried acad-
eme. No telephone was to bring a sense of the insistent
present; the room contained only a conference table
quietly flanked by floor-to-ceiling bookshelves. But
whatever the original plan, in the spring of 1947 the
present was bursting into the thinking of the policy
planners like a fire bell. The group had not even formally met for the first time when, on April 29, Secretary Marshall sent the PPS chief, George Kennan, a
written instruction to draw up a specific recommendation of moves to be made by the United States.

The next day Marshall talked with Kennan. The European situation was so bad, the Secretary said, that
Congressmen would soon be coming up with all kinds
of unworkable schemes. The Secretary wanted a
sound program and he wanted it within ten days or
two weeks. As the conference closed Kennan asked the
Secretary if he had any further instructions. Marshall
replied: "Avoid trivia."

George Kennan took his place at the head of the
policy planners' table a slender, casually dressed figure
with a preoccupied smile and quick-darting words,
who somehow suggested both the skeptical man of
affairs and the dedicated scholar. The early years of
Kennan had been routine enough—a comfortable Mil-

waukee lawyer's home, a strict Midwestern military academy, a reading of Fitzgerald's *This Side of Paradise* which sent him applying to Princeton in 1921. At college one part of the unusual combination in the man began to develop. Shy, oversensitive, sure that he was crude in manner, he was probably the most obscure and lonely student on the Princeton campus. This very lack of social success threw him together with a rebellious minority who were defying campus conventions, reading with avid excitement the products of the American literary flowering that accompanied their years in college, and arguing philosophy, religion, and politics from dusk to dawn in one of the battered ground-floor rooms of Witherspoon Hall. Twenty-one years in the Foreign Service, years that were concentrated especially on Russian affairs, only developed further the intellectualism of Kennan. Of equal importance, the years added a tough-mindedness and the two qualities—the worldliness and the bookishness—blended into a pattern of thinking.

George Kennan proved the scholar-diplomat, if the United States has ever had one. To him being a Foreign Service man came to mean studying thoroughly the nation to which he was accredited, not simply its politics and its economics but its history, its music, its mores, everything which would permit him to lay hold of its inner nature. At the same time Kennan grew impatient with any diplomacy based primarily on academic theorizing or moral and legalistic considerations; the crusadings and the One Worldism of the Roosevelt era particularly bothered him. Kennan sought, as he said later, the diplomacy of "reality"—a diplomacy which demanded a hardheaded handling of a rigorously appraised situation. The job of the Foreign Service man was to be a diplomat "in the most old-fashioned sense of the word." He was not to make the world wonderful but to save it from the worst consequences of its follies. For civilization was

in "a constant state of change and flux" and the major
function of the diplomat was "to ease its transitions,
to temper the asperities to which . . . [the constant
change] often leads, . . . to see that these conflicts do
not assume forms too unsettling for international life
in general."

When World War II ended, Kennan was the
number-two man in the American Embassy at Moscow and growing more and more disturbed by the
American policy toward the Soviet Union. In February, 1946, just as Churchill was to make his "Iron
Curtain" speech, Kennan took the occasion of some
queries from the State Department to speak his mind
in an eight-thousand-word cable. The American people, he declared, did not remotely understand the Soviet Union and the policy of the government itself
was marked by "wishful thinking." Reaching into his
profound knowledge of Russian history, he saw the
Soviet as dominated by a "neurotic view," a "traditional and instinctive sense of insecurity" stemming
from the days when the Russians were an agricultural
people living on a defenseless plain amid fierce no-
madic tribes. As Russia grew and came into contact
with the West centuries ago, its rulers acquired another fear, a disquietude about the societies they were
encountering. They "sensed that their rule was relatively archaic in form, fragile and artificial in its psy-
chological foundation, unable to stand comparison or
contact with political systems of Western countries.
For this reason they have always feared foreign penetration. . . . And they have learned to seek security
only in patient but deadly struggle for the total destruction of rival power, never in compacts and compromises with it."

After Communism took power, that dogma became
a perfect vehicle for the sense of insecurity of the new
Russian rulers. It pictured them as defending idealism
against menacing forces within and without, and thus
justified the "dictatorship without which they did not

know how to rule . . . [and] the cruelties they did not dare not to inflict." In addition, Bolshevism attached to traditional Russian expansionism the whole apparatus of an international revolutionary force. Soviet Communism, in short, was another expression of the centuries-old "uneasy" Russian nationalism and imperialism but in a much more powerful and insidious form.

From such an analysis, one could only deduce that it was useless to try to establish normal relationships with the Soviet Union by compromises, another meeting of the Big Four, or some other reasonable form of give-and-take. The Kennan cable was harsh and disillusioning doctrine, much too disillusioning for early 1946 when the United States was not even ready for Churchill's Iron Curtain speech. Only during succeeding months, as the Soviet acted ever more plainly the dark role which Kennan had assigned it, did his words begin to count. His cable was studied and re-studied in Washington until it was accepted as something of a classic among American diplomatic analyses. Kennan was summoned home, assigned to lecture to two hundred military and civilian leaders at the newly reactivated National War College, then given the vital chairmanship of the Policy Planning Staff.

In working out their recommendations for Secretary Marshall, the policy planners drew upon a number of analytical studies previously made for the State Department, particularly an over-all report written by Clayton after a trip to Europe, and on the judgment of many experts, especially Charles Bohlen, a Counselor of the State Department whose experience in Russian matters was as great as that of Kennan. Using these materials within the framework of Kennan's analysis of Soviet policy, they agreed that the United States had only three alternatives in dealing with the problem presented by Communism: to fight the Soviet in the hope of destroying the center of revolutionary activity; to permit an indefinite expansion of Bolshevism; or to regulate American foreign policy so as to halt Red gains. To Kennan and his group, this third approach was the correct one both because it avoided war or indefinite Communist expansion and because it held out the hope of the disappearance of the Bolshevik disturbance. In ten or fifteen years, the Policy Planning Staff believed, Stalin would die and the leaders of the Soviet dictatorship would be fighting among themselves or their rule would be mellowing into a more tractable form.

But meanwhile what kind of a foreign policy would halt Communist expansion? The policy planners did not see the problem as primarily a military one. They were sure that American saber-rattling would only strengthen the Soviet argument that capitalism was spoiling to deprive the masses around the world of their just social advances. Mere anti-Communism in any form was not the wise approach; the world-wide disturbances basically came not from Red activities but from economic maladjustments and "a profound exhaustion of spiritual vigor" which would be exploited by some other variety of totalitarianism even if no Communists existed. The sensible program for the United States was a positive effort to create healthy societies, primarily through economic aid. The thinking of the policy planners emphasized heavily that American economic aid alone would not stop any country from going Communist. It could only serve as a spark to recovery, and only for those nations which had the will to remain non-Communist and an economic situation capable of improvement without fundamental surgery.

Kennan and his group gave considerable attention to the Chinese civil war. They concluded that China, under the corrupt and inefficient rule of Chiang Kai-shek, lacked the kind of economic system which could be saved by American aid and that further help from the United States would simply find its way to the

Red armies. They were particularly concerned about western Europe because of the key importance of its military-industrial potential. They thought that China, in view of its poverty in coal, iron, oil, and developed sources of water power, could not become an industrial power, and hence a major menace, in the foreseeable future. (Later, when the Communists had taken over China, Kennan remarked: "I am sure that the Russians would gladly exchange our control of Japan for their control of China. China is a drain on them and is likely to remain one for a long, long time. Europe is different. Germany's potential, added to that of Russia, could tip the scales of world power within a decade.") To the Policy Planning Staff, the vital areas to keep free of Communist control were Japan and western Europe, two great industrial centers which also formed a pincers around the Soviet. And in the circumstances of the spring of 1947, with Japan firmly under American rule while much of western Europe neared chaos, their eyes were fixed steadily westward.

On May 23, Kennan submitted the recommendation of the Policy Planning Staff to Secretary Marshall. The proposal was clean-cut: a massive offer of American resources, directed toward all of Europe with no ideological overtones, in a positive effort to restore the economy of the continent. There were two important provisos. The Europeans had to take the initiative in working out all details, and the program the Europeans submitted had to give promise of doing the "whole job. . . . [of being] the last such program we shall be asked to support in the foreseeable future."

Secretary Marshall sent this memorandum to a number of his top-level assistants, then summoned a series of conferences. On every major point, the memorandum of the policy planners stood. For all hesitancies, all questionings, Kennan was ready with his relentless pragmatism. Was there doubt whether the United States or the European nations should draw up the recovery plans for the various countries and make the initial estimate of the amount of aid to be given each? By all means the European nations, Kennan argued successfully. This would weaken charges of American domination; avoid a long parade of petitioners before Congress, exacerbating feelings that America was pouring out too much money; and create a situation in which the European nations, arguing among themselves, would become irritated at each other rather than the United States.

At another stage in the discussions, Secretary Marshall raised the most tortuous question: "Are we safe in directing such a proposal to all of Europe? What will be the effect if the Soviets decide to come in?"

Again Kennan carried his point. What better way to emphasize that the program is not mere anti-Sovietism? he maintained. And why not make the American proposition one which said to Russia: "You, like ourselves, produce raw materials which western Europe needs, and we shall be glad to examine together what contributions you as well as we could make. This would mean that Russia would either have to decline or else agree to make a real contribution, herself, to the revival of the western European economy."

One point Kennan did not argue too directly; he had not been a diplomat for twenty-one years for nothing. The policy planners' memorandum spoke of "misconceptions" that had arisen concerning the Truman Doctrine, which the proposed program would correct. Actually Kennan had been deeply disturbed by the whole approach of the Truman Doctrine and the memorandum represented a sharp and conscious break with it. Specifically, he sought to get away from the President's earlier hurried message by discarding the implication that American offers of aid were a defensive reaction to Communism; by withdrawing the blanket support which Truman had offered to all nations resisting the Reds, regardless of the quality of their own governments; and by removing from American policy any air of truculence toward the Soviet Union or world Communism.

Pressure, harsh pressure, always the pressure of the onrushing chaos in Europe. A little more than a week after the policy planners' memorandum first reached Secretary Marshall, Bohlen and others were hurriedly preparing a speech which Secretary Marshall would deliver. The Secretary was scheduled to deliver the address at the Amherst commencement exercises on June 16 but the European situation was deteriorating so rapidly that Marshall asked Harvard to revive a former invitation to give him an honorary degree so that he could take advantage of their earlier commencement date. On June 4 the Secretary left for Cambridge. Deeply convinced of the significance of the words he was to speak the next day, Marshall sat in the plane making penciled changes until the last moment.

"Our policy," he declared in the authentic tone of the new program, is "directed not against any country or doctrine, but against hunger, poverty, desperation, and chaos. Its purpose should be the revival of a working economy . . . so as to permit the emergence of political and social conditions in which free institutions can exist. . . . Any government that is willing to assist in the task of recovery will find full cooperation, I am sure, on the part of the United States Government."

No one in the State Department anticipated immediate important results from the speech. The haste was to get the idea in circulation, to begin what was expected to be a slow process of having it sift through the minds of European leaders. But the State Department had not reckoned with British Foreign Minister Ernest Bevin. The Foreign Minister first heard of the speech when already in bed and leaped out, elephantine frame and all, to put his office to work with the words: "This is the turning point." French Foreign

Minister Georges Bidault reacted with almost as much decision. Just twenty-two days after the Marshall speech, a meeting was assembling in Paris to discuss the American idea.

At the conference the Soviet Union soon made plain that it wanted no part of the program, but in a way that leaves a haunting question. American observers had long noted that Foreign Minister Molotov had a bump on his head which swelled when he was under emotional strain. Molotov was discussing the plan, raising only minor objections, when he was handed a telegram from Moscow. The bump swelled high; his manner suddenly became harsh and intractable. Did Molotov believe that his masters in the Kremlin were being stupid? Did he think that the Soviet, as Marshall had uneasily wondered that it might do, should have gone along with the program and sabotaged from within?

As a practical matter, the proposal which went to the American Congress asked for an appropriation of seventeen billion dollars, to be spent in approximately four years beginning in 1948, for the purpose of bolstering the economies of all the European countries outside the Iron Curtain and of Turkey. Officially, the legislation established a "European Recovery Program" to be handled by an "Economic Cooperation Administration" but soon most Americans and Europeans were escaping the jumble of ERP and ECA to refer simply to the "Marshall Plan."

By early 1948 the Secretary of State had his own idea about what the program should be called. He told reporters he wished they would drop the term "Marshall Plan" or at least change it to "Marshall-Vandenberg Plan" and his attitude did not come solely from modesty. As soon as the Eightieth Congress began serious debate of ERP in January, 1948 the program ran into heavy weather. Some of the trouble came from the pressure on Congress of liberal or pro-

Communist groups who were following Henry Wallace in denouncing the whole idea as a war-breeding, anti-Soviet "Martial Plan." Far more serious difficulties were caused by Taft and a group of like-minded Senators. Usually without directly opposing the bill, they complained that it represented some more "global New Dealism" on the part of the State Department, called for a sum which threatened bankruptcy for the United States, and foolishly ignored Asia. The stronger the winds of criticism blew, the more Senator Arthur Vandenberg proved the dexterous skipper of ERP.

Using his full powers as chairman of the Senate Foreign Relations Committee, calling on all the sidewise techniques of a legislative artist, Vandenberg nudged the legislation ahead. So my distinguished colleague is disturbed by this or that aspect of the bill? Of course, of course. Vandenberg was ready for endless compromise—for any amendment that did not affect the substance of the legislation. No doubt seventeen billion dollars was a staggering sum of money; why not merely appropriate five billions for the first year, with an assurance to Europe that further sums would be forthcoming? The State Department certainly could do queer things; let the Marshall Plan be administered by an independent agency, headed by a man who would have to be confirmed by the Senate. And Asia—Vandenberg himself agreed that China was being neglected. The Policy Planning Staff stoutly maintained that any money for Chiang Kai-shek was just so many dollars thrown away, a sop to domestic political prejudices. The Senator was highly interested in domestic political prejudices. He induced President Truman to recommend, outside of ERP, 338 millions in economic help and 125 millions in military aid for Chiang Kai-shek.

Before long Vandenberg acquired a persuasive ally, the impatient men in the Kremlin. In February, 1948 a Communist coup sucked Czechoslovakia under the

Iron Curtain, recalling to the least-informed Americans memories of Munich, 1938. Russian moves to the north made it look as if Finland were next. The Italian elections were coming on April 18 and newspapers in the United States agreed that the Communists were at least a fifty-fifty bet to win.

President Truman appeared before his press conferences making little pretense of chipperness. His faith in ultimate world peace, the President admitted, was being shaken. Reports went out that Secretary of Defense James Forrestal was meeting in Key West with heads of the Army, Navy, and Air Force to iron out their roles in the event of fighting. Two Republican members of the House, Charles Kersten of Wisconsin and Richard Nixon of California, expressed an attitude rapidly spreading in Congress. They presented a resolution giving "solemn warning to the conspiracy in the Politburo that any further step of aggression, internal or external, will be actively resisted by every means at our disposal."

Throughout the country war fears ran rampant. In New England, "wait until the Russians hit" and "when we fight Stalin" were becoming clichés. In Atlanta, friends were greeting each other with: "Well, boy, break out that old uniform." A Seattle newspaper summarized: "Generally, people here have come to feel that war is very definitely on the way."

A Chicago reporter caught the national mood in its fuller nuances. "Cold fear is gripping people hereabouts. They don't talk much about it. But it's just as real and chilling as the current 11-degree weather. Fear of what? Most people don't know exactly. It's not fear of Russia alone. For most think we could rub Joe's nose in the dirt. It's not fear of Communism in this country. Few think there are enough Commies here to put it over. It's not fear of the atom bomb. For most think we still possess a monopoly. But it does seem to be a reluctant conviction that these three relentless forces are prowling the earth and that somehow they are bound to mean trouble for us. Not many months ago, these forces were something to be thought about only in off moments—like when you turned in some commentator by mistake. . . . But all winter, confidence in peace has been oozing away. With the Czech coup, it practically vanished."

On March 1 Vandenberg rose from his second-row desk in the Senate. Observers noted a special poignance: the desk where Vandenberg stood once belonged to Senator William E. Borah, the foreign-affairs powerhouse in a day when Americans could, with a contemptuous toss of Borah's mane, tell the world to go to hell any way it chose. This time the speech contained no histrionics, only the dogged practicality that had marked the preliminary discussions of the Marshall Plan. The legislation, Vandenberg said, "seeks peace and stability for free men in a free world. It seeks them by economic rather than by military means. . . . It recognizes the grim truth—whether we like it or not—that American self-interest, national economy, and national security are inseparably linked with these objectives." And every word Vandenberg spoke only underlined the unspoken argument. Indefinite Communist expansion would mean atomic war; what sounder way to halt the expansion than by revivifying the economic life of that crucial area, western Europe?

As Vandenberg finished, dozens of Senators lined up to shake his hand. His compromises and the mounting Communist threat had undercut any serious blockage to the Marshall Plan. The remaining critics had no broad-based support, no powerful leaders; Senator Taft was now definitely saying that he would vote yes. Working against the deadline set by the Italian elections, the Senate met in night sessions and passed the bill by the resounding majority of sixty-nine to seventeen. The House, with a brief scuffle occasioned by an attempt to include fascist Spain in ERP, quickly followed suit. On April 2, 1948, the Marshall Plan was law with no vital change from the form in which it was first presented to Congress.

So the Administration's basic foreign-policy proposal was turning into fact. Its domestic recommendations were being almost totally ignored. In defeat and in victory, the Administration of Harry Truman, after all the confusion of the early period, was taking on a coherent shape. The post-1946 policies for home or abroad were certainly not conservatism in any sense which Americans had been giving to the word. They carried no tone of Taftism and, at least in their domestic phases, were sharply antagonistic to most business thinking. The Truman programs scarcely resembled liberalism of the 1930's; the dawn-world plannings of Harry Hopkins would have been jarringly out of place amid the restrained vistas of Clark Clifford or George Kennan's wary pursuit of reality. The man named to administer the Marshall Plan, Paul Hoffman, may have been a Republican but he was a faithful replica of the Administration he was serving in at least one respect. Asked for his political philosophy, Hoffman looked puzzled, then expressed the bankruptcy of the old terms: "I would describe myself as a Republican responsible—that means, on some things I'd be liberal and on other things, well—something else."

Shortly after the Marshall Plan was first publicly announced, in July, 1947, the semi-scholarly journal *Foreign Affairs* ran an article entitled "The Sources of Soviet Conduct" by "X." The newspapers quickly identified X as George Kennan and spread across the country the key phrase of the article, "the containment" of Communism. Containment—here, better than any other term, was the expression of the emerging Truman policies in foreign and domestic affairs. Abroad, Communist expansion was to be halted and prevented from affecting American life any further. At home, the basic outline of the America created by the Half-Century of Revolution was to be accepted, to be consolidated, to be carried forward only where some situation was out of line with the larger pattern. "We aim," Truman put it, "to keep America secured inside and out"—to contain a general situation which, the President was sure, could much more easily get worse than better.

It rained frogs, little green frogs in New Bedford, Massachusetts; citizens were sure they saw them. In Spokane, a butcher shop put up a sign: "Choice Meats —The Management Will Accept Cash, First Mortgages, Bonds, and Good Jewelry." The Midwest was telling the story about the farmer who went to the bank to pay off an eight thousand dollar mortgage, discovered that he had handed in ten thousand dollars, and said: "Oh, I must have brought the wrong bucket." The war scare of spring, 1948 was giving way to a relieved, flopdoodle summer.

Whether anybody cared or not—and the nation showed no signs of being transfixed—July brought the Presidential nominating conventions. The Republicans played it safe. Passing by Robert Taft, they named Thomas Dewey, an early friend of the Marshall Plan, an inbetweener on domestic affairs, a carefully disciplined political figure who, if he did not make friends easily, was without the Ohio Senator's formidable talent for making enemies. ("You have to know Dewey well to really dislike him," the faithless chose to put it.) The problem of the Democrats was not so easily solved. They already had their man in the White House and he emphatically wanted to stay there. The trouble was that in all the United States there was scarcely a politician, a pundit, or plain citizen who believed that Harry Truman could, by the remotest chance, under any foreseeable circumstances, win the election of 1948.

Powerful segments of opinion in the South, that usual bedrock of Democratic strength, were furious at the Administration for its civil-rights drive and by convention time were moving toward a third, "Dixiecrat Party." In the North, devotees of Henry Wallace were launching a "Progressive Party" and were talking—not without evidence—of taking at least six million votes from the Democratic column in crucial states. North or South, among Democrats or Republicans, the mention of Truman for another four years was likely to produce a sad shaking of the head if not a snort of protest.

A large part of the country had unquestionably developed a certain affection for the perky, obviously well-intentioned man in the White House. Yet there was a widespread feeling that, however much the President had pulled his Administration together, he was right when he remarked at the beginning of his term that he simply was not a big enough man for the job. The usually Democratic *St. Louis Post-Dispatch* spoke the attitude in explaining why it would support Dewey against a ticket headed by Truman. The newspaper, its editorial ran, liked Truman personally and did not particularly like either Dewey or the policies he would probably push. The *St. Louis Post-Dispatch* simply believed that the President had proved he lacked "the stature, the vision, the social and economic grasp, or the sense of history required to lead this nation in a world crisis."

As the Democratic convention came on, with Harry Truman announcing that it would be Harry Truman on the first ballot, leaders from all wings of the party frantically sought to escape him. Eisenhower, "Ike" Eisenhower, the war hero with a glowing smile, admired by multitudes who were sure he was an instinctive liberal and by other millions just as positive of his bedrock conservatism—Democratic politicians clustered around the honey like so many busy, contriving bees. The previous January, the General had spoken a firm, polite no. The week before the convention he repeated the no, more firmly and less politely. Still a crazy-quilt coalition of big-city bosses, New Dealish politicos, and Southern machine leaders labored away.

Claude Pepper, the ultra-New Deal Senator from Florida, sent off a telegram designed to permit Eisenhower to remove his noes without saying yes. Pepper wired the General his "opinion" that the convention should draft Eisenhower as a totally "national" candidate, permitting him to write his own platform, freeing him of all partisan obligations, and instructing the Democratic Party to confine its own activities to Congressional and local contests. At the end of the telegram was the master gimmick: "I neither expect nor desire either an acknowledgement or a reply." Back from Eisenhower came quite a reply: "No matter under what terms, conditions, or premises a proposal might be couched, I would refuse to accept the nomination."

Boss Frank Hague read the Eisenhower telegram and crunched out his cigar. "Truman, Harry Truman. Oh my God."

The Dewey "Victory Special" rolled across the country. The GOP campaign was efficient, trimly, calmly efficient. It was, even more so, magisterial, the movements of a President-elect who somehow had to go through this unseemly business of a campaign. The Victory Special engaged in no grubby vote-chasing; many stops which could easily have been fitted into the schedule were omitted. When the speeches came, they were in cathedral tones, conspicuously above any quarreling over issues. Never, from the Hudson to the Sacramento, did Dewey attack Truman by name. Rarely did he stoop to anger. "We know the kind of government we have now," Dewey would say more in sorrow than in umbrage. "It's tired. It's confused. It's coming apart at the seams. . . . It cannot give this nation what it needs most—what is the real issue of this election—unity."

At the height of the campaign, the Republican candidate hit at a few brass tacks. He spoke of his "pride" in the Republican-controlled Eightieth Congress. He talked a bit about foreign affairs, saying that during his first campaign for the Presidency in 1944 he had founded the bipartisan support which made the Marshall Plan possible. With something akin to indignation, Dewey described "the Administration which happens to be in power at the moment" as "weak" and "fumbling." But soon everything was back to the higher level. In the closing days of the campaign, the Dewey staff talked less of the final swing than of their "real concern"—what Harry Truman might do between now and Inauguration Day to hurt the country. The burdens of power already weighed on them so heavily that one newsman was moved to inquire: "How long is Dewey going to tolerate Truman's interference in the government?"

Clark Clifford was watching it all with a craftsman's eye and he was sure that there was only one strategy for Truman—attack, incessant, razzle-dazzle attack which would shake the political apathy of the country and direct attention to the Republican record on specific issues. "We were on our own 20-yard line," Clifford later recalled his analysis. "We had to be bold. If we kept plugging away in moderate terms, the best we could have done would have been to reach midfield when the gun went off. So we had to throw long passes—anything to stir up labor and the other mass votes." Once again the Presidential adviser was talking congenial doctrine to his boss. Naturally combative, smarting under the general assumption that he could never be elected President in his own right, Harry Truman was ready to throw the stadium at Dewey to win this contest.

Dewey campaigned six weeks; Truman, eight. Dewey covered sixteen thousand miles; Truman, twenty-two thousand. Dewey made 170 speeches; Truman, 271. Up and down the country the President went, clambering out of the confusion of his campaign train to talk to any crowd that gathered at 7 a.m. or 11 p.m. "Give 'em Hell, Harry," somebody would yell. And Harry Truman, the Missouri twang shrill, both hands pumping up and down, would pour it on in the roughest English spoken by a Presidential campaigner since frontier days. So Dewey was proud of the Republican Party? "Those fellows are just a bunch of old mossbacks . . . gluttons of privilege . . . all set to do a hatchet job on the New Deal." So Dewey was above mentioning Truman's name? "That's all a lot of hooey. And if that rhymes with anything, it's not my fault." So the real issue in the campaign was unity? Dewey "is talking mealy-mouthed political speeches. . . . I warn you . . . if you let the Republicans get control of the government, you will be making America an economic colony of Wall Street."

As the campaign went on, Truman concentrated heavily on one subject—"that notorious Republican Eightieth Congress." The Truman-Clifford strategy naturally climaxed in a hammering on the Republican Congressional record of 1947-8 as a consistent assault on the interests of ordinary Americans. More and more the President singled out groups and pointed to what "that bunch has done to hurt you."

To the industrial workers of the country, he said: "The Republicans . . . voted themselves a cut in taxes and voted you a cut in freedom. The 80th Republican Congress failed to crack down on prices. But it cracked down on labor all right." In the agricultural areas, Truman cried out how "they have already stuck a pitchfork in the backs of the farmers by cutting down on funds for crop storage. . . . I warn you, that's their real attitude. First the little cuts, then all price supports would be thrown out." Campaigning among the first- and second-generation voters of the urban centers, he flailed at the "insulting" refusal of the Eightieth Congress to admit DP's and the "anti-Semitic, anti-Catholic" immigration bill it passed. With respect to the Negro issue, Truman's campaign talk was relatively vague; there were those angry Southern states. But he underlined his civil-rights program in unspoken ways—most notably, by being the first major-party candidate for the Presidency who really stumped Harlem.

The night after the Harlem rally Truman appeared at Madison Square Garden in New York City. Dewey was on his final leisurely swing, touching a number of places where the President had already campaigned. The Madison Square Garden speech, the traditional written-out address winding up the Democratic campaign, was a little stodgy, a little weary. Near its end, Truman deviated from the prepared text. He had made this point before, day after day, publicly and privately, from his deepest personal conviction. Now he had another way of saying it.

The President's tone was grave. "I have had a consultation with the White House physician," he began and the crowd stirred uneasily.

"I told him," Truman speeded up his delivery, "that I kept having this feeling that wherever I go there's somebody following behind me. The White House physician told me not to worry. He said: 'You keep right on your way. There's one place where that fellow's not going to follow you and that's into the White House.' "

"Mighty game little scrapper," people said. "Too bad he doesn't have a chance." Elmo Roper had long since stopped taking public-opinion polls; two months before election day science declared the election over. Leading Democratic politicians, students of another science, were publicly offering their Washington homes for sale. Bookies quoted odds they would have refused on Joe Louis at his prime—fifteen-, twenty-, even thirty-to-one. Families planned an early election evening, until nine or so when President-elect Dewey would make his victory statement, and then off to a good night's rest.

Until nine or so Truman was leading in the popular and in the electoral votes. This was as expected, the radio commentators explained; wait until the rural returns came in. By ten o'clock a good many of the farm areas were reporting. The figures were not particularly Republican, while Truman went on rolling up majorities in the cities. The voices of the commentators were as authoritative as ever; wait until there were enough rural returns to show the inevitable pattern. The *Chicago Tribune*, no journal for shilly-shallying, was out on the streets with its extra:

DEWEY DEFEATS TRUMAN

Some people stayed up. Ten-thirty, eleven, eleven-thirty—chairs hunched closer to the radio, conversation was shushed, somebody would dart off to telephone and wake up a friend. The Dixiecrats were carrying only three or four states in the South and Henry Wallace was showing no real strength except in California and New York. The Truman majorities in the cities remained substantial and the farm areas were reporting slim Dewey victories or Democratic sweeps. H. V. Kaltenborn of NBC, the voice that had reported Munich, 1938 to America, the voice that had been news incarnate to a large part of a generation, kept saying, crackling and definitive, wait until the full rural returns come in. But the litany was breaking. On the ABC network George Gallup was a shattered man. He could only sigh and tell his audience: "I just don't know what happened."

Later and later the lights burned in living-rooms. It was clear that Truman was holding most of the South and a sizeable bloc of Midwestern and Western states. Would this weird night end without a majority of electoral votes for either the Republican or the Democrat, in the use of a long-forgotten Constitutional provision which gives the selection of the President to the House of Representatives under such circumstances? Would it end—and here the commentators broke into shrill incredulity—in the election of Harry Truman? By dawn the issue was California, New York, or Ohio; the electoral votes of any one of these states would push the Democrat over. New York, with Wallace taking a half-million votes from Truman, went Republican. California and Ohio swung crazily back and forth, with majorities of fifteen hundred this way, twenty-five hundred the other, in states that had well over two million voters apiece.

At breakfast time the Ohio result became definite. After a long twenty minutes, Harry Truman came out of his Kansas City hotel suite. The strut of the bantam cock was gone; the eyes were misty. The President and President-elect of the United States walked slowly into the lobby, arm-in-arm with his brother Vivian, and reporters overheard him whisper tremulously: "I just hope—I hope so much I am worthy of the honor."

Up from the country came a long loud guffaw. Even many Dewey voters went about grinning at strangers, gathering in scoffing clusters with friends. The people of the United States had made fools of all the experts. They had knocked down the smooth and the smug and lifted up the shaggy, spunky underdog. They had brought off the most spectacular upset in American political history. But in those first half-real hours after Ohio came in, nobody had the slightest idea how in the world the Truman victory had happened.

Only gradually, as the experts finished their mouthfuls of crow and studied the situation, did the pattern become clear. The turnout of voters was much heavier than the political apathy at the time of the conventions would have indicated; Truman's shock tactics did not fail. So far as those who voted were concerned, the public-opinion polls had been right up to a point. Until very late in the campaign—when the pollsters had stopped taking soundings—the country was overwhelmingly ready to remove Truman. But then a vast swing had set in—a swing which came so late thousands said they had walked into the polling places intending to vote Republican and ended up casting a Democratic ballot.

To a small extent the swing was involved with foreign policy. Here Truman plainly represented the Marshall Plan and full-measured steps to check Communism. Whatever Dewey's personal position on ERP had been, the public mind inevitably associated him to some degree with the Republican Taftite reluctance to act vigorously abroad. To a much greater extent, the swing came from domestic concerns. The Truman-Clifford strategy had projected the President into everyone's view as the enthusiastic exponent of the Half-Century of Revolution. Dewey, rarely discussing specific issues and expressing general approval of the Eightieth Congress, easily appeared a Taft without the Senator's willingness to say what he meant. The very personalities of the candidates and the nature of their campaigns underlined the public impression of their attitudes toward the workaday hopes and worries of ordinary people. "I kept reading about that Dewey fellow," said Charles Crenshaw of New Lebanon, Ohio, "and the more I read the more he reminded me of one of those slick ads trying to get money out of my pocket. Now Harry Truman, running around and yipping and falling all over his feet—I had the feeling he could understand the kind of fixes I get into."

Millions of farmers were like the citizens of Guthrie County, Iowa, which had turned in regular Republican majorities even during the 1930's and proceeded to go Democratic in 1948. "I talked about voting for Dewey all summer," one Guthrie farmer put it, "but when voting time came, I just couldn't do it. I remembered . . . all the good things that have come to me under the Democrats." Scores of urban communities resembled Arlington, a suburb of Boston, which startled itself by giving Truman a majority. "I own a nice house," an Arlington resident remembered his thinking as he made up his mind how to vote, "I have a new car and am much better off than my parents were. Why change?" A breakdown of the national figures showed that basically Truman won because he received overwhelming backing from labor, Negroes, and most white minority groups, and at least fifty-fifty support from the farmers and all of the newer middle classes—precisely the segments of the population which had benefited most from the Half-Century of Revolution.

Senator Taft sat shaking his head incredulously. "I don't care how the thing is explained. It defies all common sense for the country to send that roughneck ward politician back to the White House." The election did defy sense in Robert Taft's world, where men worried over established patterns of American life and measured the manner of politicians by the yardstick of the big houses on the hill. But this was an America of Jackie Robinson's aspiring cleats and Communist lunges around the world and farmers proudly watching their sons off to college. A nation in economic and social upsurge could have its own defensiveness— against Communism abroad and against Taftism at home. The millions eager to preserve their new-found comforts and opportunities had felt their way, through all their political apathy, through all their misgivings about Harry Truman, to pull the lever for the surest available leader of containment foreign and domestic.

America aim to contain Communism by aiding Europe economically = Marshall Plan

V

Year of Shocks

INAUGURAL DAY was just right. The weather experts predicted clouds and the skies were brilliantly clear. Harry Truman had an old-home breakfast with his buddies of Battery D ("I don't give a damn what you do after the Inaugural speech but I want you to stay sober until then") and went off to the huge, folksy celebration. For seven and a half miles, almost three hours of marching time, the parade stretched out. Up front was the honor guard from Battery D, at the tail end was a calliope tooting "I'm Just Wild about Harry," and in between were Montana cowboys and a trick dog from California and Missouri mules and a Virginia band that played "Dixie" over and over again, switched to a few bars of "Hail to the Chief" at the reviewing stand, then hurried back to "Dixie." The President grinned; he was almost always grinning and raising his paper coffee cup in acknowledgment of a salute. And the crowds, well over a million men, women, and children, yelled "Hi, Harry," " 'Ray Harry," as if they were welcoming the local boy who had hit the big one out of the park.

When the car of the Dixiecrat candidate, Governor Strom Thurmond, approached the reviewing stand, Truman suddenly discovered that he had something very important to say which required turning to the man beside him. A Presidential guest, Tallulah Bankhead, hardly a woman for indirection, let out a foghorn of boos. It was all quite appropriate. On orders from the White House, for the first time in American history Negroes were invited to the top social events of the Inaugural. Even some of the attempts at unofficial Jim Crow were defeated. When the New York delegation arrived at its hotel, rooms were assigned to the whites but refused the Negroes. New York City's Deputy Commissioner of Housing, J. Raymond Jones, insisted that all or none of the delegates would stay at the hotel. The Negroes were registered and immediately telephone trouble developed in their rooms. Deputy Commissioner Jones had an idea. Noting that the owners of the Washington hotel also controlled New York establishments, he mentioned that a reinspection of Manhattan hotels was then in progress. Suddenly all the telephone difficulties disappeared. The attacks on racial segregation, Walter White, head of the NAACP, enthused, "seemed part and parcel of an Inauguration which had about it a special tone of recognizing the new place of all ordinary Americans."

President Truman had a fresh name for his domestic policy now, one he himself had invented in the exhilaration of the election victory. The "Fair Deal" he called his program in a State of the Union message delivered shortly before Inauguration Day, and Truman was soon explaining that the Fair Deal was "an extension of the New Deal; fundamentally, both mean greater economic opportunity for the mass of the people. There are differences, not of principle but of pace and personnel; the New Deal in the beginning, because of the times and its very newness, was marked by a tempo at times almost frenetic. Now there is a steady pace, without the gyrations of certain early New Dealers"—the certain New Dealers whom Truman continued to dismiss as "professional liberals."

The President's foreign policy introduced not only a new phrase but an additional idea. A number of friends had been saying to Truman that some State Department men were taking too much credit for the

Marshall Plan and that the Inaugural Address should direct the foreign policy spotlight back on the White House. Apart from any such consideration, the feeling was growing in the United States that the country should embark on a striking, world-wide offensive against Communism. A former reporter for the *Atlanta Journal*, Benjamin Hardy, now in the Public Affairs division of the State Department, agreed emphatically with this opinion, and he had a quite specific idea what the offensive should be. For a number of years the United States government had been giving technical assistance to Latin American countries and had been encouraging private investment which would speed industrialization. Why not expand this program to all non-Communist under-developed areas of the world?

Two weeks after the election of 1948, Hardy put his idea in a memorandum to his immediate superior in the State Department. Nothing happened. In mid-December Hardy wrote an expanded form of the memo, took it to a White House aide, George Elsey, and a great deal happened. When Clark Clifford prepared the next draft of the Inaugural Address, the speech revolved around four points in foreign policy and number four was Benjamin Hardy's proposal. Two State Department powers, Undersecretary Robert Lovett and the Counselor of the Department, Charles Bohlen, vigorously urged deleting the passage on the grounds that the idea was vague and premature. But Truman was enthusiastic and insisted that it remain in his address.

On Inaugural Day, the President's voice took on a special clipped emphasis as he read his fourth point. The United States was embarking on "a bold new program for making the benefits of our scientific advances and industrial progress available for the improvement and growth of under-developed areas." Much of the money, Truman plainly implied, would have to come from the United States government.

But so far as possible, the enterprise, financially and otherwise, would be co-operative and would be carried out through the United Nations. Private investment would be encouraged. "Our aim," the President summarized, "should be to help the free peoples of the world, through their own efforts, to produce more food, more clothing, more materials for housing, and more mechanical power to lighten their burdens. . . . Only by helping the least fortunate of its members to help themselves can the human family achieve the decent, satisfying life that is the right of all people."

"Point Four," the American newspapers immediately dubbed the proposal. In time peoples around the world would talk of *Punto Cuatro* or *Astle Charom* and American offices in Jordan received an enthusiastic letter addressed to "The Master of the Fourth Spot." Benjamin Hardy would be killed in a plane crash over Iran while serving as chief of the information division of an intensely active Point Four program. More than two thousand Americans from Seattle, Sioux City, and Birmingham were to be explaining sewage disposal or more efficient ways to teach reading in Tegucigalpa, Shiraz, and Djokjakarta, starting rivulets of change down unpredictable centuries. Before many years Jonathan Bingham, an enthusiastic administrator of the program, would write: "What makes Point 4 different from the ordinary concept of economic aid and makes it so infinitely appealing is that it emphasizes the distribution of knowledge rather than of money. Obviously there is not money enough in the world to relieve the suffering of the peoples of the underdeveloped areas, but . . . there is, for the first time in history, enough knowledge to do the job. This is indeed an exciting, even a revolutionary idea." All of this was to happen, but during the period immediately after the Truman Inaugural, Point Four was only a proposal slowly and laboriously turning into reality—so slowly that Congress did not pass its first Point Four legislation until May, 1950.

Meanwhile there was today, the today of jobs and Communists and grocery lists. Less than a month after the Inaugural ceremonies, Americans knew a strange sensation. Prices were going down. The nickel beer returned to Manhattan, the $1.99 shirt to Kansas City, and a Des Moines newspaper discovered that a basket of groceries which cost $4.19 in 1948 could be bought now for $3.29. Here and there people rubbed their eyes at old-fashioned price wars. In Los Angeles police were called to handle the crowds when steak dinners went down to sixty-five cents, women's panties to a quarter, and pie à la mode to one cent. With the deflation came the postwar's first real unemployment—some four million by the summer of 1949.

The more emphatic because of the threatened depression, President Truman urged the enactment of a long list of domestic measures modeled after his demands on the Eightieth Congress. During 1949 the Eighty-first Congress passed a comprehensive public-housing program, revised upward Social Security benefits and extended the coverage, increased the minimum wage, tightened price supports for farmers, and expanded programs for soil conservation, flood control, rural electrification, and public power. But the Congress huffed and puffed and did nothing about the most dramatized issues of the day—civil rights, Taft-Hartley, aid to education, and health insurance. The "ho-hum session," the more eager Fair Dealers were calling the Eighty-first Congress as 1949 ended.

The most important aspect of the Eighty-first Congress lay precisely in what it did not do; it made no significant attacks on the Half-Century of Revolution. The most important aspect of Fair Dealism in general was not what it did but what it threatened. It hung over business, speeding up still more the tendency of industrialists to try to outbid the welfare state by welfare capitalism; over the Republicans, causing even Senator Taft to view more kindly social measures; over the South, bringing a rash of voluntary moves to open educational and economic opportunities to Negroes lest civil-rights legislation should force them open still more widely.

The recession of 1949 halted well short of a depression. Supports on farm prices and the battery of social legislation prevented the deflation and unemployment from setting off a chain reaction; increased military expenditures helped; the Administration resorted to some hasty deficit spending. By the fall of 1949 the economic decline ended. The country was headed back to mounting prices and mounting incomes, high employment, and wide opportunities for climbing the ladder of status—back to more successful operation of the postwar pattern of containment domestic.

Just as surely the containment of Communism in Europe was working. The Marshall Plan did its job; Italy and France skidded past Communism and the economies of all the western European nations swung upward. In the spirit of the Marshall Plan, a series of moves brought the countries of western Europe into closer economic, political, and military relationships. Most importantly, in March, 1949 ten nations of northwestern Europe, Canada, and the United States signed the pact creating the North Atlantic Treaty Organization, under which the signatory countries began coordination of their military organizations and agreed to joint action in the event that any one of the nations was attacked by Russia. By the end of 1949 western Europe showed signs of once again becoming a region able to support itself and able and willing to resist Red blandishments if not Red armies.

It was all fine—and it was all terrible. During 1949 containment foreign might be working effectively in Europe and plans might be forming to project it around the world through Point Four programs; containment domestic might be continuing the miracle of America's social revolution. But for most Americans, Communism as a world force, far from being contained, seemed a much greater, a much more insidious menace than ever before.

Year after year the Chinese Communist armies had been advancing from their northern bases. Year after year the American newspapers had been telling of the shouts going up for Mao Tse-tung, he of the peasant's squatness and guile, incessantly smoking or chewing on melon seeds, unceremoniously stripping himself to the waist in hot weather, for

> *Chairman Mao who can be compared to the*
> *sun in the east,*
> *Which shines over the world so brightly, so*
> *brightly.*
> *Heigh-ai-yo, heigh-heigh-heigh-yo.*
> *Without Chairman Mao, how can there be*
> *peace?*
> *Heigh-ai-yo.*

Late 1948 had brought more ominous reports. Mao's armies, having overrun Manchuria, were pushing southward. January, 1949 and Chiang Kai-shek's Nationalist government fled to Formosa. May, 1949 and the Reds had swept all the way to Shanghai.

A number of Americans were exercised. In particular a group of Republican politicians kept up a loud outcry to do something. But China was far, very far away. American newspapers had been carrying news of wars and civil wars in China for eighteen monotonous years, ever since the Japanese invaded in 1931. Much more clear-cut and dramatic events were happening inside the United States and across the Atlantic. Suddenly, on August 5, 1949, every newspaper, radio station, and television outlet in the nation directed garish floodlights on the Far East. A "White Paper" of the Department of State was officially announcing that China, vast China, had fallen to the Communist armies.

The preface to the White Paper was a strong defense of American policy by Dean Acheson, who had taken over as Secretary of State from the ailing George Marshall. The Truman Administrations, Acheson emphasized, had given large-scale aid to Chiang Kai-shek since V-J—more than two billion dollars in grants and credits, not counting more than a billion dollars in surplus American war stock which had been left with the Nationalists for $232,000,000. "It has been urged that relatively small amounts of additional aid—military and economic—to the National Government would have enabled it to destroy communism in China. The most trustworthy military, economic, and political information available to our Government does not bear out this view. . . . The only alternative open to the United States was full-scale intervention in behalf of a Government which had lost the confidence of its own troops and its own people."

Acheson put the blame for the fall of China squarely on the Chiang Kai-shek government, which he described as corrupt, inefficient, and utterly purblind to the just aspirations of the masses of Chinese people. "The unfortunate but inescapable fact is that the ominous result of the civil war in China was beyond the control of the government of the United States. Nothing that this country did or could have done within the reasonable limits of its capabilities could have changed that result. . . . It was the product of internal Chinese forces, forces which this country tried to influence but could not."

The Acheson explanation was blunt; it was, at least in some important respects, persuasive. Yet no explanation could explain away the fact that China was gone, that with her fall the closely linked Communist leaders of Russia and China ruled almost a quarter of the earth's surface and more than a quarter of its people, and that, as the White Paper itself pointed out, grave danger now existed that Mao's regime would "lend itself to the aims of Soviet Russian imperialism." From one end of the United States to the other the shocked question was asked: Had Communism been checked in Europe only to spread rapidly in Asia?

Just forty-nine days after the White Paper, in the late morning of September 23, reporters were summoned to the big walnut desk of Presidential Press Secretary Charles Ross. "Close the doors," Ross said. "Nobody is leaving here until everybody has this statement." Then he passed out mimeographed sheets of paper. Merriman Smith of the United Press was the first to read enough to catch the gist. Whistling in astonishment, he edged for the door. In a moment all the reporters were tearing through the lobby, smashing the nose of a stuffed deer on their dash to pressroom telephones. The President of the United States had announced: "We have evidence that within recent weeks an atomic explosion occurred in the U.S.S.R."

Having filed their stories, the newsmen hurried to the front of the White House, hoping to question Cabinet members who had just been meeting with the President. Secretary of Defense Louis Johnson was the only one who had not disappeared and the reporters clutched at him with questions as he made his way to the waiting automobile.

Had any change been ordered in the disposition of American armed forces since this fact was learned? No, Johnson said serenely.

Was there more to the situation than had been revealed? No, Johnson replied smilingly.

The Secretary of Defense was smiling and serene throughout and as he got into his car he said: "Now, let's keep calm about this. Don't overplay the story."

The whole Truman Administration labored hard to keep the report from setting off hysteria and most news media followed suit. In his original announcement, President Truman sought to soften the news by stressing that "the eventual development of this new force by other nations was to be expected." Most commentators and editorialists underlined the point; they also emphasized that it was one thing to have a bomb or two and quite another to be able to produce them in large quantities or to deliver them where they would hurt. Yet playing down the Soviet bomb was even more difficult than cushioning the impact of the fall of China. Since Hiroshima almost all American scientists had predicted that the Russians would not be able to perfect the weapon until 1952, and some had not expected the Soviet to succeed before 1955. Here was the fact at least three years ahead of schedule, stripping the American people of whatever security they had felt behind their atomic stockpile, jangling nerves still more because the timetable of the trusted scientists had been wrong.

In Chicago Harold C. Urey, the Nobel Prize leader in atomic research, managed to phrase what so many Americans were feeling. He was "flattened" by the announcement, Urey told reporters. "There is only one thing worse than one nation having the atomic bomb—that's two nations having it."

Weekly, daily, the furor over Communism mounted. The trial of the top Communist Party leaders in the United States went ahead while Judith Coplon was trying to persuade another jury that she had trysts with Valentin Gubitchev for love, not to hand over Justice Department secrets. Congressional investigators, FBI investigators, State Department investigators, Bureau of Entomology and Plant Quarantine investigators thrashed through Washington. At an Omaha businessmen's luncheon, a speaker told a story about an Irishman who insisted on being buried in a Church of England cemetery because "that's the last place the Divil would look for an Irishman." Officials of the Catholic War Veterans who were present got an idea, opined that the last place anybody would look for

Communists would be within the Roman Catholic fold, and started looking. Harold Taylor, president of Sarah Lawrence College, noting the way that charges of Communism were being used to beat down any independence in thinking, got off a definition of a patriotic American as "one who tells all his secrets without being asked, believes we should go to war with Russia, holds no political view without prior consultation with his employer, does not ask for increases in salary or wages, and is in favor of peace, universal military training, brotherhood, and baseball." And month after month during 1949, goadingly, explosively, there was the case of Alger Hiss.

The case had been news as early as August, 1948 when the ex-Communist, Whittaker Chambers, standing in the glare of the House Un-American Activities Committee, first publicly accused Hiss of being a member of the Communist Party at least from 1934 to 1938. The succeeding months brought sensational developments but the affair as yet had little of the momentous about it. Chambers had produced nothing to back his charge except his own thoroughly tainted word. The $75,000 libel suit which Hiss lodged against Chambers seemed the natural act of an innocent man. The President of the United States was dismissing the whole series of Congressional investigations as a political red herring—designed, Truman told his press conference two days after Chambers's first public accusation of Hiss, to distract public attention from the failure of the Republican-controlled Eightieth Congress to cope with inflation. (The President also made a formal statement at the press conference which explained in a different way why he believed the committees could be brushed aside—he said that they were not uncovering anything which was not known to the New York grand jury investigating Communism or to the FBI. But it was the phrase of utter dismissal, red herring, which was left in the public mind.)

After the Democratic victory in November, 1948,

many newspapers carried reports that the House Un-American Activities Committee would probably let the Hiss case lapse, indeed that the Committee itself might disappear. After all, the Democrats now controlled the House, two of the seven members of the Committee had been defeated, and Representative J. Parnell Thomas, the chairman at the time of the Chambers charges, was under indictment for having padded his Congressional payroll.

As 1948 ended, the affair suddenly took a far more serious turn. Whittaker Chambers broadened his charge: Alger Hiss had not only been a member of the Communist Party but had been part of an espionage ring in the 1930's, taking home confidential documents to be copied so that Chambers could pass them on for Soviet eyes. Chambers also produced evidence to back both his old and his new accusations. He turned over copies of classified State Department papers; some of them, he said, were in Hiss's handwriting and some were typed on a machine that had belonged to Hiss. Then Chambers took two House Committee investigators to his Maryland farm. He led the way to a pumpkin patch, reached into a pumpkin that had been scooped out and carefully restored, and pulled forth a wad of microfilm of more classified State Department documents.

After the news of the pumpkin microfilm, a reporter asked at the White House press conference: "Mr. President, do you still feel, as you did in August, that the investigation has aspects of being a red herring?"

Truman shot back: That's what the people thought [by re-electing him].

But, the reporter pressed, did the President still think so now that it had been revealed that the documents were stolen?

He certainly did, Truman replied. The committee was prosecuting nobody and was just seeking headlines.

Four days later, on December 15, 1948, a New York grand jury indicted Hiss for perjury on two counts—his statement that he had not passed "numerous secret, confidential and restricted documents" to Chambers and his statement that he had not seen Chambers after January 1, 1937. The most casual newspaper reader knew what these indictments really meant. The statute of limitations made it impossible to bring in an indictment for espionage. But morally and in common sense, Alger Hiss was being indicted for spying against the United States in behalf of the Soviet Union.

The first trial began in May, 1949 and ended in a hung jury; the second, taking up in November, wound on into January, 1950. No case in American history has offered more in sheer human interest. The lawyers were a fascinating study in contrasts. The testimony wound through a rococo variety. Witnesses discussed light serifs on typewriters, a rickety Model-A Ford, and prothonotary warblers. A tired swarthy man named Touloukian talked of Oriental rugs. Felix Frankfurter, Associate Justice of the Supreme Court, sat like an alert bird in the middle of the big witness chair, and handyman Raymond Sylvester Catlett, very black and very loyal to Hiss, shook his finger at the prosecutor and told him that when he was young he was "taught a lot of things, like God and about fellows like you." Always there were Whittaker Chambers and Alger Hiss, the brilliant editor of *Times vs.* the high-level New Dealer and head of the august Carnegie Endowment for International Peace, the accuser fat and heavy-lidded and brooding, the accused trim, handsome, and so urbane he seemed almost another spectator of the proceedings. One of these extraordinarily gifted men was lying—not the workaday lies of all men's lives but some gigantic contrivance built out of the shambles which Communism had brought to so many able minds in Western Civilization.

It was all fascinating and the Hiss case crowded American dinner-table conversations. But as 1949 went on the color and drama of the trials gave way to a different type of impact. Whittaker Chambers receded into the background; the specific testimony was less and less discussed. Even the figure of Alger Hiss the individual blurred. Everything was turning into Alger Hiss the symbol.

Looking back on the period, Chambers has written: "No feature of the Hiss Case is more obvious, or more troubling as history, than the jagged fissure, which it did not so much open as reveal, between the plain men and women of the nation, and those who affected to act, think and speak for them. It was not invariably, but in general, the 'best people' who were for Alger Hiss and who were prepared to go to almost any length to protect and defend him." That was the way it looked to the man who had left *Time* Magazine's world of glamour and power to fight out some lonely convulsion within himself, who, as Communist or anti-Communist, seemed desperately to need a sense that he was the chosen instrument to save the common man. Yet Chambers's picture, however overdrawn, points to a salient feature of the emerging Hiss symbolism.

Every casual fold of Hiss's Ivy League clothing, every modulation of his perfectly controlled voice spoke the fact that he was a product of genteel Baltimore, Harvard '29, a onetime member of a law firm with the name Choate in it, a New Dealer who was simultaneously in the Washington *Social Register*. He was being assailed by a man who, in appearance, in manner, and in fact, had risen through the demimonde of flophouse days in New Orleans, radical litterateuring, and self-confessed Communist spying. Established America did not entirely desert its beleaguered representative. A striking number of socialites and corporation executives who hated the New Deal, not to speak of Communism, doggedly defended the image of Alger Hiss the respectable success against the image of Whittaker Chambers the grubby upstart.

At the same time the Hiss symbolism was taking a quite different and far more important form. If part of established America rallied to the defense, the larger segment did not. Many upper-status Americans were joining with the general Taft Republican movement in finding a Devil. Irritated at the Half-Century of Revolution in domestic affairs, seeing the world crisis as the result of years of Democratic softness toward Communism, they turned Hiss into a representation of the whole period of New Deal—Fair Deal rule and identified the era with muddle-headedness and susceptibility to treason. On the other side of the political fence, Americans were finding a martyr, if not a hero. Many Democrats, particularly those of a New Dealish persuasion, proud of the Half-Century of Revolution, sure that Democratic foreign policy had been basically correct, associating New Dealism with the brilliance and social-mindedness Hiss had shown, also turned him into a representation of the Roosevelt-Truman years and pictured the achievements of that era as now under assault from dark reactionary forces. For both these groups, the Hiss symbolism provoked fierce, blinding emotions.

Distinguished university professors of the pro-Hiss school, ignoring the damaging evidence against Hiss, stated flatly that it was impossible for him to be guilty. Leading attorneys and businessmen of the anti-Hiss faction, disregarding Chambers's general record of unreliability, baldly stated that the case for conviction was incontrovertible. Members of both the pro- and anti-Hiss groups, anxious to bolster their prepossessions, took up rumors for which there was no visible evidence.

Alger Hiss was shouldering the blame for his wife, the pro-Hiss group would say. Or homosexuality explained any enigmas of the case. Or Hiss was a counter-Communist agent reporting directly to Franklin

Roosevelt; as a counter-agent, he was sworn never to reveal his role and with Roosevelt's death the only man who could reveal it for him was gone.

The anti-Hiss faction had its own rumors, equally satisfying and equally unsubstantiated. The Truman Administration had moved heaven and earth to block Hiss's indictment; if the accused ever testified fully, other important ex-New Dealers would be involved in espionage. The expenses of the Hiss defense, the talk went on, were being met by a huge fund raised by pro-Communists. The rumor most widespread in anti-Hiss circles was that the judge at the first trial, Justice Samuel H. Kaufman, was pro-Hiss. Shortly after the trial ended in a hung jury, Representative Richard Nixon declared that Kaufman's "prejudice for the defense and against the prosecution was so obvious . . . that the jury's 8-4 vote for conviction came frankly as a surprise to me."

Near the end of the second trial, the symbolism took, or was made to take, a heightened form. During most of Chambers's testimony in the first trial, a well-known psychiatrist, Dr. Carl Binger, had sat in the audience intently following the proceedings. The Hiss attorneys tried hard to put the doctor on the stand but Judge Kaufman, citing the fact that there was no precedent for psychiatic testimony in federal cases, refused the requests. The judge at the second trial, Henry W. Goddard, was ready to set a precedent. Any evidence bearing upon the credibility of Chambers, he ruled, belonged before the jury. The Hiss defense attorneys took on the air of men who were about to play their ace card.

Dr. Binger, tall and deep-voiced and very professional, started his testimony in a calmly authoritative way. He discussed "a condition known as psycho-pathic personality, which is a disorder of character, of which the outstanding features are behavior of what we call an amoral or an asocial and delinquent nature." The symptoms of this condition "include chronic, persistent, and repetitive lying; they include stealing; they include acts of deception and misrepresentation; they include alcoholism and drug addiction; abnormal sexuality, vagabondage; panhandling; inability to form stable attachments, and a tendency to make false accusations. May I say that in addition . . . there is a peculiar kind of lying known as pathological lying, and a peculiar kind of tendency to make false accusations known as pathological accusations, which are frequently found in the psychopathic personality." For most of a morning the physician testified in a way that connected a number of these symptoms with Whittaker Chambers. The purport of the psychiatrist's words was inescapable: All of Chambers's accusations against Hiss were pathological lies.

The man who rose to do the cross-questioning for the prosecution was six feet, four inches tall, with a longshoreman's shoulders, a full, florid face, and a king-size mustache straight out of the beer halls of the Gay Nineties. It was not hard to believe that Thomas Murphy was the grandson of a New York cop, the son of a clerk in the Water Supply, Gas, and Electricity Department, a brother of the "Fireman" Johnny Murphy who had been cherished by Yankee fans as their stoppingest relief pitcher. "He's terribly normal," Mrs. Murphy used to say of her "Murph," and Assistant United States Attorney Murphy began his cross-questioning of Dr. Binger every inch the simple, puzzled layman.

To try to get at something an ordinary man could understand, what about the witness's qualifications? Plain Mr. Murphy brought out that Dr. Binger had been a physician for thirty-five years but a "certified" psychiatrist for only three. To anyone who knew much about the field of psychiatry—to, for example, Mr. Murphy who had been giving long hours to studying the profession—it was hardly unusual to find psychiatrists who had practiced for years and were highly esteemed without such certification. The court-room Mr. Murphy let the apparent point sink in.

And what about psychoanalysis? Had Dr. Binger himself ever been psychoanalyzed?

The physician, trying to fend off the implications, replied: "Certainly. Nobody can do psychoanalysis without having been psychoanalyzed."

Plain Mr. Murphy was bothered. "Would you try, doctor, just to say 'yes' or 'no' and we will go much faster?"

Plain Mr. Murphy was particularly bothered by the fact that he had difficulty in getting the physician to give a simple yes or no answer to questions about whether any individual characteristic of Chambers was, in itself, evidence of a psychopathic personality. "I have to consider the totality of the picture," the doctor kept saying, his calm ruffled. "I can't isolate my judgment according to specific parcels of information." But plain Mr. Murphy kept wanting to know about those characteristics. Lying, for example. Surely there was some particular kind of lie that would serve as a symptom of an abnormal personality. What if a man told a lie to his wife to avoid an argument? Pretty normal, Dr. Binger thought. Telling children that there is a Santa Claus? No symptom, the doctor said, just a part of folk mythology. Well, would Dr. Binger say "that telling the children for many, many years that the stork brings the baby—would that indicate that the parent perhaps was manifesting a symptom of psychopathic personality?"

This was the doctor's moment. "If the parents believed the story," Dr. Binger said with a twinkle, "I would think it might," and everybody, including Judge Goddard, had a good laugh. But plain Mr. Murphy was still seeking a plain definition of abnormality. If the parent believed the stork story, he wanted to know, would that be a symptom *merely* of a psychopathic personality?

"Oh no; it would be a symptom of much else."

"You said it," remarked Mr. Murphy, taking back the day.

But to get on with the statements of this puzzling doctor—Dr. Binger had made a point of the way that Chambers on the stand seemed to establish little contact with his questioner and frequently looked up at the ceiling. Mr. Murphy allowed that he had kept a check on Dr. Binger and found that the physician looked toward the ceiling fifty-nine times in fifty minutes. "And I was wondering, doctor, whether that had any symptoms of a psychopathic personality?"

"Not alone," Binger said once again, his calm strained still more.

And those lies of Chambers's—the psychiatrist had counted up what he considered the real ones and arrived at a total of twenty lies over a period of thirty-six years. Doctor, Mr. Murphy wanted to know, what's par for a normal person? The physician expressed the thought that Mr. Murphy had more experience than himself as a basis for answering that question and Mr. Murphy was hurt, very conspicuously hurt, at this slur by a highbrow doctor on a simple American trying to do his duty. Plain Mr. Murphy went right on being conspicuously hurt until Judge Goddard explained, what was not too difficult to see, that the doctor was referring to Mr. Murphy's experience as a prosecutor.

Finally recovered, Mr. Murphy ranged through other symptoms Dr. Binger had found in Chambers. Take this business of bizarre behavior—this bringing up the fact that Chamber had hid the documents in a pumpkin. Was that so queer? Didn't the colonial Founding Fathers put the Connecticut charter in the Hartford oak—were the Founding Fathers bizarre, doctor? Dr. Binger made it testily plain that he did not believe the Founding Fathers were bizarre. Well, Mr. Murphy went on, you say normal people put things in banks for safekeeping; didn't the mother of Moses hide him in the bulrushes?

Then, too, what about personal sloppiness as a symptom? Had the doctor ever seen Albert Einstein walking around in his sweat shirt? Or Will Rogers, Heywood Broun, and Thomas Edison? Was sloppiness really evidence of a psychopathic personality, doctor?

No, not alone, he never said it was, Dr. Binger snapped, his calm completely shattered.

Plain Mr. Murphy was more and more bewildered. He would try to make sense out of all this a different way. The psychiatrist had stressed the fact that Chambers rarely answered questions directly and often prefaced his statement with expressions like "it must have been" or "it could have been." Well, Mr. Murphy was no brilliant doctor but by golly he could count. And during the weekend he and his assistants had gone through 717 pages of official transcript and found that Chambers had used phrases like these a total of ten times. Would the doctor like to know how often Alger Hiss used similar expressions? The doctor showed no overwhelming desire to know. But Mr. Murphy told him anyhow: 158 times in 590 pages of testimony.

Plain Mr. Murphy was at his wit's end. He would presume to ask the learned doctor only a few more questions. Dr. Binger didn't know Chambers, did he? And the psychiatrist said he had analyzed the witness partly from his writings—especially Franz Werfel's *Class Reunion*, which Chambers had translated and which the physician intimated had provided Chambers with a morbid model for his attack on Hiss. Mr. Murphy shook his head in utter befuddlement. Did Dr. Binger find a model in *Bambi*, which Chambers had also translated?

"Who's the Psycho Now?" the headlines asked. Plain Mr. Murphy, who had never lost a case or an appeal in seven years as a government lawyer, had shown why with his tour de force; however unfair to psychiatry he may have been, he had plodded his way brilliantly to trump the defense's ace card. The Murphy handling of Binger had the larger effect of

sharpening the Hiss symbolism to a far more provoca-
tive point. Now the images of Hiss and anti-Hiss were
not only New Dealism *vs.* Taftism in domestic affairs,
a difference in foreign policies, a clash between two
general ways of looking at public problems. More than
ever, the conflict took on an aura of the highbrow and
the heretical *vs.* God-fearing, none-of-your-highfalu-
tin-nonsense, all-American common sense.

And the Hiss symbolism was heightening as most
Americans reached a decision on Alger Hiss the man.
By the close of 1949—nearly the end of the second
trial—it was clear that Chambers was hardly a saint
and that Hiss had led a distinguished career. Neither
fact was half as compelling as the battered old Wood-
stock typewriter sitting in the courtroom—a typewriter which both sides agreed had once belonged
to Hiss and which the FBI categorically stated had
typed many of the classified State Department documents handed over to Chambers. Fervid devotees of
the pro- or anti-Hiss images might go on insisting that
Hiss was a total martyr or a total scoundrel. For most
Americans the reaction was different—a growing belief that Hiss had carried on espionage activities with
Chambers and with this belief a mounting sense of
questioning. If a man of Hiss's background, achievements, and reputation for character had spied for Communism, who could be trusted? If the New Deal had
promoted Hiss, if President Truman had continued
to call committee activities which were exposing him
a red herring and a good many New Dealish people
went on backing him even after the unfavorable evidence was coming in, if the whole defense of Hiss led
down murky paths, how comfortable could an ordinary citizen feel in the middle of it all?

How comfortable indeed—1949 was proving the
most nerve-racking of all the disquieting periods the
United States had known since V-J. Some years in a
nation's history blur into a long-continuing story.
Some mark a fateful turn. There was, for example, a

period somewhere before 1776 when a strategic number of Americans passed over from thinking like colonists to thinking like rebels. There was a period too when the North and the South decided to draw the sword. The year 1949 was such a turning point. August, the concession of China to the Communists; September, the announcement of the Soviet atom bomb; August and September and the months before and after, the explosive questions raised by the Hiss case—1949 was a year of shocks, shocks with enormous catalytic force.

The shocks were hurtling a good deal of the nation into a new mood. The emotions forming the mood were the more powerful because they tied back into feelings deep in the postwar, deep in the whole modern history of the United States.

Summation ↑

VI

The Great Conspiracy

THE SHOCKS of 1949 loosed within American life a vast impatience, a turbulent bitterness, a rancor akin to revolt. It was a strange rebelliousness, quite without parallel in the history of the United States. It came not from any groups that could be called the left, not particularly from the poor or the disadvantaged. It brought into rococo coalition bankers and charwomen, urban priests and the Protestant farmlands of the Midwest, longtime New Deal voters and Senator Robert A. Taft.

Most directly the restiveness resulted from the foreign policy of the Truman Administration. As the Democratic leadership moved after 1946 to meet the Soviet menace, it broke in a jarring way with deep-seated American attitudes. During all the previous decades, the United States had known its internationalist and its isolationist phases but it had never really departed from certain bedrock assumptions. The business of America was America. It was to get on with this business without dependence on other nations and without interference from them. At times, of course, there would be an interruption when some foreign nation, acting in a way that foreigners persist in doing, went berserk. Then the matter was to be settled by diplomacy or war but whatever the technique, quickly and finally.

We are a people whose history has made us the land

of the swift, total solution, brought about by ourselves alone. We faced a wilderness; we hacked it down. We were vexed by slavery; we cut it out of our system. We fought Britishers, Mexicans, Spaniards, Germans, Germans plus Japanese, and licked them all with short shrift. No wonder our movies have a happy ending, and in ninety minutes. No wonder we are the only country in the world which has produced a popular saying like: "The difficult we do immediately, the impossible takes a little time."

Americans were the more inclined to believe in the quick, total solution of any world problem because they were sure that the world was no great problem anyhow. Republicans and Democrats, New Dealers and anti-New Dealers, they tended to assume a general international trend, a trend so certain that it took on the cast of a law of history. Human beings everywhere and at all times, the law ran, seek peace and democracy, want to get ahead to a farm of their own or a house on the right side of the tracks, prefer to do it all gradually and with a decent regard for the amenities. The history of man is consequently a long slow swing toward a world consisting entirely of middle-class democracies. Once in a while, the trouble comes when some country falls under an evil leader, who forces it along a road forbidden by the law of history. Then it is only necessary to remove the leader and let things flow back along their proper path. (Quite characteristically, the United States fought its wars not in the name of fighting a whole people but against a wicked leader or group of leaders—the tyrannical King George III, the militaristic Kaiser, the brutal fascist dictators.) If the natural swing of the world was toward peaceful, democratic middle-class ways, how could foreign policy be a problem requiring anything except the occasional surgical removal of an unnatural growth?

The containment policy which the Truman Administration adopted in 1947 represented the first fundamental break with these attitudes. Dean Acheson, George Kennan, and the other chief foreign-policy advisers of the President assumed no comforting law of history. Instead they were reconciled to a situation in which history, with a mocking toss of her head, seemed off on a roar with shaggy and disreputable suitors. The East-West clash, as they saw it, came fundamentally from a long-running, world-wide social revolution. They doubted whether the resulting problems could ever be totally solved; they were positive that they could not be solved quickly. They were not even sure that the United States should try to solve them by simply smashing Communism because they were plagued by the feeling that the Red surge represented, in a viciously distorted way, the legitimate aspirations of millions for independence, social reform, and self-respect.

Containment was to be no swift, clean-cut process; it was to move along its complicated path for at least a decade, probably over many decades. The containers relied principally on the long-range effects of economic aid to non-Communist countries, not on the more direct method of arming the free world and certainly not on any hope of destroying Communism by war. They promoted co-existence, with its implication that Communism would be powerful for an indefinite period. They showed no faith that America could solve the problem alone, and sought to bolster the American position by strong support of the United Nations and by general coalition diplomacy.

As soon as the containment policy emerged in 1947, the signs of restlessness with it were plain. Did the container insist that millions of men and women, far from moving gradually toward middle-class democracy, were hurtling off in an entirely different direction? Did scores of commentators point out that history was racing along the wrong path? Then the United States was to yank it back and have done with the business. Many Americans, continuing to think along traditional lines, assumed that all the ordinary people of the world wanted peace and democracy and hence the Soviet-American clash could be solved quickly, finally, and with no great dependence on other nations. They spurned co-existence, and put much more emphasis on direct military moves than on the complex processes of economic aid. Though few actually advocated preventive war, thousands showed a marked receptivity to the argument that the disturbance could be ended once and for all by smashing its center, the men in the Kremlin. A considerable part of the population evidenced little enthusiasm for the United Nations, coalition diplomacy, coalition war, or anything else which placed the United States in a position of relying on others.

Nowhere did this way of thinking take more characteristic form than in its attitude toward Asia. For many decades a feeling had been growing in America that the Asiatics were the special mission of the United States under the law of history. It was our duty to help feed them, educate them, convert them, nudge them along toward the middle-class life. The sentiment was plain in President William McKinley as he expressed his conviction that "there was nothing for us to do but to . . . educate the Filipinos, and uplift and civilize and Christianize them." Over the years the attitude was spoken from a thousand pulpits by missionaries returning from China with fervid reports of how many more Chinese had chopped off their pigtails, learned to wear pants, or marched to the baptismal font. The emotion made its way into endless speeches by politicians of the modern era, not to speak of the dictum of Senator Kenneth Wherry, who told a wildly cheering crowd in 1940, "With God's help, we will lift Shanghai up and up, ever up, until it is just like Kansas City."

As a result of this attitude, the swing of Asia toward Communism proved a particularly sore point with many Americans. The Chinese not only proceeded to violate the law of history by going to the extreme left; they brought the added irritation of thumbing their noses at American patronage. Hundreds of thousands of Americans were irreconcilable, above all, to the Chinese revolutionists or to any other Red movements in Asia. In their thinking about American foreign policy, they believed in Asia First; some came close to believing in Asia Only. As a group they had a view of the world deeply colored by the feeling that Communism in Asia was peculiarly intolerable.

For these Americans, the shocks of 1949 were the last straw. The containment policy was upsetting enough; it was downright infuriating when it failed to contain. Western Europe may have been saved but what of the facts that vast China was now in Communist hands, that the Soviet Union could dangle an atomic bomb over American heads, that the Hiss case easily raised the question whether Communist infiltration into the American government was ended?

Some actions and attitudes of the Democratic leaders had not created a situation conducive to quieting the uproar. Ardent followers of Roosevelt and Truman might point out that sweeping world forces had been at work, far longer-running and more powerful than the rule of any one party in Washington. They could emphasize the incontestable fact that Roosevelt in his wartime negotiations with the Soviet had given the Russians little which they could not have taken themselves. With entire accuracy they were able to stress that Chiang Kai-shek's government had been a miserable remnant of feudalism; that the pumpkin microfilm which convicted Alger Hiss was dated not 1949 but 1937-8; and that the Truman Administrations had a long, consistent anti-Communist record, including the brilliantly successful Marshall Plan and a program for removing security risks from the government so sweeping and at times so overzealous that Dean Acheson later apologized for it. Yet there were other, quite different aspects of the situation.

Only the most partisan Democrat could really believe that Roosevelt would have carried on relations with the Russians as he did had he not been proceeding on the misplaced hope that the Soviet would be a co-operative power in the postwar. President Truman hardly strengthened public confidence by his use of the phrase "red herring" in connection with the Congressional investigating committees, particularly after Chambers's charges against Hiss were backed by the pumpkin microfilm. Although Communist sympathizers certainly did not fill any sensitive government post as late as 1949, some Democratic leaders brushed the whole problem of Red infiltration aside with a conspicuous casualness. Under the circumstances, it was inevitable that part of the public would get the impression that these men would not be too disturbed if they did discover a Soviet sympathizer in, say, the State Department. Most important, the Administration's policy in China was a plain failure. Perhaps, as Secretary of State Acheson contended, there had been no way to succeed but if that was the case, the Department of State had done little to prepare public opinion for the inevitable fall of China.

Whatever the merits and deficiencies of the Roosevelt-Truman handling of the Communist problem, the Democratic leadership was a perfect devil to be flayed. What party had been in power while Communism made progress inside and outside the United States? Franklin Roosevelt, New Dealers, Harry Truman, Fair Dealers—the words came out in a hiss of exasperation and fright. The New Deal, Fair Deal Democrats, who had received so much support because of the widening economic and social opportunities, were learning the force of the political maxim of old Senator George Moses of New Hampshire: The party that receives credit when the sun shines also gets the blame for the rain.

In itself the fury over the Communist advances would have created a powerful discontent but Communism was not the whole story. The man who was middle-aged in 1949 had lived through transformations of life within the United States more swift and sweeping than any previous generation of Americans had known. He grew up in a land where free economic enterprise was the normal way; white, Protestant, old-stock families dominated the community; and the whole of everyday activities moved within a basically fixed pattern. In 1949 this American made his living in a crazy-quilt system of free enterprise, the welfare state, welfare capitalism, and the patches of socialism represented by public power. Negroes, Catholics, Jews, and the sons of recent immigrants jostled the one-time elite for jobs and status. Wherever the American turned, whether to the details of the home or the mores of the Presidency, nothing seemed unchanging except change.

"All the standards are harum-scarum," the chronicler of a more stable America, Mark Sullivan, sighed in 1950. "Children running the homes or the President of the United States barnstorming up and down the country—it's all the same dissolution of traditional, dependable ways." The more the sense of quicksand came, the more the disturbed citizen could find evidence of it on all sides. By the heavens, at least there was still such a thing as moral good and bad. But then, come to think of it, was there still such a thing? Hadn't the corrosives of all the old sure standards seeped even into this rock? When the American criticized the man next door for cocktailing with other women, his own wife was likely to quote Dr. Kinsey and ask: "Don't you know that moral codes are relative to social class?" His denunciation of juvenile delinquents was inevitably followed by a news item in which an expert insisted that the fault should be assigned not to the delinquent but to a vague complexity called maladjustments in the home. Well, at least he was sure how to raise his own children. But then, matter of fact, was he really sure what closing hour to impose on his daughter's dates? And when he raised his hand to thwack Junior's bottom, the blows were unsteadied by a crisscross of child-raising theories in his own mind.

Even the type of national leadership had been shifting. As a people, Americans traditionally have put their faith in the man of action, particularly in the man of action who has done the democratic thing of being born poor. An overwhelming percentage of Presidents have been practical politicians, lawyers, generals, or businessmen who made their own ways up in the world, and Presidential advisers generally came from the same groups. But the complexities of the welfare state had begun bringing into prominence a quite different type—the highly educated man, decidedly intellectualish in manner, with a marked, often wisecracking, impatience for the certitudes of the man of action. To top off their ability to arouse suspicion, many of these Brain Trusters were the sons of wealth and the products of Eastern universities which had long been associated in the popular mind with snobbery.

The Half-Century of Revolution in domestic affairs had reached a climacteric—in social changes and in the dissolution of old ways and old ideas which accompanied the changes. "New Dealism" people called it all and the term was appropriate despite the fact that Franklin Roosevelt was long dead and the New Deal as a specific program had ended years ago. In its simplest form, New Dealism may have been a set of domestic policies but it was also, in just as important a sense, an emphasis, a climate of opinion, a collection of attitudes. It was the assumption that the new was better than the old; that intellectuals ought to be leaders; that morals and religion as well as economics and politics were constantly to be re-examined; that progressive education and Freudianism and planned parenthood were to be furthered; that the cocked eye was man's most proper expression. The Truman Administration broke with many of these attitudes but it never really disassociated itself from them in the public mind. The New Deal and the figure of Franklin Roosevelt loomed over anything a Democrat might do.

No nation can go through such rapid changes in its domestic life without backing up an enormous amount of puzzlement, resentment, and outright opposition. Revolutions provoke counter-revolutions; drastic change, a weariness of change. In this case the reaction was the greater because of the prosperity and enormous social and economic opportunities which had come to exist by 1949. In social movement, nothing quite fails like too much success. New Dealism, having labored mightily to lift low-income Americans, found that it had created a nation of the middle class, shocked at New Dealism's iconoclasm and especially annoyed at its insistence on placing the values of change above those of standard middle-class thinking. Nobody believes more in self-made men than the man who has been made by distant social legislation. No group is more annoyed by reform than those who have benefited from it and no longer need it.

Any irritation with domestic New Dealism was stoked by the Communist threat. The joining of New Dealism and Communism in a troubled American mind was easy, almost axiomatic. Was it not the New Dealers, like the Communists, who talked of uplifting the masses, fighting the businessman, establishing economic controls over society, questioning the traditional in every part of living? Was it not the reformers at home who had called during the war for linking hands with the Bolsheviks abroad? Was not Alger Hiss just the type of which the New Dealers had been so proud? As the postwar went on, Franklin Roosevelt, labor unions, Harry Truman, progressive education, the Marshall Plan, Alger Hiss and a thousand other aspects of New Dealism were becoming jumbled into a bitter thinking which amounted to a theory of conspiracy.

In 1933, so the theory ran, Franklin Roosevelt put into control of the nation a group of men whose ultimate aim was a Communist world. They did not say they were Communists. Instead they called themselves by the sweet-smelling words, "New Dealers," "progressives," "humanitarians," and worked deviously toward their goal. They hurried the destruction of free economic institutions in the United States by manipulating the tax structure and by strangling free enterprise in bureaucracy and controls. When World War II came, they maneuvered American foreign policy to strengthen the forces of world Communism. Roosevelt and his aides propagandized America into a picture of the Soviet Union as a peace-loving democracy, hurried over quantities of lend-lease far beyond military needs, then sold out eastern Europe and China at Yalta. Under Truman, the Communizers went on undermining the American economic system while bringing about the confirmation of Soviet control of eastern Europe at Potsdam and making sure of the final delivery of China to the Reds.

And the conspirators were not only operating in American economic affairs and on the world scene. Their wily hand reached into every aspect of life in the United States, inculcating attitudes destructive of the truly American way of living and thinking. The shocks of 1949 loosed not only a sweeping anti-Communism but a tendency to denounce anything associated with the different or disturbing as part of a Communist conspiracy. With the end of 1949, many an American was attacking Sigmund Freud in the same breath with his denunciation of Alger Hiss. Ladies' committees that stalked the bookstores for pro-Communist writings also wanted to burn John Steinbeck's *Grapes of Wrath*. Textbook boards, setting out to protect the schools from Communism, shielded the young from any praise of minimum-wage laws along the way.

People were beginning to use the word "intellectual" as if it meant some compound of evil, stupidity, and treason.

The heart of the emotional drive behind this whole conspiracy theory lay precisely in the fact that it *was* a theory of conspiracy. The hated developments could all have been prevented; they were all the work of a few wicked men, operating behind a cloak of hypocrisy. The American who was so annoyed at the fact that a Negro sat down beside him in a bus rarely saw the social upsurge in the United States as an ineluctable part of the democratic process. The Negro was there because New Dealers had plotted to put him there. The rise of Communism around the world did not result from long-running historical forces; the Red advances came from the Alger Hisses, who had contrived to bring them about. The sense that any unwanted development could have been prevented was strongest and most bitter with respect to the Communist menace. The danger had been and was within the United States, not from the outer world. It was not really the Russian and Chinese Communists but Reds in the United States who had brought the crisis and who now direly threatened America.

As the sense of conspiracy mounted, its hottest emotions centered on the State Department. In a way this was natural. After all, the State Department played a major part, or was assumed to have played a major part, in the negotiations with the Soviet and the handling of the Chinese problem which were being so much criticized. Yet the excoriation of the State Department involved much more than this. Back in 1889 the *New York Sun* declared: "The diplomatic service . . . is a costly humbug and sham. It is a nurse of snobs. It spoils a few Americans every year, and does no good to anybody. Intead of making ambassadors, Congress should wipe out the whole service." Throughout American history, the State Department has been the subject of intense suspicion in times of

international stress. Manned for the most part by products of upper-status families, it aroused charges of
aristocracy. Calling more and more upon specialists, it
rubbed wrong the faith in the man of action. Above
all, its very function—the carrying on of continuous
relations with other powers—easily annoyed a nation
which believed in its heart of hearts that somewhere,
somehow there must be a foreign policy which had
the supreme virtue of making foreign policy unnecessary.

As long ago as 1906, that sensitive analyst of American society, Henry Adams, remarked: "The Secretary of State has always stood as much alone as the
historian. Required to look far ahead and around him,
he measures forces unknown to party managers, and
has found Congress more or less hostile ever since Congress first sat. The Secretary of State exists only to
recognize the existence of a world which Congress
would rather ignore. . . . Since the first day the Senate existed, it has always intrigued against the Secretary
of State whenever the Secretary has been obliged to
extend his functions beyond the appointment of Con-
suls. . . ." And to crown the vulnerability of the
State Department in 1949, its chief was Dean Acheson.

One afternoon a staid Washington affair reached the
point where the Secretary of State was to make a few
remarks. Dean Acheson tweaked his perfectly
groomed mustache and began in the most cultivated
of voices: "All that I know I learned at my mother's
knee and other low joints. . . ." There it was—a man
in the so easily suspected post of Secretary of State
who was the New Dealish type down to the last item
of irrepressible kidding. To capsule Acheson is to sum-
marize the things which provoked the devotees of the
theory of conspiracy. He was born to the Social Register and he was Groton, Yale, and Harvard Law
School. He had been a New Dealer in domestic affairs
despite some differences with Franklin Roosevelt,
operated as a let's-be-friends-with-Russia man during

the war, and when he shifted in his attitude toward the Soviet after V-J, did it with a conviction that the world revolution called for a basic change in traditional American ideas. Acheson and Alger Hiss were longtime associates; Alger's brother, Donald, was a member of the law firm of which the Secretary had been a senior partner. Acheson was not only the Secretary of State who had to announce the fall of China but he had been a high officer in the State Department during most of the period when Communism made its chief advances. And always there was Dean Gooderham Acheson the man, a goadingly adventurous mind in irritatingly handsome tweeds.

"Our name for problems is significant," Acheson declared as early as 1946. "We call them headaches. You take a powder and they are gone. These pains . . . [brought by the world situation] are not like that. They . . . will stay with us until death. We have got to understand that all our lives the danger, the uncertainty, the need for alertness, for effort, for discipline will be upon us. This is new for us. It will be hard for us."

It was hard, infuriatingly hard, for a good many of Acheson's fellow Americans. "I look at that fellow," Senator Hugh Butler of Nebraska exploded for them, "I watch his smart-aleck manner and his British clothes and that New Dealism, everlasting New Dealism in everything he says and does, and I want to shout, Get out, Get out. You stand for everything that has been wrong with the United States for years."

To some extent the mounting restiveness simply represented an intensification of feeling on the part of a long-running opposition. After all, since 1933 millions of people in the United States had been listening sympathetically to speakers who charged that New Dealers were socializing the economy, leading the nation to ruin in foreign affairs, and leaving the whole of American life prey to radical intellectuals. Men who felt this way were usually Taft Republicans and such Republicanism easily slid over into a theory of conspiracy under the pressure of the events of 1949.

Most Taftites were either upper-income Americans or middle- or lower-middle-class people who were relatively old stock. To wealthy Taftites, the economic leveling of New Dealism was infuriating. To rich and poor Taftites, the social leveling and the disruption of old ideas associated with New Dealism were just as exasperating. They were ready to believe the worst of the long years of Democratic rule and when the advances of Communism offered a chance to believe that New Dealers had plotted its successes, a good many Taftites eagerly seized the opportunity.

Taft Republicanism moved in this direction the more easily because of the nature of its own central doctrine. Long before the crisis of 1949, Senator Taft had emphasized repeatedly his conviction that the United States was far less menaced by any foreign foe than by conditions at home. New Dealism—particularly its great expenditures of money, its economic controls, and its approval of strong executive actions—was bankrupting the United States, crushing free enterprise, and generally stifling the atmosphere of sober, solvent liberty which was the source of America's power and its surest protection against foreign threats. Taft argued this way in refusing to support the large appropriations and the executive moves called for by New Dealers in the face of rising Nazi power. He repeated the arguments—particularly his opposition to huge expenditures—in explaining his reluctance to go along with the Marshall Plan. "Keep America solvent and sensible," the Senator put it in 1947, "and she has nothing to fear from any foreign country." From this way of thinking to a belief that America's worries came not from Red armies without but from New Dealish conspirators within was not a long step—certainly not too long a step to be taken in the heated atmosphere of 1949.

Yet to see the emerging bitterness as simply an accentuation of Taft Republicanism is to misunderstand seriously what was happening in American life. Angry suspicion of New Dealism was building in groups which had been largely Democratic since the 1930's and had generally supported the domestic and foreign policies of both Roosevelt and Truman. It was not only that prosperity was releasing groups from their long-time emotional loyalty to Democratic reformism; the shocks of 1949 were so severe that all old alignments were being shattered. These ex-New Deal dissidents, unlike most Taftites, did not assail social legislation which was already enacted. But they joined in the sense of evil pro-Communist plotting and they were likely to snap and snarl at the whole mood of New Dealism. Of the one-time New Deal supporters, three groups were particularly susceptible to some variety of the conspiracy theory because of special historical circumstances—Midwesterners, relatively recent immigrants, and Catholics.

The history of the western part of the United States, particularly of the Midwest, is a confusing one. The Midwest was a great center of Populist social reformism in the 1890's and it gave powerful support to progressivism in the various forms which it took before and after World War I. Yet this Midwestern liberalism contained elements which could easily turn it into anti-New Dealism. It was anti-Eastern America and anti-"aristocracy." To some extent, it was against new immigrants and against any movement with an air of freewheeling cosmopolitanism. In foreign affairs, it was filled with a particularly strong aversion to Europe, a fear and hatred of Britain, and a deeply emotional concern over Asia. There is a direct line from the Midwestern Populist leader, Ignatius Donnelly, denouncing "the oppression of farmers by a devilish conspiracy of bloated Easterners and Britishers" to the *Chicago Tribune* of 1949 with its assault on Dean Acheson as "another striped-pants snob" who "ignores the people of Asia and betrays true Americanism to serve as a lackey of Wall St. bankers, British lords, and Communistic radicals from New York."

Another important part of support for New Dealism had come from recent immigrants living in the great urban centers across the country, most of whom were in the working class during the 1930's. These people had a special sensitivity, to which they could afford to pay little attention during depression times. As the 1940's and 50's moved many of them into the middle classes in income or in actual jobs, the sensitivity became a vital part of their reaction to public affairs. Americans, just because they are so mixed in background, are one of the few peoples in modern history who have shown a great concern with aspiring to full nationality—with being "100% Americans." By 1949, the nature of the population had changed so much that only a minority could feel genuinely old stock; the typical American, if such a person could really be found, was a third-generation immigrant. Rising to the middle class left the Italian-American worker, the Slovak-American accountant, the Russian-American teacher only the more anxious to achieve the further respectability of unhyphenated Americanism. Under the circumstances, he was the more likely to want no part of the New Dealism and the Democratic foreign policy which were being assailed as an un-American conspiracy and he was the more ready to accept that view himself.

A large number of the first- and second-generation immigrants were Roman Catholics, and most of the Catholics were city dwellers and working class or just moving into the middle class. American Catholicism is a vast and complex subject; almost any generalization about it is likely to contain at least some inaccuracies. Yet it can be said with reasonable factuality that millions of these Catholics were subject to all the aspirations for unchallengeable Americanism which were influencing other recent immigrant groups, and they were also under influences that were peculiarly their own. The Catholics may have been prime supporters of the New Deal in the 1930's but the support had an undertone. Basic in the philosophy of the Church is the tenet that Catholicism has its own unique attitude toward all problems, and a part of the American Church, while rarely breaking with Roosevelt, was often standoffish about the government's increasing invasion of the life of the individual.

The phase of New Dealism that was not directly concerned with legislation—its whole pragmatic, iconoclastic approach—provoked still more resistance. In 1864, Pope Pius IX had expressed the Church's flat opposition to such tendencies, and his encyclical blended easily with the natural tendency of many of the priests and diocesan newspapers in the United States. American intellectualism as it was commonly practiced provoked much the same reaction. In 1955 the unabashedly intellectual Bishop John J. Wright, of the diocese of Worcester, looked back over the post-World War II period and summarized: "There have been grave reasons in recent years to fear that in our [Catholic] newspapers and our forums, not to say even on our campuses, we have frequently revealed a nervous spirit of impatient and sullen anti-intellectualism."

After World War II, some parts of the Church led in identifying non-Communist liberal agitations with Communism. Many diocesan papers gave fervid support to the House Committee on Un-American Activities, which was denouncing scores of liberals as Reds. Priests in various parts of the country carried on their own un-American investigations. Typical of many of these efforts was a Cleveland episode of 1948. The priest who was director of the diocesan Holy Name Society attacked a candidate for the Ohio state senate on the ground that he had knowledge that the candidate was "of the left-wing variety," " 'pink,' at least." Specifically, the knowledge was that the candidate had "sought to have the movie censorship lifted, one of the Communist activities."

Toward Communism itself, many American Catholics had long had an attitude of fear and intransigence much deeper than that of the general population. The position of the Church had been made militantly clear in 1937. The encyclical of Pius XI, *Atheistic Communism*, ruled out all co-operation, conferences, or compromises between Communists and non-Communists. "See to it, Venerable Brethren," Pope Pius XI declared, "that the Faithful do not allow themselves to be deceived. Communism is intrinsically wrong, and no one who would save Christian civilization may collaborate with it in any undertaking whatsoever." During World War II, while much of the United States was thinking of the Soviet as a friendly ally, a good part of the American hierarchy was sharply anti-Soviet. When the East-West clash developed after V-J, Francis Cardinal Spellman, the most publicized spokesman of the American Church, delivered address after address which had the tone of war and which directly charged the existence of a powerful Communist conspiracy in American life.

As early as 1946 the Cardinal was talking of the grave need of combating the "aggression of enemies within" the United States. "The fear weighs upon me that we may fail or refuse to realize that Communists, who have put to death thousands of innocent people across the seas, are today digging deep inroads into our own nation. . . ." During 1947-48 the tone heightened. Cardinal Spellman spoke of "this hour of dreadful, desperate need. . . . Once again while Rome burns, literally and symbolically, the world continues to fiddle. The strings on the fiddle are committees, conferences, conversations, appeasements—to the tune of no action today." By 1949 the Catholic prelate was declaring in the bluntest possible language that America would not be safe "until every Communist cell is removed from within our own government, our own institutions, not until every democratic country is returned to democratic leadership. . . ."

In February, 1949 the Cardinal appeared in the pulpit of St. Patrick's Cathedral to speak one of the most passionate sermons ever delivered from an American pulpit. America was in imminent danger of "Communist conquest and annihilation. . . . Are we, the American people, the tools and the fools for which the Communists take us?" The situation called for an immediate end of all "ostrich-like actions and pretenses," particularly in halting the "Communist floodings of our own land."

Throughout the later postwar period, Catholic anti-Communism sometimes took on an emotional tone close to the hysterical. The year before the crises of 1949, the Catechetical Guild of St. Paul distributed a comic-strip pamphlet called *Is This Tomorrow?*, in which Communist mobs were depicted as attacking St. Patrick's Cathedral with torches and nailing the Cardinal to the door. When a widely read Catholic magazine carried the publication as a supplement, the Detroit police banned the issue on the ground that it might provoke violence. The editor of the journal told the police commissioner: "Then you'll be arresting twenty or thirty pastors who will be selling it next week." The Detroit police backed down; other police departments chose not to move. A single New York priest sold more than seven thousand copies of the booklet from the pamphlet rack of his church.

Some leading Catholics deplored this publication, and throughout the postwar era prominent Catholics publicly criticized the extreme positions taken by particular Church figures. The American Church did not respond with one voice to the problems raised by 1949, just as there has rarely been a monolithic Catholic opinion on any issue in the United States. So too, millions of Midwesterners and Taft Republicans did not fit into sweeping generalizations about their attitudes. Yet as the shocks of 1949 took their full

effect, it was clear that the mounting restiveness was
disproportionately centered in these groups.

In January, 1950 Clark Clifford resigned his White
House post; with three growing daughters, Clifford
explained, it was time for him to return to the high
income of private law practice. Shortly before,
George Kennan left the chairmanship of the Policy
Planning Staff and soon headed for a post at the Institute for Advanced Study in Princeton. Kennan,
friends said, was disappointed with the Administration's foreign policy, not too well, and anxious for
time to think and study. The resignations were
scarcely noticed in the press. At the close of 1949,
attention was hardly centered on Clifford's containment domestic or the containment of Communism in
Europe associated with Kennan.

New faces were prominent. Everybody was now fa-
miliar with intense, scowling young Congressman
Richard Nixon; when the House Un-American Activities Committee was about to give up on Alger Hiss,
had Nixon not kept on pursuing him? Old figures of
prominence were talking differently. Arthur Vandenberg, for so long a rock of bipartisanship in foreign affairs, was wondering out loud if "bipartisanship
means more Chinas and more Hisses and more messes
with Russian bombs hanging over us." Robert Taft's
face no longer took on a pained look when the discussion turned to international affairs. He had a fresh
major theme—"the great problem of Asia" and the
"wreckage that is our Far Eastern policy."

President Truman was troubled, testy. He rode over
to Arlington to attend a dinner honoring Harry
Vaughan, lost his temper completely, told the startled
guests that he didn't care about "any s.o.b." who criticized Vaughan. He stood before his press conference
talking grimly of the "great wave of hysteria" that was
building. It would subside, Truman added stanchly.
We had gone through this sort of thing before and

"the country did not go to hell, and it isn't going to now."

Presidential Press Secretary Charles Ross went away from the session rubbing his chin reflectively. "Well," he said to a friend, "it all depends on the way Harry defines that word 'hell.' "

America restless — against
New Deal + Communism —
Said ND was conspiracy
against US

Americans were frightened
and embittered

VII

Dinner at the Colony

1949 GAVE way to 1950 and nothing changed except the calendar. For the frightened and embittered, there was only more incitement to fright and bitterness.

Early in the afternoon of January 21, 1950, a plump Bronx widow, Mrs. Ada Condell, gave the news in a nervous, almost inaudible voice. "Guilty on the first count and guilty on the second," she said. Alger Hiss could only stand before Judge Goddard and explain lamely: "In the future all the facts will be brought out to show how Whittaker Chambers was able to commit forgery by typewriter." When the onetime New Deal luminary was led to the station wagon handcuffed to a common thief, it was the thief who hid his face from the photographers.

Four days after the conviction, Secretary of State Acheson held his weekly press conference and Homer Bigart of the *New York Herald Tribune* asked: "Have you any comment on the Alger Hiss case?"

Acheson refused to discuss the legal aspects of the trials. Then he edged forward in his chair and with considerable feeling added: "I take it the purpose of your question was to bring something other than that out of me. I should like to make it clear to you that, whatever the outcome of any appeal which Mr. Hiss or his lawyer may take in this case, I do not intend to turn my back on Alger Hiss." The Secretary's face flushed as he continued. "I think every person who has known Alger Hiss . . . had upon his conscience the very serious task of deciding what his attitude is and what his conduct should be." His own conduct would be determined by the twenty-fifth chapter of Matthew, beginning at verse thirty-four, the lines in which Christ called upon His followers to recognize that the man who turned his back on anyone in trouble also turned his back on Him.

Of course the Secretary of State did not mean that he was questioning the verdict of the court or that he intended to remain in friendly association with a man convicted of perjury and, by implication, of espionage. He was simply saying, as Acheson explained later, that he was following "Christ's words setting forth compassion as the highest of Christian duties." In its way, the Secretary's statement spoke as courageous and as genuinely Christian an attitude as American politics has ever produced and it will no doubt earn him a special garland when the furies of recent years have completely died away. The sentence about not turning his back on Hiss was also a remark which, like Truman's red-herring comments, was easily misunderstood or deliberately misconstrued. In the atmosphere of 1950, it was a tremendous and totally unnecessary gift to those who were insisting that the foreign policy of the Truman Administration was being shaped by men who were soft toward Communism. The tone of the outcry was expressed by Congressman Richard Nixon who, in the course of a speech treating the Acheson-Hiss relationship, declared: "Traitors in the high councils of our own government have made sure that the deck is stacked on the Soviet side of the diplomatic tables."

Ten days after the Hiss conviction, on January 31, Presidential Press Secretary Charles Ross handed reporters a statement from President Truman: "It is part of my responsibility as Commander in Chief of the armed forces to see to it that our country is able to defend itself against any aggressor. Accordingly I have directed the Atomic Energy Commission to continue its work on all forms of atomic weapons, including the so-called hydrogen or super-bomb." Once again a terrifying announcement had been made with all the studied toning down of a mimeographed sheet —this time the President even saw to it that he was casually lunching at Blair House when Ross met the reporters. Once again nothing could really cushion the news. Not only would a hydrogen bomb have one hundred to one thousand times the power of the largest atomic weapon. Twelve distinguished scientists immediately issued a joint statement which pointed out that "in the case of the fission bomb the Russians required four years to parallel our development. In the case of the hydrogen bomb they will probably need a shorter time."

Some Americans talked tough. Secretary of Defense Louis Johnson told an alumni gathering at the University of Virginia: "I want Joe Stalin to know that if he starts something at four o'clock in the morning, the fighting power and strength of America will be on the job at five o'clock in the morning." Other Americans raised harsh, portentous questions. Senator Brien McMahon, chairman of the Joint Congressional Committee on Atomic Energy, brought solemn handshakes from both sides of the chamber by a speech in which he asked: "How is it possible for free institutions to flourish or even to maintain themselves in a situation where defenses, civil and military, must be ceaselessly poised to meet an attack that might incinerate fifty million Americans—not in the space of an evening, but in the space of moments?" The most authoritative voice of all talked doom. Albert Einstein went on television, the simple sweater jacket, the scraggly gray hair, the childlike face with the brilliant eyes all adding to the aura of an otherworldly wisdom beyond the power of ordinary mortals. With the order of President Truman to produce an H-bomb, Einstein said, "radioactive poisoning of the atmosphere and hence annihilation of any life on earth has been brought within the range of technical possibilities. . . . General annihilation beckons."

Another four days and another jolting headline. On February 3 the British government announced the confession of Dr. Klaus Fuchs, a high-level atomic scientist. The descriptions of Fuchs sitting behind the cast-iron grill of the prisoner's dock in Bow Street police court, plainly dressed, bespectacled, quiet-mannered, gave him every inch the appearance of the dedicated scientist—"the last man in the world you would expect to be a spy," as one English reporter commented. Yet Fuchs's confession stated that from 1943 through 1947, while engaged in government atomic research in the United States and Britain, he had systematically passed over to Soviet agents the inmost scientific secrets of the Western powers. "I had complete confidence in Russian policy," he told the police, "and I had no hesitation in giving all the information I had." The knowledge Fuchs handed over, his superior, Michael Perren, stated, had been "of the highest value to a potential enemy," and no doubt speeded up the Russian production of an atom bomb "at least a year."

Senator Homer Capehart of Indiana stood up in the Senate and stormed: "How much more are we going to have to take? Fuchs and Acheson and Hiss and hydrogen bombs threatening outside and New Dealism eating away the vitals of the nation. In the name of Heaven, is this the best America can do?" The applause was loud and long, from the floor and from the galleries.

That afternoon the regular plane from Washington to Wheeling, West Virginia, began loading. The stewardess did her duty, noted a United States Senator on the passenger list, and greeted him with a smiling, "Good afternoon, Senator McCarthy." The reply was a bit plaintive. "Why, good afternoon—I'm glad somebody recognizes me."

Getting recognized was no new concern of Joseph McCarthy. The Irish settlement in northern Wisconsin where he grew up respected money and looks; the McCarthys were a struggling brood of nine and Joe was the ugly duckling, barrel-chested and short-armed with thick eyebrows and heavy lips. Mother Bridget McCarthy threw a special protective wing around the shy, sulky boy and when the rough teasing came, he sought out her big warm apron. "Don't you mind," she would console. "You be somebody. You get ahead."

Joe took heed. He would get back; he would show everybody. The shy sulkiness turned into a no-holds-barred ambition curiously mixed with a gawky, grinning likability. The boy worked so furiously on the family farm that neighbors joked he must have spent his babyhood wearing overalls instead of diapers. Starting his education late, he talked, wheedled, and shoved his way through Marquette University with so much corner-cutting that Wisconsin educators still gasp at the record.

Associates noted the fierce, blinding drive in everything McCarthy did. When he boxed and his awkwardness was getting him cut to pieces, he would keep coming in, slashed and bleeding but flailing away in the hope of striking a knockout blow. When he played poker, he played all-or-nothing. He had the "guts of a burglar," one friend remembers. "He was brutal. He'd take all the fun out of the game, because he took it so seriously." When he ran for office in college, he dropped his homework, cut school for weeks at a time, devoted night and day to buying coffees and cokes and making lavish promises. He and his opponent agreed that each would vote for the other until the election was decided. The first ballot was a tie. On the next McCarthy won by two votes.

"Joe," the defeated candidate said, "did you vote for yourself?"

McCarthy grinned his big, disarming, tail-between-the-legs grin. "Sure. You wanted me to vote for the best man, didn't you?"

Once out of Marquette, he bashed his way to a Wisconsin Circuit Judgeship and soon converted it into a political stump, knocking off divorces in five minutes or less, racing around to please people by trying as many cases as possible. After Pearl Harbor he entered the Marine Corps, turning the whole Pacific Theater of War into a headquarters of McCarthy for United States Senator, blithely giving himself the name of "Tail-gunner Joe" although most of the time he was actually serving as an intelligence officer and doing the paper work for a squadron of pilots. Elected to the Senate in 1946, he thrashed about for ways to secure his political hold. McCarthy served the interests of the Pepsi-Cola Company so faithfully he became known to fellow Senators as the "Pepsi-Cola Kid." He delighted the real-estate interests in Wisconsin by battling public housing and he pleased some of his large German-American constituency by defending the Nazis on trial for the murders of Malmédy.

It was a great life, this being a United States Senator. "Pretty good going for a Mick from the backwoods, eh?" McCarthy would grin at the cocktail parties and the ladies thought he was awfully cute—"such an engaging primitive," as one debutante put it. But there was a problem and the engaging primitive was no more patient with a problem than he had ever been.

On January 7, 1950 McCarthy sat having a troubled dinner at the Colony Restaurant in Washington. The get-together had been arranged by Charles H. Kraus, a professor of political science at Georgetown University, and William A. Roberts, a well-known Washington attorney. Kraus in particular had been seeing a good deal of the Senator and had been suggest-

ing books for him to read—especially the potent anti-
Communist volume *Total Power* by Father Edmund
A. Walsh, vice-president of Georgetown and regent
of its School of Foreign Service. (McCarthy was
hardly a booklover but he did like to skim hurriedly
and he had spoken of his desire "to read some meaty
books.") The prime purpose of the dinner was to permit the Senator to meet Father Walsh, whom both
Kraus and Roberts profoundly admired.

McCarthy soon brought the conversation around to
what was uppermost in his mind. His situation was
bad, the Senator said. Here it was already the beginning of 1950, with his term running out in two years,
and he had neither the national publicity which would
attract Wisconsin voters nor any specific issue likely to
stir them.

Within months Kraus, Roberts, and Walsh were all
to repudiate McCarthy but at this time they were
well disposed toward the youthful Senator. Kraus and
Roberts were also Marine veterans of World War II;
everyone at the table was a Catholic; the Senator's
shaggy affability could attract men as well as women.
Eager to help McCarthy, the group threw out suggestions.

"How about pushing harder for the St. Lawrence
seaway?" Roberts proposed.

McCarthy shook his head. "That hasn't enough appeal. No one gets excited about it."

The Senator then thought aloud about a Townsend-
type pension plan for all elderly Americans. Why not
start a campaign to pay one hundred dollars a month
to everybody over sixty-five years of age? But the
three other men agreed that the idea was economically
unsound.

After dinner the group went to Roberts's office in
the adjoining DeSales Building and continued the discussion. McCarthy and Roberts, both voluble men,
did most of the talking but at one point Father Walsh
spoke at length. He emphasized the world power of

Communism and the danger that it would infiltrate any democratic government. He was sure, Walsh declared, that vigilance against Communism was of such importance that it would be an issue two years hence.

The Senator's face brightened. Communist infiltration—wasn't this what everybody was talking about? And wasn't this, after all, a *real* issue? The priest's remarks touched chords that reached far back into McCarthy's life. In the 1930's, the Irish settlement of northern Wisconsin voted for Franklin Roosevelt; the farms were in too desperate a condition for anything else. But the New Dealism had its own Midwestern, new-immigrant, Irish-Catholic coloration. It was filled with suspicion of Easterners, "radicals," "aristocrats," the British, and the "striped-pants fellows" of the State Department. McCarthy had started in politics a New Deal Democrat but as soon as the prosperity came he shifted to a more congenial Taft Republicanism. Whether a Democrat or a Republican, he had always more or less consciously assumed that the big trouble with America, as his boyhood neighbor Jim Heegan used to put it, was "those Leftists."

McCarthy cut in on Father Walsh. "The Government is full of Communists. The thing to do is to hammer at them."

Roberts, a longtime liberal attorney, spoke a sharp warning. Such a campaign would have to be based on facts; the public was weary of "Wolf! Wolf!" cries about "Reds." The Senator said offhandedly he would get the facts.

Lincoln's Birthday, the traditional time for Republican oratory, was approaching, and McCarthy—probably at his own request—was assigned by the Senate Republican Campaign Committee to speak on the topic, "Communism in the State Department." The Senator's office put together some materials drawn mostly from hearings and staff investigations of a House Appropriations subcommittee. Three weeks after Hiss was convicted, ten days after President Truman ordered work on the H-bomb, six days after the British announced the Fuchs confession, on February 9, 1950, McCarthy took the plane to deliver his speech before the Women's Republican Club in Wheeling, West Virginia. He would give it a try. He would see if he could not get someone besides polite airline stewardesses to recognize the name Joseph McCarthy.

"The reason why we find ourselves in a position of impotency [in international affairs]," the Senator told the club, "is not because our only powerful potential enemy has sent men to invade our shores, but rather because of the traitorous actions of those who have been treated so well by this Nation. . . ." Where was the situation most serious? "Glaringly" so in the State Department. And what kind of men were the offenders? "The bright young men who are born with silver spoons in their mouths are the ones who have been worst. . . . In my opinion the State Department, which is one of the most important government departments, is thoroughly infested with Communists." Most dangerous of all was Dean Acheson, that "pompous diplomat in striped pants, with a phony British accent."

McCarthy had always believed that a speaker had to get specific in order to make his points stick. Near the end of his speech he talked about a list "I hold here in my hand." Exactly what he said about the list will probably never be known with certainty. James E. Whitaker and Paul A. Myers, news editor and program director respectively of the Wheeling radio station that broadcast the speech, WWVA, later swore in an affidavit that McCarthy's words were: "I have here in my hand a list of 205—a list of names that were known to the Secretary of State as being members of the Communist Party and who nevertheless are still working and shaping the policy in the State Department." The Senator's friends later insisted that his point was something like: "I have here in my hand 57 cases of individuals who would appear to be either card-carrying members or certainly loyal to the Communist Party, but who nevertheless are still helping to shape our foreign policy." One man who would never be sure what he had said was Joseph McCarthy. Frederick Woltman, the responsible reporter for the Scripps-Howard newspapers, has described how "on a number of occasions—mostly in my apartment at the Congressional—I heard McCarthy and his advisors wrack their brains for some lead as to what he said in that Wheeling speech. He had no copy; he had spoken from rough notes and he could not find the notes. . . . The Senator's staff could find no one who could recall what he'd said precisely. He finally hit on the idea of appealing to ham radio operators in the area who might have made a recording of the speech. He could find none."

For the moment there was no such interesting problem. There was only another plane to catch, another polite stewardess to greet Senator McCarthy. The speech seemed to disappear; it was not even reported except in the Wheeling newspapers and in the *Chicago Tribune*. The Senator kept flailing away. On February 10, in Salt Lake City, he made a speech similar to his Wheeling talk and charged that there were "57 card-carrying members of the Communist Party" in the State Department. The next day he repeated substantially the same talk in Reno and wired President Truman demanding that the White House do something.

Things began to happen. Newspapers in many parts of the country headlined the Salt Lake City and Reno charges. President Truman and Secretary of State Acheson issued angry statements of denial. The Senate stirred, authorizing a subcommittee of the Foreign Relations Committee to investigate the Senator's statements.

But what was happening did not seem to bode well for Joseph McCarthy. The materials that he had used for his speeches were largely old and none too sturdy charges. The Senate subcommittee, chairmanned by the militantly Democratic Millard Tydings of Maryland, kept McCarthy pinned in the worst possible light. Veteran Republican Senate leaders were plainly hesitant about backing this rambunctious upstart.

Then, gradually, support came. By an instinct born of the whole climate of ideas in which he had grown up, McCarthy was attacking precisely in the way most likely to capture the groups in America who were most disturbed about foreign policy—the whole conspiracy theory of international affairs down to the last suspicion of Dean Acheson's striped pants. By the same instinct, he kept broadening the sense of conspiracy, catching more strands of the rebelliousness abroad in the country. Within a month after his Wheeling speech he was assailing as Communists the "whole group of twisted-thinking New Dealers [who] have led America near to ruin at home and abroad." Many others had been saying these things. No one had kept naming names, dozens of specific, headline-making names. And no one had attacked with such abandon— McCarthy politicking as he had done everything else, ignoring the rules, always walking in, taking his beatings, endlessly throwing wild, spectacular punches. Shortly after the Tydings subcommittee did its most telling job on the charge of fifty-seven card-carrying Communists in the State Department, the Senator closed his eyes completely and swung so hard he shook the country.

He would "stand or fall on this one," McCarthy let it be known. He was naming "the top Russian espionage agent" in the United States and a man who had long been "one of the top advisers on Far Eastern policy"—Owen Lattimore. In the ensuing uproar only the most informed Americans could make out the fact that Lattimore was a non-Communist liberal who had been called into consultation infrequently by the State

Department and whose suggestions had been almost totally ignored.

By late March private contributions were pouring into the Senator's office. The awards began. The Marine Corps League of Passaic, New Jersey, announced that it had selected Joseph McCarthy to receive its 1950 citation for Americanism. Leading Taft Republicans, including Senator Taft himself, the two powerhouses, Senators Kenneth Wherry and Styles Bridges, and the chairman of the Republican National Committee, Guy Gabrielson, were giving a respectful and cooperative attention to the rambunctious upstart. Various groups which had their own special uses for McCarthy's kind of anti-Communism came to his support—including the potent manipulators who were soon known as the "China Lobby."

Now the grin was as broad as Mother Bridget's apron. The Senator was affable, endlessly affable. In the course of a discussion in McCarthy's apartment, Mrs. Frederick Woltman asked testily: "Tell me, Senator, just how long ago did you discover Communism?"

The Senator grinned. "Why, about two and a half months ago."

In the office of Herbert Block, the strongly New Dealish cartoonist of the *Washington Post*, there was no grinning. Herblock angrily sketched a harassed Republican elephant, being pushed and pulled by Taft, Wherry, Bridges, and Gabrielson toward a stack of buckets of tar with an extra big barrel of tar on top. The cartoonist hesitated for a moment, thinking over possible one-word labels. Then he was satisfied. On the large barrel of tar he printed the letters, McCARTHYISM.

Immediately, and so naturally that people promptly forgot where the term had first been used, the word McCarthyism passed into the language. The revolt set off by the shocks of 1949 had its name and the expression of its most violent, most reckless mood.

VIII

Suspended Moment

THE SUMMER of 1950 came over the eastern seaboard hot and drowsy. Saturday, June 24 found most of America's top foreign-policy men weekending away from thoughts of Joseph Stalin or Joseph McCarthy. President Truman was enjoying a family reunion in Independence. Secretary of State Dean Acheson was at his lovely old farm, "Harewood," in Sandy Spring, Maryland. The U.S. Representative to the United Nations, Warren Austin, walked through his apple orchard near Burlington, Vermont, pruning a bit here, stopping to admire a particularly fine specimen there. Austin's deputy, Ernest Gross, was overwhelmed with a different kind of specimen. In an expansive mood his teen-age daughter had invited twenty of her girl friends to come out and party in the cool of their Manhasset, Long Island, home.

That Saturday evening W. Bradley Connors, the Officer in Charge of Public Affairs for the State Department's Far Eastern Bureau, was relaxing with his wife and children in their Washington apartment. Shortly after 8 p.m. Connors received a telephone call from Donald Gonzales, of the United Press Washington office. Gonzales said that Jack James, the UP man in Korea, was cabling that fragmentary reports indicated a large-scale North Korean attack on South Korea (the Republic of Korea). Could the State Department confirm this bulletin? Connors tried to place a telephone

call to the American Embassy in Seoul, the capital of
South Korea, but it was early Sunday morning on the
other side of the Pacific and the overseas circuits to
Korea were closed. He hurried to the State Department and by 9.26 p.m. Connors no longer needed a
connection to Seoul. From John J. Muccio, American
Ambassador to the Republic of Korea, came an official
cable: "North Korean forces invaded Republic of Korea territory at several places this morning. . . . It
would appear from the nature of the attack and the
manner in which it was launched that it constitutes an
all-out offensive against the Republic of Korea." An
astonished Bradley Connors reached for his phone to
alert an astonished officialdom.

The American government had long known that
Korea was a trouble spot. The 38th parallel separating North and South Korea made no sense geographi-
cally or economically; it was simply an arbitrary line
hastily drawn to define the areas in which Japanese
military commanders would surrender to American or
Soviet forces. By June, 1949 the occupation armies of
both the United States and Russia had withdrawn but
efforts of the UN to conduct free elections for a
united Korean government had foundered on the refusal of the Communist leaders of North Korea to co-
operate. The UN did sponsor elections in South Korea,
which resulted in the "Republic of Korea" headed by
the fire-eating old nationalist Syngman Rhee. Rhee's
government, recognized by the General Assembly of
the UN as the only legitimate one in Korea and bolstered by American funds, was nevertheless beset by
economic and political troubles and it showed a constant restlessness to bring North Korea under its control. Because of the danger that Rhee might try to use
force to bring all Korea under the jurisdiction of his
government, the United States, though it kept a military advisory group in South Korea, sent only light defensive arms. North of the 38th parallel the tight Communist dictatorship went on ruling and it persistently

proclaimed its intention to "liberate" the south. Periodically North Korea would stage raids across the border, sometimes using as many as fifteen hundred men. In the spring of 1950, the American Central Intelligence Agency was reporting that the North Koreans were continuing to build up their military machine with Soviet assistance and might launch a full-scale offensive.

Yet whatever the tensions in Korea, Washington's attention was not concentrated on that area. If Central Intelligence indicated the possibility of an aggression in Korea, it also indicated an equal possibility at a number of other points in the world. As a matter of fact, when Connors's telephone call reached his superior, Assistant Secretary of State Dean Rusk, the Assistant Secretary was at the house of the columnist Joseph Alsop, where the conversation centered on the threat to Yugoslavia resulting from the build-up of the Rumanian and Bulgarian armies.

Dean Rusk hurried to his office. Lights were going on all over the State and Defense Departments. Rusk conferred with the Secretary of State in Sandy Spring by phone, and Acheson put in a call to the Truman home in Independence. The phone rang just as the President and his family were entering the library after a leisurely dinner.

Truman's impulse was to fly back to Washington immediately but Acheson dissuaded him. It was still not certain whether the North Korean attack was a big raid or the real thing; besides, a dramatic return by the President could precipitate the world into a war scare. Truman and the Secretary of State discussed bringing the invasion formally before the United Nations and agreed that, for the moment, they would merely alert UN headquarters at Lake Success, Long Island.

John Hickerson, Assistant Secretary of State in charge of relations with the UN, put in the call to the Long Island home of UN Secretary-General Trygve Lie. The Secretary-General, who was just about to tune in a news broadcast, had heard nothing of the North Korean move and the news Hickerson spoke profoundly shocked him. "My God, Jack," Lie ejaculated, "this is war against the United Nations."

All Saturday night cables kept coming into Washington from Ambassador Muccio and from General Douglas MacArthur's headquarters in Tokyo, each one more ominous. The attack looked less and less like a mere raid; still more disturbing, evidence mounted that the invaders were fighting with Russian-made tanks and guns. At 2 a.m. Acheson put in another call to the President. They quickly agreed that the United States should formally bring the invasion before the Security Council and in the strongest possible manner. The United States would not present a resolution which merely called the attack a "dispute." It would urge the Security Council to categorize it under the "last resort" clause of the UN Charter—"threats to the peace, breaches of the peace, and acts of aggression." Under this heading the Security Council was empowered to take a further step and use economic sanctions, a blockade, or all-out military action against the aggressor.

Again, it was John Hickerson's turn for action. Vermont was too far away in terms of an emergency Security Council meeting at Lake Success and Hickerson did not contact the senior American representative to the UN, Warren Austin. Instead the call went to Long Island, where Deputy Representative Ernest Gross picked his way through a living-room full of sleeping teen-agers to get to the phone. Shortly before 3 a.m. Gross roused Secretary-General Lie from a none too restful sleep to tell him that the United States was requesting a Security Council meeting at the earliest possible time. Calls went out all over the area surrounding UN headquarters, summoning Security Council delegates from their weekend retreats.

When the Council assembled at 2.20 on Sunday afternoon, one of the big green chairs was glaringly vacant. For five months the Soviet representative had been boycotting the Council because of its refusal to replace the Nationalist Chinese delegate with a representative of Red China, and the Russian did not appear now. An added figure sat at the glistening horseshoe table, there by request of the United States. He was bespectacled little John Chang, the Republic of Korea's UN Observer.

Secretary-General Lie, shifting his huge body restlessly as he talked, opened the session with a firm statement: "The present situation is a serious one and is a threat to international peace. . . . I consider it the clear duty of the Security Council to take the steps necessary to reestablish peace in that area." Ernest Gross, his gray pin-stripe suit falling trimly over his solid build, heavy brows capping large, clear eyes, looked and talked like a highly successful attorney who was particularly sure of his case this time. The attack on South Korea, Gross declared, was of "grave concern to the governments of all peace-loving and freedom-loving nations" and "openly defies the interest and authority of the United Nations." The resolution which Gross asked the Council to adopt accused North Korea of "armed invasion," demanded that she cease fire immediately and order her troops back across the 38th parallel, and called upon all UN members "to render every assistance to the United Nations in the execution of this resolution."

In quick succession John Chang of South Korea and the representatives of Britain, Nationalist China, France, Ecuador, and Egypt supported the American resolution. But the French delegate and, more emphatically, the Egyptian representative indicated that they wanted time to suggest revisions and at 4.15 the Council recessed. Moves were made to change "armed invasion" to "armed attack" and to direct the cease-fire order not simply at North Korea but at both sides. These and other minor alterations were accepted by the United States without serious argument and the Council convened again at 5.25.

Throughout the session the nervous figure of Djura Nincic had been darting in and out of the chamber. Nincic's lot was hardly a happy one. His superior had not been able to get back to Lake Success in time and Nincic had little authority to act without telephone instructions. Nincic's country, Yugoslavia, was in a scarcely better position. It had broken with Stalin and was moving toward alignment with the West, but it was also looking into Soviet guns. After the recess, the Yugoslav made his move—the presentation of a compromise resolution which merely called for a cease-fire and invited North Korea to state its case before the UN. The only hand that went up for Nincic's proposal was his own (although Egypt, India, and Norway abstained). By 6 p.m. Sunday the American resolution had been adopted with the support of all the representatives except Nincic. Once again he compromised and abstained.

In Independence, Harry Truman had been trying hard to keep the appearance of calm. His original plan had called for having Sunday lunch at the farm which he and his brother Vivian owned in Grandview, near Kansas City. Sunday morning he drove over to Grandview and duly fiddled with a new milking machine, but that morning his interest in milking machines was minimal. By 11.30 he was back in Independence, awaiting further word from Washington.

At 12.35 Secretary Acheson telephoned. The North Korean attack, the Secretary of State informed the President, was undoubtedly an all-out offensive. American advisers in South Korea were asking for emergency supplies of ammunition and General MacArthur was sending arms from Tokyo. The UN, Acheson predicted correctly, would probably vote a cease-fire and the North Koreans, the Secretary went on just as accurately, would no doubt ignore the UN.

Harry Truman had heard enough. He told Acheson that he would order his plane, the *Independence*, readied immediately and asked the Secretary of State to get together with the military chiefs and prepare recommendations. The departure of the *Independence* was so abrupt that aides with clotheshangers over their shoulders were still running for the plane as the motors were tuned up. The President took care to say to newsmen at the airport: "Don't make it alarmist. It could be a dangerous situation, but I hope it isn't. I can't answer any questions until I get all the facts." The reporters noticed other things. Bess Truman waved good-by to her husband with a look very much like the one she had on that eerie evening when Vice-President Truman suddenly became President Truman. Margaret stood a bit apart from the airport crowd, staring at the plane with her hands clasped under her chin as if in silent prayer.

While the *Independence* sped toward Washington on the sunny Sunday afternoon, Truman had the plane's radio operator send a message to Acheson asking him to summon an emergency supper conference at Blair House that evening. For most of the three hours of the flight, the President kept to himself, mulling over the crisis.

During the hectic late 1940's, the Administration had been feeling its way toward a policy for the Far East and in the months immediately preceding the North Korean invasion, Truman and Acheson spelled out their program in a series of public statements. Basically the policy was containment, but with special twists intended to meet the circumstances of the Orient. The fundamental sources of unrest in the Far East, Truman and Acheson declared, were poverty and the hatred of being treated as colonial peoples. Military intervention in Asia by the United States would provoke bitter resentments which the Communists could exploit. America should be particularly careful

not to associate itself too closely, militarily or otherwise, with the Nationalist government of Chiang Kai-
shek, who was identified in the minds of millions of
Asiatics with the old, hateful ways of poverty and
Western domination and who was now holed up in
the only territory he had been able to keep from the
Communists, the island of Formosa.

So far as the mainland of China was concerned,
Acheson said for the Administration, the American attitude would be to keep hands off and to encourage
the Chinese leaders to realize that their real enemy
was the Soviet Union. In the case of Formosa, the
United States would from now on provide only limited economic assistance and would not send further
arms or military experts. With respect to the rest of
non-Communist Asia, the policy would be to seek to
win the goodwill of the masses through economic aid
while bolstering their ability to resist Communism by
the shipment of arms.

Five months before the North Korean invasion, as
part of a speech before the National Press Club of
Washington on January 12, Acheson approached the
Far Eastern problem in terms of military strategy. The
Secretary spoke of the "defensive perimeter" of the
United States in the Pacific and described it as running
from the Aleutian Islands off Alaska, to Japan, to Oki-
nawa south of Japan, and on to the Philippines. If any
of these points or any areas east of them were attacked,
Acheson made plain, the United States would fight.
Korea and Formosa lay west of this perimeter and of
this outer area the Secretary said: "So far as the military security of other areas in the Pacific is concerned,
it must be clear that no person can guarantee these
areas against military attack. But it must also be clear
that such a guarantee is hardly sensible or necessary
within the realm of practical relationship. Should an
attack occur—one hesitates to say where such an
armed attack could come from—the initial reliance
must be on the people attacked to resist it and then

upon the commitments of the entire civilized world under the Charter of the United Nations which so far has not proved a weak reed to lean on by any people who are determined to protect their independence against outside aggression."

Did these sentences say that the United States would permit Formosa, South Korea, or similar areas in the Far East to fall to the Communists? The Acheson speech obviously did not state that the United States would go to their defense. On the other hand, it did not state that the United States would refuse to defend them—provided that the United Nations sponsored the action. So far as the whole American attitude toward the Orient was concerned, the Secretary of State stressed in a number of statements, it could be radically changed by war in the region.

Well before the invasion of Korea, this Far Eastern policy of the Truman Administration had been the subject of a mounting attack. The Pacific was the area where Communism had made its most frightening postwar advance—China. It was also the area which aroused all the emotional furies of Asia Firstism. Devotees of the theory of conspiracy saw in the Truman-Acheson Far Eastern policy shocking proof that pro-Communists were guiding American affairs. Angrily they had been demanding that the United States throw its unqualified support behind Chiang Kai-shek, guarantee that Formosa would not be taken by the Chinese Reds, and encourage the Nationalists to attack the mainland. They were inclined to call for unreserved support of all anti-Communists in the Orient, whatever else the anti-Communists represented, and to place the United States on record as ready to fight rather than acquiesce in any further territorial advance of Communism. They found their hero in General MacArthur who, they said, stood for their whole position. These attitudes, so strongly felt by men who held to the theory of conspiracy, marked the thinking of many Republican leaders to a greater or lesser degree. Most notably, Senator Robert Taft had been moving closer and closer to such a position in the months before the North Korean invasion.

There was all this past debate over policy to move through the President's mind as the *Independence* flew east. There were also stark considerations of the present. In or outside any defense perimeter, the Republic of Korea had been set up by the United Nations. If the North Korean invasion overwhelmed the little country, the prestige of the UN would be undermined if not destroyed. And what of the effects on world opinion? Wouldn't millions of Asiatics say that the march of Communism was inevitable? Wouldn't many European leaders, already highly skeptical of the extent to which the United States would go in defending collective security, believe that America was ready to go no further than talk? Above all, the North Korean attack bore a haunting similarity to the fascist aggressions of the 1930's. In his thinking on the flight to Washington, the President had very much in mind the opinions of many experts who believed that World War II could have been prevented if the early aggressions of the 1930's had been stopped.

The *Independence* landed in Washington at 7.15 p.m. Sunday and Truman hurried off to Blair House, where Acheson had assembled the chief State Department aides, the Secretary of Defense, the Secretaries of the three branches of the military, and the Joint Chiefs of Staff. The White House maître d'hôtel Alonzo Fields, was rather proud of the dinner he and his staff managed to get together by calling on the frying-chickens in the freezer, but minds were scarcely on the food. The meal was doubly quick because the President asked that no real discussion of the situation should begin until the servants were out of the room.

After dinner the long mahogany table was cleared and served as a conference board. The President, as was his usual practice, listened to the views of his advisers before expressing his own but it was soon obvious that Truman's thinking on the plane had taken him far. He was the clear-cut leader of the group, grim and decisive. This was no time, Truman made his attitude plain, for worrying over what Administration policy might have been up to now. The world-wide Communist threat was getting out of hand. In the Far East, particularly, the situation was deteriorating to the point where the national security of the United States, the future effectiveness of the UN, and the ability to avoid World War III were gravely endangered. The hour was at hand, the President's whole manner emphasized, for boldness.

Truman asked Acheson to present the joint recommendations of the State and Defense Departments and the Secretary listed a number, of which three were most immediate. MacArthur should be ordered to continue what he was already doing—rushing ammunition to South Korea. The General should be told to furnish ships and planes to protect the evacuation of Americans. American policy toward Formosa should be altered by having the Seventh Fleet sail from the Philippines and protect the island from invasion by the Chinese Reds. At the same time the fleet should see to it that Chiang launched no attack on the mainland.

The Formosa proposal provoked considerable discussion—just how much and how heated the available evidence does not make certain. The conferees also made varying estimates as to how far the United States might have to go in order to check the aggression in Korea. At least two of the military men present brought up the possibility that American ground forces would have to be used. On one point there was absolutely no disagreement. The President has recalled "the complete, almost unspoken acceptance on the part of everyone that whatever had to be done to meet this aggression had to be done. There was no suggestion from anyone that either the United Nations or the United States could back away from it."

Before the meeting broke up, Harry Truman made his decisions. He ordered the ammunition sped to Korea and the evacuation of Americans protected; the latter order followed the general tenor of the discussion and permitted MacArthur wide discretion in defining how much action by American air and naval units was needed to "protect" the evacuation. The President issued no instructions about Formosa but he did order the Seventh Fleet to leave the Philippines and proceed toward the island.

On Monday, June 26, the news from the battlefront steadily darkened. Far from obeying the UN ceasefire, the North Koreans were sweeping ahead in a six-pronged blitz. By late afternoon the reports were so bad another emergency council was summoned at Blair House, this time for 9 p.m. Once again Secretary of State Acheson presented the joint recommendations of the State and Defense Departments. The key proposal was that the United States Navy and Air Force should be ordered to provide cover and support for the South Korean armies although they were not to operate north of the 38th parallel. The Secretary also repeated the recommendation that the Seventh Fleet should neutralize the island of Formosa. He added that the UN Security Council would meet the next day, Tuesday, and urged that the United States press for a resolution calling on members of the UN to give armed assistance to South Korea. In the ensuing discussion, no one raised any important objection to the recommendations. Harry Truman made his affirmative decisions on the spot. Forty minutes after the conference began it was over.

All during Sunday and Monday, opinion in the capitals of the free world had been growing increasingly restive. No real news leaked from the Blair House conferences. A Presidential statement of Monday, which consisted merely of generalities, left most observers with the feeling that another Munich was in

158 THE CRUCIAL DECADE

the making. Friends of collective security in Washington and the other Western capitals were downcast. They were inclined to agree with the European diplomat who cabled his government from Washington: "The time has come when Uncle Sam must put up or shut up, and my guess is he will do neither." At UN headquarters, delegates smiled wryly at the signs on the bulletin boards which announced: "Monday, June 26 is the fifth anniversary of the signing of the United Nations Charter." June 26 so easily could be the wake of the United Nations.

Early on the morning of Tuesday, June 27, word began to get around Washington that the President would announce he had pledged American arms to the defense of South Korea. Most reporters were astonished. At 12.30 the official statement was released. Washington gulped, then reacted with a massive closing of ranks. The *Christian Science Monitor*'s Washington bureau chief, Joseph C. Harsch, a resident of the capital for twenty years, reported: "Never before in that time have I felt such a sense of relief and unity pass through the city." James Reston of the *New York Times* added: "The decision to meet the Communist challenge in Korea has produced a transformation in the spirit of the United States Government. . . . There have been some differences in the last seventy-two hours over how to react to the Communist invasion, but . . . these differences have apparently been swept away by the general conviction that the dangers of inaction were greater than the dangers of the bold action taken by the President."

When the Truman statement was read in the House of Representatives, the whole chamber rose cheering except Vito Marcantonio of New York, long a fellow traveler of the Communist Party. In the Senate, a few Republicans asked irritably—to use the words of James Kem of Missouri—whether the orders to the Navy and Air Force meant that Truman "arrogates to himself the power to declare war." A scattering of other questioning remarks were made. While the Democratic leader, Scott Lucas of Illinois, was answering the criticisms, Senator William Knowland of California, a rising figure in the Taft group, interrupted to say: "I believe that in the very important steps the President of the United States has taken to uphold the hands of the United Nations and the free peoples of the world, he should have the overwhelming support of all Americans regardless of their party affiliation." Both sides of the Senate broke into loud, sustained applause.

Throughout the United States opinion rallied to the support of Harry Truman. Telegrams and letters, some of a highly personal nature, flooded the White House, running ten-to-one in favor of the Presidential action. Truman was especially pleased by a wire from his 1948 opponent, Thomas Dewey, which read: "I wholeheartedly agree with and support the difficult decision you have made." The *Chicago Tribune* was unhappy, but most Republican opinion across the country went at least as far as the head of a Warren County, Iowa, organization, who said to reporters: "We don't know who told him [Truman] to do it, but for once he made the right decision." The nation's most respected Republican newspaper, the *New York Herald Tribune*, gave center front page to an editorial that declared: "The President has acted—and spoken—with a magnificent courage and terse decision. . . . It was time to draw a line—somewhere, somehow. . . . The jubilation in the Soviet satellite press over the first successes of the Korean invasion, the dispirited reaction from all peoples who have looked to United States support in their battle for freedom, is sufficient indication of what would have been bound to follow if the United States had supinely accepted this as one more victory for Communist armed infiltration. The President has refused so to accept it; his is an act of statesmanship and this newspaper believes that it is a basic contribution toward genuine peace in our disturbed and distracted world."

As Truman's words went out on Tuesday, an air of intense excitement gathered around UN headquarters. The President's statement declared that he had ordered the use of the American Navy and Air Force in support of the UN resolution of Sunday. The resolution could be interpreted to sanction armed intervention but it certainly did not explicitly call on America or any other member nation to enter the shooting war. Now the Administration, anxious to have clear-cut UN endorsement for its move and to bring other nations to the military support of South Korea, was pressing for a resolution that unequivocally summoned the member nations of the UN to "furnish such assistance to the Republic of Korea as may be necessary to repel the armed attack and to restore international peace and security in the area." Passage of this resolution would mark an epochal step. For the first time in the five thousand years of man's recorded history a world organization would be voting armed force to stop armed force.

Since early Tuesday morning the United States had been pressing hard for a quick assembling of the Security Council. From the point of view of American and overseas opinion every hour counted, but the President of the Security Council, the veteran Indian diplomat Sir Benegal Rau, was not to be rushed. The new American policy presented problems for the countries of Asia and the Middle East, which were becoming more and more neutralist in their attitude toward the East-West struggle. Sir Benegal and the representative of Egypt both wanted fresh instructions from their home governments before they took a position and they were having trouble getting the instructions. Apparently the home governments were none too sure what they wanted to do in the ticklish situation. Besides, the overseas telephone lines on this particular day were filled with squawks and fadeouts.

The minutes and the hours went by and still the Security Council was not called to order.

Lunch hour brought a curious scene in the Stockholm Restaurant on Long Island. The UN Secretary-General, Trygve Lie, had a long-standing date to eat with a group including Ernest Gross and the Soviet delegate, Jacob Malik. Gross and Malik sat on either side of Lie and the three men talked at length about the Korean situation. The Russian insisted that the first, June 25, resolution was "illegal" because no Soviet delegate was present at the meeting and because the Security Council had not seated a representative of Red China. He also charged "intervention by the United States" in Korea. About the time the meal was reaching coffee and dessert, the Secretary-General performed his duty as an international officer and urged the Russian to end his boycott of the Security Council and attend the meeting that afternoon. "Won't you join us?" Lie urged. "The interests of your country would seem to me to call for your presence."

Malik shook his head vigorously. "No, I will not go there."

Lie and Ernest Gross left the luncheon together and got into the Secretary-General's car. Gross's relief was unconcealed. "Think," he said to Lie, "what would have happened if he had accepted your invitation."

It was a moment that recalled the day in Paris when the bump on Molotov's head swelled and he made plain that the Soviet would have no part of the Marshall Plan. What, indeed, would have happened if Malik had attended the Security Council, vetoed the resolution, and left the American Navy and Air Force fighting without explicit UN sanction until the cumbersome machinery of the UN General Assembly could have been brought into action?

By mid-afternoon the Egyptian and Indian representatives were still without instructions and at 3.16

p.m. Sir Benegal gaveled the Council to order. Each country had its first team in now. The senior American delegate, ex-United States Senator Warren Austin, was back from his apple orchard, looking very pink-cheeked and very fatherly and very agitated. The number-one Yugoslav, slim and swarthy Ales Bebler, sat in ramrod alertness. Spectators filled every seat in the Security Council chamber and overflowed into the usually sacrosanct delegates' lounge, where a television set was tuned to the proceedings (more than 5,000 people were being turned away). The summer prints of the women were gay and the men's seersuckers casual, but a tense, hushed atmosphere surrounded the crowd.

Action came in a rapid fire. With a brief speech, Austin presented the American resolution. Bebler immediately countered with a proposal that would have left the United States far out on a limb—a resolution calling merely for a repetition of the cease-fire order and the institution of mediation proceedings.

The crowd strained irritably as it heard the translation of Bebler's words, then returned to complete quiet. John Chang of South Korea was talking now. He had not been to bed since the first news of the invasion and his short speech dragged with weariness. "Moral judgment," Chang said, was not enough. It had to be backed with force sufficient "to expel the invader from our territory and act directly in the establishment of international peace and security." Chang's drawn face seemed to relax as, in quick succession, the representatives of France, Britain, Nationalist China, Cuba, Norway, and Ecuador rose to support the American resolution. When Egypt's turn came shortly after five o'clock, Mahmoud Fawzi could only say that he expected "shortly to receive . . . instructions on this matter of extreme urgency and importance." Sir Benegal, who was in no better position, proposed an adjournment to 6.15.

As Austin walked from the Council chamber to the

delegates' lounge, reporters surrounded him. One newsman asked if he thought there was any chance Jacob Malik might show up for the later session.

Austin chewed hard on his cigar. "Oh, Lord, don't ask me such questions."

Another reporter wanted to know whether the next step after passing the American resolution would be the establishment of a permanent United Nations military force. "Now, boys," Austin said, "don't take me too far. Remember that a big country has to be careful. It's so easy for a big country to give offense."

The spectators were jamming the bar, watching two children's puppets named Foodini and Pinhead on the television set, drifting out into the corridors. At 6.25 it was announced that the Council would stay adjourned until 9 and a large part of the crowd gave up and went home for supper. At 9.22 the session was postponed again, and at 10.20 the delegates finally filed into the chamber. The seat of Jacob Malik was still glaringly vacant; Egypt and India were still without instructions from home. The balloting, first on the American and then on the Yugoslav resolution, followed its preordained course. Egypt and India abstained. Every other country except Yugoslavia voted for the U.S. resolution. Yugoslavia alone voted for the Yugoslav proposal.

As the balloting ended, there was a stir at the delegates' table. Sir Benegal turned over the Presidency to his alternate, Gopala Menon, and the Indian and Egyptian delegates hurried from the room. "New Delhi and Alexandria are on the phone," Menon told the Council. Five minutes went by and it was just past 11 p.m. A messenger whispered to Menon and the Acting President said: "I understand it has not been possible to get the phone calls through. The meeting of the Security Council is adjourned."

The UN was backing Harry Truman; the U.S. was cheering him. There was still that special principality, armed and formidable, which went by the name of

Senator Robert A. Taft. He had sat through the Senate discussion on Tuesday, head resting in his hand, wrapped in quiet inscrutability. Not until Wednesday afternoon did Taft take the Senate floor.

In many ways the speech spoke the strongest feelings of the devotees of the theory of conspiracy. The fall of China and the succeeding troubles in the Far East were all the fault of the Administration, "of the sympathetic acceptance of communism." The Democrats had "invited" the North Korean attack. The acceptance of the 38th parallel meant "giving the Russians the northern half of the country, with most of the power and a good deal of the industry, and leaving a southern half which could not support itself, except on an agricultural basis." The "Chinese policy of the administration gave basic encouragement to the North Korean aggression. If the United States was not prepared to use its troops and give military assistance to Nationalist China [Formosa] against Chinese Communists, why should it use its troops to defend Nationalist Korea against Korean Communists?" Taft declared that Acheson's speech of 1950 in which he described the Pacific "defensive perimeter" of the United States as running on the American side of Korea and Formosa offered an especially obvious green light to the Communists. "With such a reaffirmation of our Far Eastern policy, is it any wonder that the Korean Communists took us at the word given by the Secretary of State?"

In the manner of the whole revolt against the Administration foreign policy, the Senator singled out Acheson for his heaviest blows. "The President's statement of policy [on Tuesday] represents a complete change in the programs and policies heretofore proclaimed by the Administration." It meant a "reversal" of Acheson, and "any Secretary of State who has been so reversed by his superiors and whose policies have precipitated the danger of [world] war, had better resign and let someone else administer the program to which he was, and perhaps still is, so violently opposed." In the scattering of applause which followed this statement, the enthusiasm of Senators Joseph McCarthy and the emerging McCarthyite leader, William Jenner of Indiana, was particularly conspicuous.

Taft then went on to question Truman's right to order armed intervention without consulting Congress, whether the intervention was in support of the UN or not. The Senator had not "thoroughly investigated" the matter. But after all, the Constitution gave Congress the exclusive right to declare war and "his action unquestionably has brought about a de facto war. . . . So far as I can see, and so far as I have studied the matter, I would say there is no authority to use armed forces in support of the United Nations in the absence of some previous action by Congress dealing with the subject. . . ."

Yet the questioning and the attack were only one phase of the Taft speech. Throughout he made plain that "I approve of the changes now made in our foreign policy. I approve of the general policies outlined in the President's statement." Had the question of armed intervention in Korea been brought before Congress, the Senator emphasized, he would have voted affirmatively. The seasoned newspaperman William S. White, who was covering Washington politics at the time, has commented: "While Taft was sharp . . . [his] speech was welcomed by the internationalists; they felt that, for him, it was remarkably soft toward the President and toward the whole enterprise."

Truman's press secretary, Charles Ross, put it another way. Told of the Senator's speech, he shook his head incredulously and said: "My God! Bob Taft has joined the UN and the U.S."

At 7 a.m. on Thursday, June 29, the news from Korea took another sharp turn for the worse. General

MacArthur's headquarters, communicating by tele-con with the Pentagon, reported that the South Ko-rean casualties were nearing a staggering fifty per cent. The capital city of Seoul had fallen and the Re-public of Korea troops (ROK's) were trying to form a line at the Han River, south of Seoul, but it was questionable whether they could. Other disturbing information followed. By late morning Secretary of Defense Louis Johnson was on the phone to the White House, suggesting another top-level conference and the hour was set for 5 p.m.

At 4 p.m. the President held his first press confer-ence since the North Korean attack. Quickly one of the reporters got to the inevitable: "Mr. President, every-body is asking in this country, are we or are we not at war?"

"We are not at war," Truman replied and he granted the newsmen the unusual privilege of directly quoting a President's words at a press conference. Truman also permitted direct quotation of his phrase that the United States was trying to suppress "a ban-dit raid" on the Republic of Korea.

Another reporter asked: "Would it be correct to call this a police action under the United Nations?"

Yes, the President replied, that was exactly what it amounted to. (Thus, indirectly, Truman became as-sociated with the phrase that was to be so bitter a part of later foreign-policy debate.)

Reporters did not push the President on the defini-tion. They, like the nation, were not pushing him on anything these days. Later in the conference a news-man asked about Taft's demand for Acheson's resig-nation and Truman brushed it aside with a disdainful remark about political statements in the middle of an emergency like this. The reporter subsided.

From the press conference the President turned to the five o'clock meeting of his advisers, which assem-bled this time at the White House. The council con-sisted of all the men present at the Sunday and Monday meetings and some additions, including John Foster Dulles, Republican adviser to the State Department who had been in Korea as recently as June 21, and W. Averell Harriman, chief of American economic activities in Europe, who had been summoned from Paris the day before. Defense Secretary Johnson opened the conference with a gloomy review of the military situation. Circumstances were such, he pointed out, that even American naval and air aid were not proving of great help.

Johnson then read a proposed directive to General MacArthur, which had been prepared by the Defense Department and concurred in by the State Department during the day. The order authorized the use of American service troops (primarily signal-corps and transport units) throughout South Korea, and the use of American combat troops for the limited purpose of protecting the port and airfield at Pusan on the southeastern tip of the peninsula. American ships and planes, previously forbidden to strike at Communist supplies and reinforcements until they came south of the 38th parallel, were permitted to attack military targets in North Korea. The directive did not permit MacArthur to send American combat troops into the combat area, which was still nearly two hundred miles north of Pusan.

The President hesitated. He was particularly disturbed by the thought of committing ground troops anywhere in Korea. During the ensuing discussion Secretary of State Acheson contributed the news of the Soviet reply to an American note which had asked Russia to use its influence with the North Koreans to get them to cease fire. The important aspect of the Soviet note, Acheson said, was not the fact that Russia refused. It was rather that the Soviet reply seemed to indicate that the Russians did not plan direct military intervention in the war. This estimate removed some of the President's reluctance to commit American ground troops; the unanimous urging of his military advisers removed the rest. By 5.40 the conference was over and the new orders were being hurried to Tokyo.

That evening Acheson returned to the White House with a communication from Chiang Kai-shek. The Nationalist leader was offering ground forces up to thirty-three thousand men, although he would need American air and naval units to transport and supply his troops. The President's inclination was to accept the offer. Wasn't this what the UN had asked its member countries to do? he said. Moreover, Truman could hardly have failed to be thinking that the more troops fighting with the ROK's, the less likelihood of need for American units in the actual battles. The Secretary of State opposed acceptance of the offer. Chiang Kai-shek's troops would need a great deal of re-equipping before they could go into combat, he argued. Besides, Nationalist China was a special case among the UN members. Formosa was being defended by the American Seventh Fleet and did it make sense for the United States to protect the island while its natural defenders went off elsewhere? The President, still unconvinced, asked Acheson to bring the matter up at a Friday-morning conference.

Before the morning came, at 3 a.m. on Friday, the Pentagon received a lengthy cable from General MacArthur. He had just returned from a personal reconnaissance at the battlefront and his words were blunt. "The South Korean forces," the General declared, "are in confusion, have not seriously fought, and lack leadership. Organized and equipped as a light force for maintenance of interior order, they were unprepared for attack by armor and air. Conversely they are incapable of gaining the initiative over such a force as that embodied in the North Korean army. . . . It is essential that the enemy advance be held or its impetus will threaten the over-running of all Korea." Then MacArthur made his recommendation: "The only assurance for holding the present line and the ability

to regain later the lost ground is through the introduc-
tion of United States ground combat forces into the
Korean battle area. . . . If authorized it is my intention to immediately move a United States regimental
combat team to the reinforcement of the vital area discussed and to provide for a possible build-up to a
two division strength from the troops in Japan for an
early counteroffensive."

General J. Lawton Collins, Chief of Staff of the
Army, had a hurried telecon connection put through
to Tokyo. The President, Collins told MacArthur, had
made it plain that he was reluctant to commit troops
to combat, and before giving such an order Truman
would probably want to consult advisers. Wouldn't
the directive of Thursday—using service troops and
moving combat units to Pusan—be enough until the
President could hold such a conference?

Time was of the essence, MacArthur answered emphatically. Immediate authorization to use American
troops in the fighting was of the highest importance
if all South Korea were not to fall.

Collins replied that he would get the President's answer with the greatest possible speed. It was Secretary
of the Army Frank C. Pace, Jr. who telephoned Blair
House. Harry Truman, always an early riser, was up
even earlier these days. Shortly before 5 a.m., already
shaved, he took Pace's call at the phone on his bedside
table. With only a flicker of hesitation the President
authorized the sending of one regimental combat team
to the combat zone. On the question of a build-up to
two divisions, he promised an answer in a few hours.
Top military and State Department officials were tumbled out of bed. There would be a White House meeting at 8.30 a.m., the Presidential message ran, and the
conferees were to be prepared to discuss Mac-
Arthur's urgent recommendation and the Chiang Kai-
shek offer of troops.

At the meeting Truman raised the question whether
it would not be wise to accept the Nationalist offer.

The number of trained American troops, he stressed, was quite limited and there was no telling where else trouble might break out. What, for instance, was Mao Tse-tung planning? And what might the Russians do in the Balkans, Germany, or Iran?

Acheson continued his opposition. To his arguments of the previous night he added the consideration that the use of Nationalist troops might provoke the Chinese Reds to enter the fighting. The Secretary was backed by all the military chiefs on military grounds. They maintained that Chiang's ill-equipped men would be helpless against the North Koreans. Furthermore, the transportation required would be more profitably used by being assigned to carry American soldiers and supplies from Japan.

Disagreements might arise about particular ways to throw back the North Korean aggression; Harry Truman was not wavering in the slightest in his determination to achieve that purpose. "I was still concerned," he has recalled the close of the conference, "about our ability to stand off the enemy with the small forces available to us, but after some further discussion I accepted the position taken by practically everyone else at this meeting; namely, that the Chinese offer ought to be politely declined. I then decided that General MacArthur should be given full authority to use the ground forces under his command"—not only the build-up to two divisions but all the combat troops he could spare from Japan. At the suggestion of Admiral Forrest Sherman, Chief of Naval Operations, a second order was added, a naval blockade of the Korean coast. At 1.22 p.m. on Friday, June 30, just short of six days after the first shots were fired by the North Koreans, the orders left Washington which put the United States irrevocably in the war—planes, ships, tanks, and infantrymen.

Late Friday afternoon the President left Washington. He had been canceling engagements all week, but now he was going to keep a date to address an international boy scout jamboree at Valley Forge. Then he would meet his daughter Margaret, who was singing at a concert in Philadelphia, and they would board the Presidential yacht *Williamsburg* for a leisurely trip back to Washington. As Truman approached the train in Washington, reporters noted that the lines in his face were receding and his step was regaining its sprightliness. The decision to fight was made and he was confident it was the right one. He was not going to let the United States and its President be pushed around, Truman remarked several times on Friday, and he was not going to let the United Nations be pushed around.

The nation was in no mood to disagree. The order to send combat troops into Korea produced even less dissent than had come with the Tuesday decision to use only the Navy and Air Force. The fact of war, of course, hushed criticism but this was hardly the complete story. A whole concatenation of emotions pulled Americans together in support of the President —a feeling of relief that the United States had at last taken an armed stand against Communism, the hope that Korea would stave off World War III and the dread that it would not, a sense of pride that American deeds were now matching American words, the natural human response to the forthright courage of Harry Truman.

The very nature of the Presidential decisions disarmed critics of the Truman-Acheson foreign policy. Devotees of the theory of conspiracy and many less extreme dissenters had insisted that Asia was being neglected; Asia was now the focus of the national effort. They had demanded American arms to protect Formosa from the Chinese Reds; the Seventh Fleet shielded the island. They had cried out for a line to be drawn against Communism, beyond this not one step further; the line was as plain as guns and bombs could make it. They had put their faith, above all, in General

Douglas MacArthur. It was at the General's recommendation—and this fact was generally known—that full intervention had been decided upon, and Douglas MacArthur was in command in Korea.

American acceptance of the Truman moves was bolstered by the reaction around the free world. Western representatives at the United Nations were jubilant. Delegate after delegate was telling reporters that the Truman leadership had saved the UN from going the tragic way of the League of Nations. Newspapers were filled with descriptions of the stiffened sense of resolution in western Europe and Asia. From all over the free world came comments like that of the high French official who said: "A few days ago I was filled with despair. I saw as in a nightmare all the horrors repeated that followed the first surrender to Hitler in 1936. Now there is a burst of sun." Even if the intervention failed, the Frenchman went on, that was not the essential point. "It is the proof of your willingness to act that makes all the difference. A continent that is emerging slowly from defeat and demoralization needs moral assurance as much as material help or proofs of military preparedness."

Most striking of all was the news from India, huge and critically important India. For weeks Prime Minister Jawaharlal Nehru had been making increasingly neutralist statements and Indian newspapers freely predicted that their country would not support the Tuesday resolution of the UN Security Council. On Friday afternoon Sir Benegal Rau finally received his instructions from New Delhi and he reported that India "accepted" the resolution. The Nehru government was "opposed to any attempt to settle international disputes by resort to aggression."

East, west, north, and south, American newspapers reported overwhelming support of the President in their areas. "The White House gang is today enormously popular, incredibly popular," even the *Chicago Tribune* found itself saying. In Congress criticism was only a growl here and there on the side aisles. Senator Robert Taft made no speech; instead he observed in the lobby that America should go "all out." Senator Joseph McCarthy found no one to applaud. As a matter of fact, the Democratic leadership had proceeded to suspend the investigation of McCarthy's charges against the State Department without a single Republican protest. The loudest cheers in either the House or the Senate followed a speech of Representative Charles Eaton of New Jersey, ranking Republican on the House Foreign Affairs Committee. Eaton was an ordained Baptist minister and he managed to convey just how much he supported Democrat Harry Truman. "We've got a rattlesnake by the tail," said the Reverend Representative, "and the sooner we pound its damn head in the better."

For one moment, suspended weirdly in the bitter debates of the postwar, the reckless plunge of the North Korean Communists and the bold response of Harry Truman had united America, united it as it had not been since that distant confetti evening of V-J.

All Taft, Republican gripes at Dems, + US for policy, were shot, because Truman's decisions were of that type — see 171-72

Americans united! glad US was taking stand against Communism

The Hills of Korea

THE NEWS was terrible. Day after day, week after week the newspapers read the same—retreat, bloody, humiliating, scarifying retreat.

The UN forces under General MacArthur's command—largely American and South Korean—were pitifully unprepared to stop the powerful North Korean blitz. They were outnumbered three to one, eight to one, even twenty to one in some areas. The light defensive arms of the ROK's bounced helplessly off the huge Soviet-made tanks advancing against them. The Americans who came rushing in from Japan were little better prepared. They had no tanks of their own and the thirty-five-ton Soviet machines laughed at their old World War II bazookas. Only ten to twenty per cent of the Americans were seasoned by combat. All of them were occupation soldiers who, as their field commander Major General William Dean remarked later, were used to being "fat and happy in occupation billets, complete with Japanese girl friends, plenty of beer, and servants to shine their boots."

The desperately needed arms and reinforcements could be sent from the United States only with agonizing slowness. The situation was the product of years of economizing in the military budget, pushed by Republican and Democratic Congresses, tolerated by President Truman, and sanctified by the Secretary of Defense, Louis Johnson, who had done that pontifi-

cating about if "Joe Stalin . . . starts something at
four o'clock in the morning," the "fighting power" of
America would be taking care of things by five. It was
way past five o'clock now and the United States was
fighting back with a feather.

From the battlefronts came the reports, stark and
heart-rending. The retreat of the UN forces was so
pellmell that three weeks after the war began headlines told of the capture of General Dean himself.
He was last seen, the accounts said, in the front lines
of the confused fighting, desperately trying to rally
his men against the tanks. Generals or privates, the debacle was the same. The story of tens of thousands of
GI's was told by Sergeant Raymond Remp, of Pittsburgh, who fled Taegu after fourteen and a half
hours of constant fire.

"Someone fired a green flare, and they saw us," the
Sergeant choked out his account to reporters. "All
around us in the hills, bugles started in blowing. . . .
They were right on top of us in the hills, firing down
on us. . . .

"Some colonel—don't know who—said, 'Get out the
best way you can.' He stayed behind to hold them. As
we went up a draw, they opened fire. I got my rifle
belt and canteen shot off. Two men following me got
hit. They were so tired they just couldn't move.

"We headed south. An officer and me split up our
ammo and rations into a couple of cans. I drank water
from the rice paddies. Got cramps—sick as a dog—and
my dysentery is awful. . . .

"Tanks fired at us from our own motor pool. We
met some more guys cut off. We climbed a big mountain. The guys had machine guns strapped on their
backs. One ran with his gun and stooped over. His
partner fired. I don't know where they got the
strength.

"They ran like goats. We took off and got on top of
another mountain. We ran across six of them mountain
tops and killed four guys. We were out of ammo. . . .

"For 10 miles outside Taegu, we were fired at. All day and night we ran like antelopes. We didn't know our officers. They didn't know us. We lost everything we had.

"These new shoes were put on me a couple of days ago. The soles were almost ripped off from running. My feet are cut to pieces. I saw lots of guys running barefooted.

"I can't stand it—seeing friends get it and not being able to help them drives you crazy. I thought the Huertgen Forest was bad and Normandy, but they were nothing like this. This was awful.

"How much can you take?

"I guess I'm lucky. I'm not hit. But what it did to me. . . . Oh my God, what it did to me."

It was not only frantic retreat. It was frantic retreat amid savagery. The fighting was not two weeks old when the authenticated stories came of American soldiers lying in ditches, their hands tied behind their backs and bullet holes in the rear of their heads. With or without butchery, almost any aspect of this war was proving peculiarly disturbing to the American reader. MacArthur's command was supposed to be a United Nations force and a scattering of other nations were soon contributing some military aid. But why, influential publications in the United States demanded to know, should America be expected to bear so heavy a share of the fighting?

For the first time ordinary citizens in Portland, Omaha, and Tuscaloosa were discovering just how complicated it was to fight Communists. Foreign correspondents kept pointing out that North Korean propaganda pamphlets emphasized things like: "Today, under the orders of a Southern U.S. President, U.S. planes are bombing and strafing COLORED PEOPLE in Korea." Almost everyone who wrote from Korea stressed that this conflict was not only a war against North Koreans but a highly complex struggle for the feelings of all Asiatics, feelings that had become ex-

traordinarily sensitive under the proddings of nationalism and of Communism.

Americans were reading daily the evidence that
even the GI was no longer his cocky, wisecracking
self. Ever-retreating, outmanned, outtanked, outsup-
plied, outflanked, and outyelled, fighting over saw-
tooth ridges, wreck-littered roads, and paddies ferti-
lized by human excrement, most of the American
soldiers were glum, bitter, confused. The average GI
had not the slightest idea why he was battling on these
far-off hills. "I'll fight for my country," Corporal
Stephen Zeg of Chicago put it, "but I'll be damned if
I see why I'm fighting to save this hell hole." After a
few flourishes at the beginning of the war, troops leaving the United States usually wanted no parades. Once
in Korea, they went in conspicuously little for jokes
and horseplay. No Kilroy announced his sovereign
presence. There was no bouncing "Mademoiselle from
Armentières," which the doughboys had marched to
in World War I, no love song like "Lili Marlene" of
World War II. The most popular GI expression was a
fatalistic, "Well, that's the way the ball bounces." The
Korean GI, if he sang at all, was likely to rasp out lines
like:

> *The Dhow, the Gizee, and Rhee*
> *What do they want from me?*

Finally, on August 6, 1950 the retreat ended. Large
numbers of reinforcements, the stiffening lines of the
ROK's, new tank-killing American arms, and the mur-
derous operations of the U.S. air forces had all told. A
defense perimeter was now stabilized around the port
of Pusan at the southeastern tip of Korea.

On September 15 the UN forces took the offensive.
In a brilliant amphibious operation conceived by General MacArthur, the troops landed at Inchon near the
western end of the 38th parallel and fought their way
east. Other UN armies struck north from Pusan. The
North Koreans, in danger of total entrapment, surren-
dered by the thousands or ran for the 38th parallel.

The UN forces swept north in hot pursuit, up to the parallel and—authorized by a hasty and vague UN resolution—into North Korea. Soon advance units of the UN armies were on the banks of the Yalu River, which separated North Korea from Chinese Manchuria. On November 24 General MacArthur launched a "final" offensive, designed to crush all remaining resistance in North Korea and leave North and South Korea united under UN supervision. "The war," MacArthur told reporters, "very definitely is coming to an end shortly."

As the UN troops had advanced toward the 38th parallel, the Premier and Foreign Minister of Red China, Chou En-lai, bitterly denounced the "frenzied and violent acts of imperialist aggression" of the United States and stated that the Chinese people would not "supinely tolerate seeing their [North Korean] neighbors being savagely invaded by imperialists." During late October and November, MacArthur's troops encountered considerable units of Chinese "volunteers" as much as fifty miles south of the Yalu.

President Truman had put the danger of Chinese intervention to General MacArthur in a conference at Wake Island on October 15. Just what was said at Wake Island and in subsequent communications between Washington and Tokyo is the subject of furious controversy (Truman and MacArthur have devoted large sections of books to the subject, the President in his *Memoirs*, the General in the authorized volume, *MacArthur: His Rendezvous with History*). What emerges as incontestable fact is that MacArthur told Truman at Wake Island that there was little if any chance of Chinese intervention and that, if the Chinese did come in, their armies would be slaughtered; that the Truman Administration approved the movement north of the 38th parallel and the "final" offensive only on the basis of this assurance; that as the evidence of Chinese fighting increased, the General appealed to Washington for permission to blow up the bridges across the Yalu and the Administration refused, partly because it was trying to stay out of war with the Chinese and partly because the river would soon freeze and be as passable as any bridge; and that McArthur launched his Yalu offensive with little thought in his own mind and no indication to Washington that it might provoke a major Chinese counter-offensive.

Late in November President Truman appeared at the door of his White House office to summon his staff for the daily conference. He put his hands on his hips in the mock impatience he loved to show and he grinned. But the little ritual had no exuberance. The President went around the group in his usual way, taking up the problems each man had on his mind. Then he moved to the middle of his desk, shifted papers back and forth, and finally spoke in a quiet, solemn way. "General Bradley called me at 6.15 this morning," Truman said. "He told me that a terrible message had come from General MacArthur. . . . The Chinese have come in with both feet."

The Chinese had come in with both feet and a roundhouse swing. On November 26 thirty-three divisions hit the UN lines. Night after night the pattern of attack was the same. Under cover of darkness, specially trained and specially armed units of five to nine Chinese crawled forward to determine just how the UN front troops were arranged, to destroy artillery positions, and to cut supply lines. Then flares lit up, bugles or cymbals sounded, whistles went off, and the mass of infantrymen charged, thousands of them, falling unexcited and apparently unafraid only to make room for more thousands. Quickly the Chinese smashed down the center of the UN forces. To the west American and other UN units were able to retreat in orderly fashion, though with heavy casualties. To the east the situation was desperate. The overwhelming Communist offensive cut off and surrounded masses of UN troops, including the First Marine Division and two battalions of the Seventh Infantry Division of the United States. The position of the First Marine Division was especially critical. It was surrounded on the frigid wastes beside the Chongjin Reservoir, forty miles from the nearest evacuation point on the east coast.

Major General Oliver P. Smith, a Marine for thirty-three years and now the proud commander of the First Division, sent out the defiant word: "Retreat, hell! We're only attacking in another direction." The Marines did fight with guts and wits that sent a thrill through the home country but the newspapers also had to describe the worst ordeal since Tarawa. Much of the escape route was a corkscrew trail of icy dirt, just wide enough for a two-and-a-half-ton truck and winding by rocky ridges and forested bluffs that were filled with Chinese. Sub-zero cold, violent snowstorms, and sudden wild gorges two thousand feet deep were as much of a menace as the Communists. A large part of the fighting was during the night and at close quarters, with pistols, grenades, and submachine guns. 2,651 wounded were flown out in only four days; once 117 bodies were buried in a single grave and a bulldozer used to push a covering over them—there was no time for anything else when a grave had to be blasted from ground frozen to eighteen inches.

Long-distance telephone lines to Washington were flooded. "What is the real situation?" "Is it true that the First Marine Division has been wiped out and the news is going to be let out slowly?" "Why doesn't somebody *do* something?" After thirteen days the survivors began to reach safety. The Marines came in so many remnants of holocaust, the uninjured with sunken, staring eyes, the wounded often grimacing from frostbite as well as their injuries, some of the dead lying grotesquely across trailers with blood frozen to their skin.

In Washington grim faces grew grimmer. President Truman confided to a memorandum pad: "We had conference after conference on the jittery situation facing the country. Attlee, Formosa, Communist China, Chiang Kai-shek, Japan, Germany, France, India, etc. I have worked for peace for five years and six months and it looks like World War III is near." Hastily the Administration, with a scared Congress going along for the most part, moved to bolster the military strength of the non-Communist world. Hurried steps were taken to enlarge the American armed forces, to improve the defenses of Formosa and of the nations in Southeast Asia, to speed the building and co-ordination of armies in the NATO countries, even —what would have seemed so wildly improbable only a few years before—to push the rearmament of West Germany.

The Chinese, stopping and starting, pushed through North Korea and a few miles into South Korea. There the UN forces, regrouped, were able to hold. Day after day, by foot, ox-cart, packhorse, and two-humped Bactrian camel, more of what MacArthur called the "bottomless well of Chinese manpower" crossed the Yalu into North Korea. No one could question that the Chinese armies, now firmly linked with the North Koreans, were getting ready for their own end-the-war offensive and would try to drive the UN troops off the peninsula. On New Year's Eve, in the dark of another night and more zero weather, the onslaught came.

The UN lines bent, Seoul fell again, but the Communists could not break through. As 1951 went on, the UN forces began a slow, punishing advance back toward the 38th parallel.

Corporal William Jensen was shot in the thigh in the first Chinese breakthrough and he was flown home to Hastings, Nebraska. The day after he arrived, he hobbled down along the stores of Second Street and delivered himself of a judgment. "Man," he said, "I never saw anything like it. This town is just one big boom."

During the Korean War the whole United States was one big boom, the boomingest America in all the prosperous years since V-J. Virtually all of the soft spots that were still left in the economy were removed by the Korean War. The most telltale sign, employment, told a tale of historic proportions. Two months after the Korean War began, employment crossed the sixty-two million mark—two million beyond the fondest dreams of New Dealers at V-J. As a matter of fact, by August, 1950 New York State had so few unemployment claims that it fired five hundred people in its compensation division.

It was prosperity, too, within the framework of continuing the Half-Century of Revolution in domestic affairs. Once the Korean War started, Congress passed little domestic legislation but the laws that did go through often inched ahead government aid to lower-income groups. Most notably, the Social Security Act underwent its first comprehensive change since enactment of the bill in 1935 and an estimated ten million Americans, largely farmworkers, domestic servants, and small businessmen, were added to the coverage. Outside the political arena, the steady leveling on the American social scene was still more evident. Once buying stocks may have been a matter for the Fifth Avenues of the nation but now the long-established brokerage firm, Ira Haupt & Co., set up a tent exhibit at the Mineola, Long Island, County Fair. Ernest E. Ruppe, the Haupt man assigned to Mineola, stood on the sodden grass and, amid a great crowing of roosters and cackling of hens, bespoke the era. "Money has changed hands in the last twenty years. The people who used to have it don't. The working-man does. . . . One of my best customers is a potato farmer in Hicksville; I've sold him nineteen thousand dollars' worth of mutual funds."

The walls of discrimination against Negroes, Jews,

and other minorities kept on lowering. The decades-old trend was at work; moreover, the argument that America could not win the Asiatic mind while discriminating against colored men at home was having its effect. In the middle of the Korean War an incident brought a flash of the attitude that was becoming more and more common. The body of a casualty, Sergeant John Rice, was brought to Sioux City for burial and just as the casket was to be lowered in the grave, officials of the Sioux City Memorial Park stopped the ceremony. Sergeant Rice, it seemed, was a Winnebago Indian; he was "not a member of the Caucasian race." The officials made an offer to Mrs. Evelyn Rice. Would she care to sign a statement stating that her husband had "all white blood"? Mrs. Rice emphatically did not care to sign the statement and the body was taken back to the funeral home. The next morning President Truman read of the incident at breakfast. Within minutes Mrs. Rice was invited to bury her husband in Arlington National Cemetery and was informed that the United States Government would be happy to dispatch an Air Force plane to bring the body and the family to Washington. Harry Truman had rarely done anything more popular. A wide variety of opinion across the country agreed that, to use the words of the *Cleveland Plain Dealer*, "it is high time we stopped this business. We can't do it as decent human beings and we can't do it as a nation trying to sell democracy to a world full of non-white peoples."

The Negro scored his most meaningful advance since the issuance of the FEPC order during World War II. Shortly before the election of 1948 President Truman had issued an Executive Order, declaring it to be "the policy of the President that there shall be equality of treatment and opportunity for all persons in the armed services. . . . This policy shall be put into effect as rapidly as possible, having due regard to the time required to effectuate any necessary changes without impairing efficiency or morale." In January,

1950 Secretary of the Army Gordon Gray issued a supplementary policy statement, reiterating the President's general position and going on specifically to direct that soldiers with special skills were to be assigned without regard to race or color. The directives were none too sweeping and they were not rigorously pushed. When the Korean War began, the Air Force was largely integrated; segregation was the general pattern in the Army, Navy, and Marine Corps. But the new currents of thinking were running strong and the practical circumstances gave an opening to the military men who wanted to end Jim Crow or had no particular feelings about it one way or another.

Brigadier General Frank McConnell was a veteran army officer simply interested in doing an efficient job at the post he was assigned when the Korean War began—commandant of the infantry training base at Fort Jackson, South Carolina. The General put into effect the customary pattern of segregation and then, during the North Korean blitz, the draftees came pouring in at the rate of a thousand a day. Treating the whites and Negroes separately in beginning the training of the men was enormously slowing the whole process. McConnell summoned his staff and proposed ignoring the color line.

An aide spoke up. Wasn't there danger that the General would be "going off the deep end"?

McConnell pulled out from his desk the directive of Secretary Gray concerning segregation. "It was all the authority I needed," he recalled later. "I said that if we didn't ask permission, they couldn't stop us." The General issued a verbal order that the next fifty-five draftees who arrived were to be put in a platoon in the order that they arrived and that was the end of segregation at Fort Jackson.

No race incidents followed. "I would see recruits, Negro and white, walking down the street off-duty, all grouped together," McConnell remembered. "The attitude of the Southern soldiers was that this was the army way; they accepted it the same way they accepted getting up at 5:30 in the morning." Word of the new way of doing things at Fort Jackson got around rapidly and some high-ranking military officials, including General Mark Clark, chief of the Army Field Forces, were anything but happy. But soon the color line was disappearing at all Army training bases.

Meanwhile the Army Chief of Staff, General J. Lawton Collins, wrote his overseas commanders a confidential letter calling for integration according to a deliberate, unspectacular program. Again the reasoning was pragmatic. As Collins's assistant, General Anthony McAuliffe, remarked later: "We didn't do it to improve the social situation. It was merely a matter of getting the best out of the military personnel that was available to us."

On the battlefields of Korea, emergency circumstances swept ahead the change. Colonel John G. Hill, another matter-of-fact military man, commanded the 9th U.S. Infantry Regiment, one of the first American units to land in Korea. Hill had ten per cent overstrength in his all-Negro 3rd Battalion but his two white battalions were short of men and battle losses quickly thinned them still further. "Force of circumstances" dictated the next move, Hill told the story later. "We had no replacements. . . . We would have been doing ourselves a disservice to permit [Negro] soldiers to lie around in rear areas at the expense of the still further weakening of our [white] rifle companies." When he ordered the integration of the Negroes, Hill continued, the whites took the situation in stride. As for the Negroes, a remarkable change occurred. The same men who had been unreliable in combat now were entirely dependable under fire. What's more, Negroes suddenly began volunteering for dangerous assignments.

After Hill's move succeeded, other Korean commanders tried integration. They found that the pattern held. Negro units were none too steady in combat. Once integrated, the Negroes fought as well as the whites and the whites accepted the change with few incidents. The discovery of this basic practical fact spurred ahead integration and by early 1951 the color line was scarcely visible among the U.S. troops fighting in Korea.

The effects of what the Army was doing spilled over into many parts of American life. It had shown that racial barriers could be removed without causing disruption and with a marked increase in the efficient use of human beings. The Army moves speeded integration in the Navy and the Marine Corps. Outside the military, they undermined segregation in scores of ways, tangible and intangible. Tens of thousands of white men left the service with an experience which otherwise they never would have had. Some acquired an increased dislike of Negroes but from the available evidence most soldiers took home a slant on race markedly different from the previous assumption of segregation. In areas of the United States near Army camps, military integration inevitably affected nonmilitary situations. North or South, here and there churches, USO clubs, cafés, and taxicabs began voluntarily to admit Negroes on an equal or near-equal basis. Just as inevitably, there were instances of military pressure to change local racial practices—like the Provost Marshal on a northern post who ended Jim Crow in a near-by bar by telling the owner that his place would be declared off limits unless all soldiers were served. Old ways were crumbling; new habits were being formed.

Perhaps most important of all, military desegregation furthered general desegragation by capturing the emotions of many people. In the atmosphere of the 1950's few crusades seemed bright and shining; here was an appealing human cause to which human beings could respond. Brigadier General Lloyd Hopwood, Deputy Chief for Air Force Personnel Planning, touched the note when he stopped one day to talk with Lee Nichols, a journalist who was examining letters from Air

Force commanders attesting the success of their integration program. "I like to go through them myself once in a while," the General said. "It kind of restores my faith in human nature."

More social revolution, more boom, and withal a vast restlessness. The prosperity itself was involved with the irritations of a sharply accelerated inflation. A month after hostilities began the government had to announce a new low in the purchasing power of the dollar; it was now worth just 59.3 cents as compared with 1939 and the value was going right on sinking. The inflation was most severe where it was most annoying—in the price of food. The sale of horse meat tripled in Portland (it tends to be sweet, the *Oregon Journal* advised, so cook it with more onions and fewer carrots). The New Jersey Bell Telephone Company put pot roast of whale on its cafeteria menu. In Toledo the Utopia Auto Laundry added a frozen-meat department with an opening-day special of filet mignon at $1.75 a pound—twenty-five cents more than a car wash. Like all wartime inflations, the Korean price spiral spurred itself upward. Throughout the country many a citizen (considering himself just as patriotic as the next fellow of course) was hoarding everything from automobile tires to metal hair curlers. "Buy Nothing From Fear" Macy's pleaded in full-page ads—and then reported sales twenty-five per cent above normal.

All the while the public was being jabbed by news of scandals of a dozen varieties. In the months before the Korean War, a subcommittee of the Senate Committee on Executive Expenditures began spreading in the headlines the story of the "five percenters" who sold actual or pretended influence with government officials. Before long the subcommittee was proving that these five percenters were no small operators—that, in fact, some of them were working with leading officers in the procurement sections of the armed forces. The investigation climaxed when testimony was given that shortly after the end of World War II a perfume company, which was eager to speed some European oils through the remaining wartime regulations, had presented a $520 deep-freeze unit to Harry Vaughan, a man with a pad of White House stationery which could expedite such matters.

The dust had not settled over these proceedings when Senator J. William Fulbright's subcommittee of the Senate Banking and Currency Committee ran into a cesspool in the Reconstruction Finance Corporation. The American Lithofold Company, thrice turned down for an RFC loan of $565,000, had suddenly received the money after it retained as its lawyer William Boyle, Jr., chairman of the Democratic National Committee. Republicans cried shame. Then the subcommittee discovered that Guy Gabrielson, chairman of the Republican National Committee, had intervened with the RFC in an attempt to get the terms extended on a large-scale loan to the Carthage Hydrocol Company, of which he was president.

Along the line, the investigators came upon a mink coat which immediately took a place alongside Harry Vaughan's deep freeze in the national symbolism. Mrs. E. Merl Young, wife of a former examiner of loans for the RFC, had a $9,540 mink, acquired with the financial help of an attorney whose firm, it so happened, had represented a company in its application for a loan of $150,000 from the RFC. After that Mrs. Blair Moody, wife of the United States Senator from Michigan, went around wearing on her fur coat a sales receipt showing that the fur was mink-dyed muskrat and that the price, including the taxes, was $381.25. The general furor was so great the mink farmers wailed it was threatening their $100,000,000-a-year industry. An "unjust stigma" had been placed on the woman with a mink, said Harold W. Reed of the Mink Ranchers' Association. He wanted everybody to know that most wearers of mink were "highly respectable people of discriminating taste."

Outside of Washington other scandals were breaking, forms of corruption that reached deep into areas of special national pride. Millions had followed the brilliant basketball team of the City College of New York as it whirled its way to consecutive national championships. Now three out of the five members of the first team admitted taking bribes up to fifteen hundred dollars to rig scores. Soon similar cases were revealed at Long Island University, New York University, Bradley University, the University of Kentucky, and Toledo University. New York General Sessions Court Judge Saul S. Streit, before whom many of the cases were tried, took the occasion to study the national sports situation and he could only report that "commercialism" in college sports was "rampant throughout the country . . . .[It] contaminates everything it touches. It has fostered bookmaking and nationwide gambling; it produces illegal scouting, recruiting, proselytizing and subsidization of athletes; it corrupts the athlete, the coach, the college official and the alumnus; it breeds bribery, fraud and forgery; it impairs the standards of integrity of the college."

What a mess, people said; something is decidedly wrong. Then the country was really rocked. West Point, proud West Point, a school that placed character-building above everything else and trained the men who were to lead everybody's son in battle, had to make an announcement. West Point announced that it was dismissing for cheating in examinations ninety cadets, including Robert Blaik, son of the football coach and an All-American quarterback, eight other students on the Army first team, and members of the varsity squads in most other sports.

The nation gulped doubly hard when the dismissed students began talking. Many of them were not contrite and they were bewildered. Everybody had been cheating, they said in puzzlement; as a matter of fact, it was the "honest" students who stated what they had been doing and the "liars" who were still cadets. Earl

H. Blaik, the colonel who had coached football at the Point for ten years, hurried down to an emotion-charged press conference at Leone's Restaurant in New York and insisted that there was "no moral reason" why the dismissed athletes, these "men of character," should not leave the Point with their reputations totally unimpaired. "Stop knocking football," Blaik said in a choked voice. "God help this country if we didn't play football. . . . Gen. Eisenhower came to West Point with his greatest desire to play football."

The national concern over the sports scandals linked closely to the jolting realization of just how serious a problem juvenile delinquency had become. From V-J on through 1948 the rate declined. But then it began to rise and after the outbreak of the Korean War it mounted so swiftly that about a million children a year were getting into trouble with the police. Just as disquieting were the incidents that did not involve actual brushes with the law. Out of small towns and cities, particularly in the Midwest and South, came story after story like those of the teen-age clubs in Borger, Texas, and Mattoon, Illinois. The Borger club staged "house-parties" at which numbers were drawn by the high-school boys and girls and the matched pairs then went off to a shack or an auto for intercourse. In Mattoon each girl was "initiated" by having intercourse with one male in the presence of another male and she pledged herself to have intercourse at least four times a month if she was to remain "in good standing."

Whatever the form of the teen-age problem, the whole situation was showing peculiarly disturbing trends. The age of the children who went astray was rapidly dropping. Housebreaking, for example, had formerly been committed largely by boys sixteen years or older; now the offender was often thirteen to fifteen or even, in a shocking number of cases, ten to twelve. The offenses were growing more serious, with burglary, drug addiction, sex attacks, and murder increas-

ingly frequent. It was no longer possible to dismiss the
child in trouble as something which did not happen
to nice people. More and more it was the son or daughter of the manufacturer or the professional man who
ended up in a jumble.

Nahant, Massachusetts, provided one of the endless
newspaper stories. Fifteen-year-old Roberta McCauley,
seventeen-year-old Eileen Jeffreys, and sixteen-year-
old Marilyn Curry were pert, cutely dressed, apparently happy daughters of middle-class America.
One fine summer's night the three girls found themselves together in the course of a baby-sitting job at the
home of Dr. Albert Covner. Things were pretty dull,
the girls agreed. So they stole eighteen thousand dollars from a box in the bedroom closet and took off on a
New York tour of buying $235 Christian Dior suits,
handing ten dollar tips to cab drivers, turning Roberta
into a blonde and Marilyn into a redhead, and picking
up prize-fighter Wayne Eckhart who chose Roberta
and registered with her at the Dixie Hotel as Mr. and
Mrs. John Daly of Cedar Rapids, Iowa.

The next day Eileen ended the episode with just the
words to comfort the parents of the United States.
"Don't say I've been smoking," she asked the reporters.
"My father would kill me if he knew I had been."

Meanwhile, starting in May, 1950, a Senate committee had been crisscrossing the United States, holding
and reholding hearings in a number of large cities. The
Special Committee to Investigate Organized Crime in
Interstate Commerce was the official name; the Kefauver Committee, people called it after its chairman,
Senator Estes Kefauver of Tennessee. In three of the
cities visited, the proceedings were televised with a
degree of local interest and when the Committee came
to the Foley Square Courthouse in New York for public hearings, arrangements were made to set up the
cameras. The independent station WPIX was to do the
televising and it prepared for a routine public-service

assignment. Charles A. Voso, who was in charge of the production crew, later remarked: "We didn't expect much of a public response. Neither did the Committee."

On March 12 Senator Kefauver rapped his gavel and started the proceedings in his mild, schoolmasterish way. The Committee counsel, youthful Rudolph Halley, went along with his questions, mostly in a singsong manner. Things slowly picked up. The convicted gambler, burly Frank Erickson, was asked his occupation and answered, with entire accuracy, "I'm in jail." Then he made his contribution to the English language; he announced he would refuse to answer a question because "it might intend to criminate me." Joe Adonis came to the stand looking cool and dapper and left it just another overdressed hood, mumbling the Fifth Amendment. And always Rudolph Halley's questions were becoming more sharply spoken, more insinuating, more concerned with the activities of one Frank Costello.

When Costello walked to the witness chair, his two hundred dollar suit was trim, his heavily lined face composed, his eyes hard and arrogant. His lawyer, George Wolf, soon insisted that the TV cameras be taken off his client. The Committee agreed to the demand and one of the cameramen had an idea. Why not turn the cameras only on Costello's hands?

While the cameras recorded hands fiddling with papers or pouring water from a glass, Halley drove hard to establish evidence that Costello was what the Committee was perfectly sure he was—head of one of two gigantic crime syndicates operating across many states. Bigger crowds were trying to get into the Foley Square Courthouse now. Thousands more New York sets were tuned to WPIX. TV stations across the country were being fed by WPIX.

Halley asked Costello about the testimony of George M. Levy, who was connected with the Roosevelt Raceway. Levy had said that in 1946 the chairman of the

New York State Harness Racing Commission threatened to revoke the track's license if he did not get rid
of the bookmakers operating there. Levy thought of
his golfing friend, Costello, paid him fifteen thousand
dollars a year for four years, and the bookmakers disappeared. Didn't this suggest, Halley wanted to know,
that Costello had at least some control over the bookies?

Costello's answer was unruffled. Of course he controlled no bookies. Levy had talked to him about the
matter and "I says, 'What way can I help you?' . . .
I says, 'Well, what I can do George, I can spread the
propaganda around that they're hurting you there
and you're a nice fellow. . . . I don't know how much
good it's going to do you, but I'll talk about it.' He says,
'I wish you would,' and I did."

HALLEY: Where did you talk about it?
COSTELLO: Oh, in Moore's Restaurant, Gallagher's Res-
    taurant, a hotel, a saloon, as you would call it, any
    place, or a night club, whenever I had the chance,
    just in general. . . .
HALLEY: What did you do in 1946 to earn $15,000?
COSTELLO: Practically nothing. . . .
HALLEY: And what did you do in the second year that
    made your services more valuable?
COSTELLO: Nothing. I did the same thing I did the first
    year, and I don't think I did a damn thing.

The Committee and Halley pursued Costello doggedly. How much money did he have in all? Well, he
had a sort of "little strong box" at home where he kept
"a little cash" but he couldn't remember how much.
Couldn't he remember roughly how much? Couldn't
he make a guess?

Senator Charles Tobey erupted. The elderly Committee member from New Hampshire had been listening to the evasion and lying with the air of a deacon
confronted by saturnalia. Now he cut in: One way to
find out how much is in the strong box is for us to send
somebody up to look.

Costello's memory suddenly improved. Yes, he thought he had about fifty thousand dollars or so in the box, another ninety thousand dollars to one hundred thousand dollars in his bank account.

The aplomb of the witness was fast disappearing. On the TV screens his hands tore up pieces of paper or jiggled the water glass. Halley shifted the subject, casually asked Costello if he ever paid anyone to check his telephone for wire tapping. "Absolutely not," the witness said. A heavy-set, graying man named James F. McLaughlin took the stand. He testified that in 1945 he checked Costello's phone two or three times a week for about three months, and Costello would hand him fifty dollars or one hundred dollars or one hundred and fifty dollars when he saw him outside the Waldorf-Astoria barbershop. Senator Kefauver's soft voice spoke the harsh words: "Somebody has committed perjury."

When Costello returned to the witness stand, his face was dark and scowling. His client felt awful, George Wolf said. His throat was inflamed, the television lights and the photographers bothered him, and he was just in no condition to testify further. In a very mild and a very firm voice, Kefauver insisted that the witness should try to answer questions.

Costello managed to sound a half-step from the hospital. "I want to testify truthfully, and my mind don't function. . . . With all due respect to the Senators . . . , I have an awful lot of respect for them, I am not going to answer another question. . . . I am going to walk out."

An estimated 30,000,000 Americans watched Frank Costello leave the courtroom—by far the biggest TV audience assembled up to that time. The routine public-service program of WPIX was turning into the nation's first TV spectacular. All the major networks were now carrying the full hearings. New York City was seized as if by some sudden hypnosis. Videodex reported that 69.7% of the city's sets were tuned to the Foley Square Courthouse—a percentage twice as high as the one for the World Series games of the previous fall. Merchants complained to the Committee that their businesses were paralyzed. Movie houses became ghost halls during the hours of the proceedings (some gave up, installed TV, and invited the public to come in free). Housewives did their ironing and fed the baby in front of the set. In many big cities business and home life were noticeably affected. One Chicago department-store manager took a look at the number of customers in his aisles and ran an ad: "Ten Percent Off During Kefauver Hours."

Other witnesses were taking the stand including, as Senator Kefauver said with quiet emphasis, *Mrs.* Virginia Hauser. She was *soignée* in a five thousand dollar silver-blue mink stole, gray suede gloves, black dress, and large-brimmed black hat. She was also annoyed. She pointed to the photographers and screamed: "Make those goddam fools stop. I'll throw something at them in a minute." The Committee had good reason to believe that this witness was the bank courier for some of the key figures in the underworld; they were anxious for her to talk. Senator Kefauver waved the photographers away and soothed her in his best Southern manner. Wouldn't she just tell the Committee something of her life?

Why, she said with drawling innocence, she was just another Alabama girl who came to Chicago, worked for a while, and met some fellows. There was Joe Adonis and Charlie Fischetti and Ben Siegel—

But what about all her money? Where did that come from?

Mrs. Virginia Hauser lolled in the witness chair. "For years I have been going to Mexico. I went with fellows down there. And like a lot of girls that they got. Giving me things and bought me everything I want. . . . Whatever I have ever had was, outside of betting horses, was given to me."

Since she knew these men well, didn't she hear things about their business operations?

Her air of innocence could no longer conceal the smirk. Know anything about their affairs? Why, when any of the fellows talked business she left the room. At Siegel's Flamingo Club in Las Vegas, "on a lot of times, people didn't even know I was there. I was upstairs in my room; I didn't even go out. . . . I was allergic to the cactus."

And with a few more drawls Mrs. Virginia Hauser shrugged her mink stole higher on her shoulders, ran a gauntlet of photographers, and left the courthouse yelling at the cameramen: "You bastards, I hope a god-damn atom bomb falls on every goddam one of you." The Kefauver Committee had not exactly proved her role as the bank courier for gangsters. But it had provided quite an education for those thirty million people at TV sets who had known the Virginia Hausers only as a product of Hollywood's imagination.

Over the weekend Frank Costello decided to come back on the stand and was maneuvered into statements that risked further perjury charges. All the while Halley kept probing the role of money in New York politics and the connections between crime and politics. Along the way the stand was taken by William O'Dwyer, the ex-Mayor of New York and at this time the United States Ambassador to Mexico.

O'Dwyer was amiable, reasonable, practical. He was an honest man, the ex-Mayor's manner said, but no bluenose and he knew the facts of life. Casually fingering a paper clip, he rambled over an account of his career ("I took 190,000 people out of slums"), soliloquized at length that organized crime was bred by Prohibition, slot machines, and too many tattered nerves in family living. O'Dwyer readily admitted that he knew Costello.

Senator Tobey interrupted in his best Biblical manner. "It almost seems to me as though you should say, 'Unclean, unclean' . . . and that you would leave him alone. . . ."

O'DWYER: You have bookmaking all over the country. They say there is a lot of it in New Hampshire, too —thirty million a year. . . .

TOBEY: Well, we haven't a Costello in New Hampshire.

O'DWYER: I wonder. . . . And I wonder who the bookmakers in Bretton Woods support for public office in New Hampshire?

O'Dwyer conceded that large-scale gambling had probably gone on in New York while he was Mayor and that it could not have existed on such a scale without police protection. But with respect to things like that, he explained, all a man who was trying to run a city of eight million could do was to try to appoint good men and then depend on them. The testimony brought out a series of interlockings between New York City politics and the underworld, including the fact that O'Dwyer had named a protégé of Frank Costello to a judgeship and that one of his Fire Commissioners, Frank Quayle, was a friend of Joe Adonis. "There are things that you have to do politically if you want to get co-operation," O'Dwyer said. They had nothing to do with his honesty or the fact that his political powers as Mayor had not been for sale.

Matter-of-factly, Halley asked O'Dwyer whether he knew John P. Crane, president of the Uniformed Firemen's Association. Yes, O'Dwyer knew Crane. Did Crane ever make any campaign contribution through you? No, he did not. Matter-of-factly, Halley went on to other matters.

The next day John Crane took the stand. Did he know O'Dwyer? Yes, Crane had kept wanting the Mayor's support for increasing firemen's salaries and once shortly before a mayoralty election he had gone to see O'Dwyer.

HALLEY: Will you tell the committee what transpired?
CRANE: I told the mayor at that time that I had pro-

mised him the support of the firemen, and I offered
him some evidence of that support on the occasion,
in the form of $10,000. . . .

HALLEY: Was that in cash?

CRANE: That was in cash. . . .

HALLEY: You gave it to the mayor . . . ?

CRANE: Yes.

Late that afternoon, the eighth day of the proceedings, the cameras were taken from the Foley Square
Courthouse. It had been quite an eight days. The New
York hearings of the Kefauver Committee made television (now TV became almost an essential of the ordinary home). They made Estes Kefauver, who the
next year was to go to the Democratic National Convention with 340 delegates pledged to him for the
Presidential nomination. But above all the televised proceedings, with their stark portrayal of the practical
Mayor who might not have been merely practical, of
the sinister arrogance of the Costellos and the Virginia
Hausers, of the endless shadowy fingers that obviously
controlled so much, catalyzed the whole vague feeling
that corruption was moving through all American
life like a swarm of maggots.

Across a full page of the New York newspapers the
advertising firm, Young and Rubicam, expressed the
national reaction:

"With staggering impact, the telecasts of the Kefauver investigation have brought a shocked awakening
to millions of Americans.

"Across their television tubes have paraded the
honest and dishonest, the frank and the furtive, the
public servant and the public thief. Out of many pictures has come a broader picture of the sordid intermingling of crime and politics, of dishonor in public
life.

"And suddenly millions of Americans are asking:
What's happened to our ideals of right and wrong?

What's happened to our principles of honesty in government?

What's happened to public and private standards of morality?

"Then they ask the most important question of all: How can we stop what's going on? *Is there anything we can do about it?*"

Was there anything Americans could do about standards of morality? Was there anything they could do about anything?

The spring of 1951 came to an America caught in a snarl of frustration. On a rain-swept Easter Sunday the UN forces in Korea fought their way north across the 38th parallel. They had crossed the line twice before—once going and once coming—and did the crossing mean any more now? General MacArthur, no man for pessimistic statements, made it unmistakably clear that he expected stalemate. The reports of the war were taking on a peculiarly meaningless quality, the killing of a hundred Communists here when there were thousands a bit further north, the taking of some hill without a name only to lose it, still unnamed, a few days later. The news on the attitude of the soldiers in Korea was that, to use the dispatch of E.J. Kahn, Jr., "the idea of this war as an endless one is almost universally accepted here"—endless war, and endless war in as cheerless a situation as American troops had ever encountered. Even money was worthless, Kahn continued, "since there is absolutely nothing to spend it on. A couple of days ago, I saw two rifle companies playing a softball game on a diamond laid out in a paddy field, for a purse of a thousand dollars."

The descriptions of Korean deadlock came back to a country filled with a sense of stalemate wherever it turned. Why couldn't America make the world realize that it wanted only peace and decency? One of the earliest books on the Korean crisis was by Mrs. Dorothy Vieman, the wife of an Army officer stationed in Korea before the invasion, and Mrs. Vieman wrote: "I believe other nationalities think we are crazy." Surely there was some way of getting people to sit down at a table and straighten out the mess? The Big Four under-secretaries of foreign affairs were sitting down at a table in Paris; they were only trying to arrange an agenda for the secretaries and at that they were getting nowhere. There was always Assistant Commissar for Foreign Affairs Andrei Gromyko, sonorous, belliger-ent, and endlessly obstructive.

Home-front problems kept taking on the same qual-ity of deadlock. Inflation, for example—the jukebox men announced an anti-inflation song *Once Upon A Nickel* as they proceeded to retool the jukeboxes to take only dimes. The hoodlums? In Los Angeles Dis-trict Court Judge Ben Harrison sentenced gangster Mickey Cohen with the statement: "His parents came from abroad . . . and the environment here produced Mr. Cohen. When he started violating the laws by be-coming a gambling commissioner, it could only have been with the acquiescence of the law enforcement agencies." The government scandals? Senator Ful-bright told the country that the problem was not really illegal conduct but unethical conduct—a lack of ethics that ran through the whole community. "How do we deal with those who, under the guise of friendship, ac-cept favors which offend the spirit of the law but do not violate its letter? What of the men outside govern-ment who suborn those inside it?" The teen-age sex clubs? When they appeared in Indiana a reporter thought of asking Dr. Kinsey. He noted that according to his studies an unmarried male beyond the age of puberty had premarital experiences at the rate of about once a week, multiplied this by Indiana's 450,000 un-married males, and got 450,000 male premarital ex-periences per week in Indiana. "And that," said Dr. Kinsey, "is why I don't get excited when the newspapers report three or four teen-agers having such experiences."

Irritation rasped through American life. The unity of the week when the country cheered intervention in Korea lay in shreds. Harry Truman was being flayed as he had not been since the "Had Enough?" days of 1946. Senator Joseph McCarthy was in the headlines again shrill and confident. Delegations trooped into Washington with block-long petitions demanding the ouster of Dean Acheson.

Irritation, anger, worry, bitterness—and through it all the sense of frustration mounted. The veteran journalist George Creel found the words for the America of spring, 1951. Entertaining a group in San Francisco, Creel tapped the table impatiently and said: "I have never seen anything like it in all my seventy-four years. On any problem it's like those damned hills of Korea. You march up them but there's always the sinking feeling you are going to have to march right back down again."

During war, US had inflation
Americans were exposed to
the scandals + immorality
that existed — were
shocked + irritated by it.

X

Yearnings and the Fulfillment

On Wednesday April 11, 1951 the United States forgot all about Estes Kefauver, Chinese infantrymen, or mink coats. The news was released at one a.m. (to coincide with the delivery of a message on the other side of the world) and most Americans did their gasping at the breakfast table. Harry Truman, Captain Harry of Battery D, had upped and fired General of the Army Douglas MacArthur, Commanding General of the U.S. Army Forces, Far East, U.S. Commander-in-Chief, Far East Command, Supreme Commander for the Allied Powers in Japan, and Commander-in-Chief, United Nations Command.

From MacArthur came magisterial silence. Aides of the General talked to reporters in a sepulchral hush. "I have just left him," Major General Courtney Whitney said. "He received the word of the President's dismissal from command magnificently. He never turned a hair. His soldierly qualities were never more pronounced. This has been his finest hour."

From the United States came a roar of outrage. By ten a.m. on April 11, Senator Taft and other major Republican figures were caucusing in the office of the House GOP leader, Joseph Martin, agreeing that MacArthur should be invited to address a joint meeting of Congress and that the whole foreign and military policy of the Administration should be subjected to a Congressional investigation. "In addition," Martin told the press, "the question of impeachments was discussed" and he emphasized the *s* on the word impeachment in a way that left no doubt he meant Secretary of State Acheson as well as President Truman. Senator McCarthy immediately staged his own impeachment of the President. "The sonofabitch," McCarthy said; the decision to fire the General must have come from a night "of bourbon and benedictine." Seventy-eight thousand telegrams or letters, running twenty-to-one against the dismissal, were assaulting the White House. The Gallup Poll sent out its interviewers and they came back with a thumping sixty-nine per cent for MacArthur and only twenty-nine per cent backing the Presidential action.

From San Gabriel, California to Worcester, Massachusetts, Harry Truman was burned in effigy. In Los Angeles the City Council adjourned "in sorrowful contemplation of the political assassination" of the General. In Charlestown, Maryland, a woman tried to send a wire calling the President a moron, was told she couldn't, persisted in epithets until the clerk let her tell Harry Truman he was a "witling." In Eastham, Massachusetts, Little Rock, Houston, and Oakland, flags went down to half-mast. People savored scores of new anti-Truman stories. "This wouldn't have happened if Truman were alive," the wisecracks went. Or "I'm going to have a Truman beer—you know, just like any ordinary beer except it hasn't got a head."

Within five days MacArthur's big Constellation, the *Bataan*, was coming in over the San Francisco Airport. The General paused at the head of the gangway, the trench coat and the frayed battle cap silhouetted in the floodlights, and the crowd roared and surged. When the police and the MP's managed to get the General's party into automobiles, almost two hours were needed to crawl through the fourteen miles to

the St. Francis Hotel and only a flying wedge of policemen got the MacArthur family into their suite.
Next day the General went to a reception in front of
San Francisco's City Hall and said: "The only politics
I have is contained in a single phrase known well to all
of you—God Bless America!" A hundred thousand
people cheered in a way San Francisco had not heard
since the visits of Franklin Roosevelt.

On to the national capital and, for a moment,
something less than tumult. At the Washington airport MacArthur was greeted by the Joint Chiefs of
Staff, who had unanimously recommended his dismissal. Everyone was very polite. Up stepped the personal representative of the Commander-in-Chief, Major General Harry Vaughan. The General and the
Major General engaged in hasty greetings and
Vaughan scurried away. He was heard muttering
"Well, that was simple."

Then the crowds took over and everything was San
Francisco redoubled. Wherever MacArthur appeared
—at a meeting of the American Society of Newspaper
Editors, riding down Pennsylvania Avenue through
300,000 people, before another quarter of a million
gathered in front of the Washington Monument—
everywhere the reception was thunderous. The DAR
was beside itself. The six thousand ladies assembled in
their Sixtieth Continental Congress at Constitution
Hall went to the ultimate; they took off their hats en
masse so that everybody could see a full Douglas Mac-
Arthur. "I have long sought personally to pay you
the tribute that is in my heart . . . ," the General said
in his three-minute talk to the DAR. "In this hour of
crisis, all patriots look to you." The next day Recording Secretary General Mrs. Warren Shattuck Currier
read from her minutes that MacArthur's speech was
"probably the most important event" in the history of
Constitution Hall. Mrs. Thomas B. Throckmorton
was immediately on her feet. She moved, and the con-

vention promptly agreed, to strike out the word "probably."

At 12.30 on April 19 the Doorkeeper of the House of Representatives intoned: "Mr. Speaker, General of the Army Douglas MacArthur." He walked down the aisle in a short army jacket, his chest bare of ribbons, the back rigid and the face stony. The packed galleries, the Senators and Representatives, the Republicans and Democrats, were on their feet applauding wildly. The General stood calmly at the rostrum and waited for complete silence. "I address you," he declared, "with neither rancor nor bitterness in the fading twilight of life, with but one purpose in mind: To serve my country." Emotion seized the chamber again; thirty times in a thirty-four-minute speech the hall broke into fervid clapping. The words went on, at times sharp with anger, at times sinking to an emotional whisper, but always controlled in a way that Congress had not witnessed since the World War II visits of Winston Churchill. MacArthur presented his differences with the Truman Administration in the most rousing possible manner. "Why, my soldiers asked of me, surrender military advantages to an enemy in the field?" He paused a long few seconds, then said: "I could not answer."

As the General neared the end of the speech, the voice dropped and the words were misty. "I am closing my fifty-two years of military service. When I joined the Army, even before the turn of the century, it was the fulfillment of all of my boyish hopes and dreams. . . . The hopes and dreams have long since vanished, but I still remember the refrain of one of the most popular barracks ballads of that day, which proclaimed most proudly that old soldiers never die; they just fade away. And like the old soldier of that ballad, I now close my military career and just fade away, an old soldier who tried to do his duty as God gave him the light to see that duty. Good-by."

MacArthur handed his manuscript to the clerk, waved to his wife in the gallery, and strode toward the exit. The din swept up, crashed against the musty ceiling of the House chamber, went on and on. More than a few Congressmen had tears in their eyes. Across the country millions snapped off their television sets in a state of high emotion, some raging against corniness, a good many more furious at a President of the United States who would fire such a man.

On to New York City and more cheers and emotion—a reception that exceeded Lindbergh Day or Eisenhower Day or the excitement of V-J. Seven million people turned out for the parade. The torn paper cascaded down until some streets were ankle-deep and TV screens blurred for long periods. Amid all the uproar a quite different kind of feeling kept expressing itself. As MacArthur's limousine went by, men and women would cross themselves. The handkerchiefs came out. And sometimes there were patches of quiet, a strange, troubled, churning quiet.

The limousine took the General to the Waldorf-Astoria for a few days' rest and the furor in New York and in the nation went right on. MP's and police turned away droves of reporters from the hotel. Special switchboard arrangements diverted three thousand telephone calls a day. Hasty recordings of "Old Soldiers Never Die" leaped up on the hit parade (the song, tracing back to a British barrack-room version of an American gospel hymn, "Kind Words Can Never Die," was out in a half-dozen versions). Any store with MacArthur buttons, pennants, or corncob pipes left over from the 1948 MacArthur-for-President flurry was hitting it rich. The flower marts of the country blossomed with a Douglas MacArthur orchid, geranium, cactus, gladiolus, day lily, bearded iris, herbaceous peony, and a hybrid tea rose (the advertisements described the tea rose as rose gold in color and "needing no coddling or favor"). "The country," said

Senator James Duff of Pennsylvania with no one to gainsay him, "is on a great emotional binge."

As MacArthur stayed holed up in the Waldorf-Astoria, reporters became increasingly inquisitive. What were his intentions? Despite his disavowals of political ambition, did he seek the Republican Presidential nomination? The General returned to a lofty silence and his aides were hardly explicit. When asked how MacArthur might react to a Presidential draft, Major General Courtney Whitney replied: "The General told me that if any such question was raised he would advise the questioner to go home and read the Bible. Especially the chapter on St. Thomas, the part pertaining to doubting Thomas." Resorting to their Gospel of John, the reporters read how doubting Thomas had questioned the resurrection of Jesus. Except for the suggestion that MacArthur might be confusing himself with Jesus, an idea that was not exactly news to many of the reporters, they had learned nothing.

After a week MacArthur emerged from the Waldorf-Astoria. A "crusade" he called his next move; a "vendetta" was the name in Democratic circles. Whatever the interpretation, the General engaged in the most substantial and noisiest fading away in history. He went to Chicago and Milwaukee to make speeches at welcome-home celebrations and attacked the Truman Administration. He returned to Washington to testify before a joint Senate Committee which was investigating his dismissal and denounced the Administration some more. Then he went off on a speaking tour that took him Truman-thwacking to the West Coast, into Texas and the South, through Wisconsin, Michigan, Ohio, Pennsylvania, and Massachusetts.

Everywhere the General spoke for an older, more conservative America frightened and irritated by the whirligig of changes which was climaxing during the post-World War II period. In his speeches on domestic affairs MacArthur was Robert Taft in a general's cap. His attacks on the foreign and military policies of the Administration amounted to a repudiation of the whole breakaway from traditional ideas which had begun with the policy of containment and been swept ahead by the Korean War.

The Truman Administration called its policy in Korea "limited warfare" and the name was correct. The American military effort was decidedly constrained by worry that both China and the Soviet might come full scale into the fighting; by concern whether the allies of the United States would support a direct attack on China; by a constant consideration of the way other countries in Asia were likely to react to American moves; and by a hesitancy to commit too large a part of American resources in the Far East lest Communism should move in Europe or in the Middle East. To MacArthur such limited warfare was simply the "appeasement of Communism." The result was "prolonged indecision" and "in war there is no substitute for victory." The quick total solution, brushing aside what other countries might think and emphasizing Asia first—here was the heart of the Mac-Arthur demands and here was an expression of deeply grooved American attitudes which had been causing so much restlessness with the Truman foreign policies since the shocks of 1949.

Apart from specific arguments about international or domestic affairs, MacArthur stood for an older America in a score of less tangible ways. His full-blown oratory recalled ten thousand Chautauqua nights. "Though without authority or responsibility, I am the possessor of the proudest of titles. I am an American," the General would say with a grandiose patriotism straight out of the days of William McKinley. In city after city MacArthur appeared with one arm around Mrs. MacArthur, another around his son Arthur, the unabashed symbol of Home and Motherhood and what he delighted in calling "the simple, eternal truths of the American way."

Like many Americans who were so disturbed by the dominant trends in the national life, the General moved closer and closer to the theory of conspiracy in explaining the developments. An aura of dark conniving surrounded MacArthur's denunciations of "the insidious forces working from within," of those who would "lead directly to the path of Communist slavery." "We must not underestimate the peril," he cried out. "It must not be brushed off lightly. It must not be scoffed at, as our present leadership has been prone to do by hurling childish epithets such as 'red herring,' 'character assassin,' 'scandal monger,' 'witch hunt,' 'political assassination,' and like terms designed to confuse or conceal. . . ."

Harry Truman played it cagily. He expected, the President told friendly reporters, an immediate stormy reaction in favor of the General, then about six weeks of rough sledding, then a swing against MacArthur. Meanwhile Harry Truman knew the uses of a storm cellar.

Gradually the Administration took the offensive. Speaking largely through the authoritative Joint Chiefs of Staff, it used the widely publicized Senate hearings on MacArthur's dismissal to make its case. The Joint Chiefs of Staff hammered on the point that the General had repeatedly and publicly challenged the Korean policies of the Administration and had thus flagrantly violated a basic principle of the American Constitution—that military men must remain subordinate to their civilian superiors. The moves MacArthur was advocating, the Administration spokesmen went on, were tragically wrong. He called for ending the Korean stalemate by permitting Chiang Kai-shek to invade the mainland, using Nationalist Chinese troops in Korea, blockading the whole Chinese coast, and bombing Chinese bases beyond the Yalu. But this, the Truman group insisted, would mean full-scale war with China. It would bring a split with America's allies who, ever since the Chinese intervention in Korea, had been making it increasingly plain that they wanted no expansion of the fighting in the Far East. It would suck American manpower and material into the vastness of China while the real enemy, Russia, stood unassailed. In the course of the hearings the mild-mannered chairman of the Joint Chiefs of Staff, General Omar Bradley, the last man anyone would pick for a spellbinder, got off the really telling phrase summarizing the Administration's case. MacArthur's program, Bradley said, "would involve us in the wrong war, at the wrong place, at the wrong time and with the wrong enemy."

By late May, 1951, the hearings were having a decided effect on public opinion. Douglas MacArthur was having decided effects too. For millions of Americans delighting in their new standard of living the General's speeches on domestic affairs sounded ominously like Herbert Hoover. For a generation including so many who were proud of their blaséness, too much talk of Motherhood and God-bless-America and too much trench coat and battered cap could pall. The polls were showing a tremendous shift away from MacArthur. The talk of MacArthur-for-President was dying down among responsible Republican leaders. The General's public appearances were losing their overpowering quality.

When MacArthur returned to New York and went to the Polo Grounds for a Giant-Phillies game, he and the management did their best. A recording of a seventeen-gun general's salute was played. MacArthur stood up in a box decorated with the Stars and Stripes and a five-star flag and told the crowd how happy he was "to witness the great American game of baseball that has done so much to build the American character." The MacArthur party left before the other spectators, walking across the whole diamond to the center-field exit while "Old Soldiers Never Die" was played. But things were different now. As the General neared the exit, the stands roared with laughter when a voice of purest Bronx vintage yelled: "Hey, Mac, how's Harry Truman?"

But if Douglas MacArthur the man was at last genuinely fading away, the impact of his dismissal was not lost. Here was an unquestionably skillful general, intimately associated with the victory in World War II, now cashiered because he insisted, regulations or no regulations, on advocating the old-fashioned American remedy of quick total victory. The MacArthur dismissal was one more event—and a tremendously jarring one—in the whole series of developments which was leaving so many Americans feeling confused, irritated, utterly frustrated.

All the situations on the home front which contributed to the feeling—the evidences of political corruption, the inflation, the signs of slackening personal standards—went on worsening. Korea was Korea and more so. Two days before the MacArthur hearings ended, on June 23, 1951, the Soviet representative to the UN, Jacob Malik, intimated in a radio speech that the Russians were ready for a cease-fire in Korea. Hopes soared in the United States only to bring the added bitterness of disappointment. Month after month the negotiators talked peace in the tent at Panmunjom and month after month the killing went on.

Christmas, 1951 was grisly. On December 18 the truce talks reached the point where the enemy handed MacArthur's successor, General Matthew Ridgway, a compilation of UN prisoners allegedly held in North Korean prison camps. The list staggered the United States. It contained the pitifully small total of 11,559 names and of these a mere 3,198 were Americans although Washington recorded 11,224 men as missing in action. Had the Communists murdered seven to eight thousand American prisoners? To add to the consternation, there was the possibility that the whole

compilation was a cruel hoax. Were the Americans
on the list really alive? President Truman had to issue
a heart-rending statement: "This country has no way
of verifying whether the list is accurate or inaccurate,
true or false, complete or incomplete. For the sake of
the families whose sons are missing in action, everyone
should treat this list with skepticism." As newspaper
pictures of anguished faces studying the names appeared during the Christmas season, no one could disagree with the statement of the *Louisville Courier-
Journal:* "This list is mocking everything Christmas is
supposed to represent."

The inevitable came and with tremendous force.
The shocks of 1949 had given Senator Joseph Mc-
Carthy his start. The frustrations of 1950 and 1951
blasted wide his road to power. With America tangled
in deadlocks at home and abroad, the man with the
simple answer, the furious, flailing answer, had his
day. In early 1951 Mickey Spillane's *One Lonely Night*
started on its way to selling more than three million
copies. The hero, Mike Hammer, gloated: "I killed
more people tonight than I have fingers on my hands.
I shot them in cold blood and enjoyed every minute of
it. . . . They were Commies, Lee. They were red
sons-of-bitches who should have died long ago. . . .
They never thought that there were people like me
in this country. They figured us all to be soft as horse
manure and just as stupid." Hammer's tough-guy certainty that he was solving the world's problems by
bludgeoning Communists hardly hurt the sales of *One
Lonely Night.* It was a day for Mike Hammerism, in
books or in politics.

Week after week Senator McCarthy became bolder
and more reckless. For years General of the Army
George Marshall, the over-all architect of victory in
World War II, had been one of the most generally esteemed figures in the United States. But Marshall was
associated with the Truman policy in the Far East and
on June 14, 1951 McCarthy stood up in the Senate and

delivered a sixty-thousand-word speech which charged that Marshall was part of "a conspiracy so immense, an infamy so black, as to dwarf any in the history of man. . . . [a conspiracy directed] to the end that we shall be contained, frustrated and finally fall victim to Soviet intrigue from within and Russian military might from without." The more reckless McCarthy became, the more his influence mounted. Fewer and fewer Senators rose to gainsay him. Pollsters found that steadily increasing percentages of Americans were ready to answer yes to questions like, Do you in general approve of Senator McCarthy's activities?

Outside of politics, the flood of McCarthyism mounted—the people who were chasing alleged Communists, the men and the institutions who were abetting McCarthyism by acquiescing in its attitudes. Some of the furor was simply ridiculous. Monogram Pictures canceled a movie about Henry Wadsworth Longfellow. Hiawatha, the studio explained, had tried to stop wars between the Indian tribes and people might construe the picture as propaganda for the Communist "peace offensive." Wheeling, West Virginia, staged the kind of comic-opera terror that was going on in scores of cities. In Wheeling the hubbub began when a policeman announced his discovery that penny-candy machines were selling children's bonbons with little geography lessons attached to the candies. The very tininess of the messages, half the size of a postage stamp, was suspicious; most rousing of all was the revelation that some of the geography lessons bore the hammer-and-sickle Soviet flag and the message: "U.S.S.R. Population 211,000,000. Capital Moscow. Largest country in the world." City Manager Robert L. Plummer thundered: "This is a terrible thing to expose our children to." Stern measures were taken to protect the candy-store set from the knowledge that the Soviet Union existed and that it was the biggest country in the world.

Much of the furor, far from being ridiculous, was

sinister. The United States Government was tainting the names of innocent men and costing itself the services of invaluable specialists. Senator McCarthy decided that Philip Jessup, a distinguished professor of international law at Columbia and a skilled diplomat, was a man with "an unusual affinity for Communist causes"; supinely a subcommittee of the Senate Foreign Relations Committee turned down Jessup's nomination as a delegate to the UN General Assembly. Trying to fight off McCarthyism, the Truman Administration adopted loyalty procedures that were increasingly dubious. In or out of government, utterly innocent people were losing their jobs. Irene Wicker, the "Singing Lady" of television, who was soon to have an audience with the Pope and be given a special blessing for her work with children, found her TV contract canceled. The McCarthy-type magazine *Counterattack*, which was connected with the pressure to dismiss her, made everything clear. The *Daily Worker* had listed Miss Wicker as a sponsor of a Red councilmanic candidate in New York and "the *Daily Worker* is very accurate; they never make a mistake."

Everywhere in the United States, the fury against Communism was taking on—even more than it had before the Korean War—elements of a vendetta against the Half-Century of Revolution in domestic affairs, against all departures from tradition in foreign policy, against the new, the adventurous, the questing in any field. Self-confident Yale University felt it necessary to appoint a committee of distinguished alumni to protect itself against a recent undergraduate, William F. Buckley, who talked, in the same burst of indignation at the Yale faculty, about the menace of Communism and the threat of "atheists" and of men who criticized "limited government" or economic "self-reliance." For most of 1951 the best-seller lists of the country included *Washington Confidential* by two newspapermen, Jack Lait and Lee Mortimer. The book was a jumble of breathless revelations about "Communism" in Washington, quotations like the one from an unnamed Negro dope peddler who told an unnamed federal agent "You can't arrest me. I am a friend of Mrs. Roosevelt," and such observations as "Where you find an intellectual in the District you will probably find a Red." In a number of cities, educators reported, anything "controversial" was being stripped from the schools—and more than a few times the "controversial" writing turned out to be factual information about UNESCO or New Deal legislation. A battle over a textbook in Council Bluffs, Iowa, produced the kind of statement that was commonplace. Ex-Congressman Charles Swanson opened the meeting with a roaring denunciation of "all these books. . . . They should be thrown on a bonfire—or sent to Russia. Why according to this book, Jefferson, Jackson, Wilson and Franklin Roosevelt were outstanding Presidents— what about William Howard Taft?"

In Washington, William Howard Taft's son Robert was in a new phase of his career. "The sad, worst period," his sympathetic biographer, William S. White, has called it. Certainly Senator Robert Taft was moving closer to McCarthyism. Even before the Korean War, in March, 1950, several responsible reporters asserted that Taft had remarked: "McCarthy should keep talking and if one case doesn't work out he should proceed with another." The Senator protested that this quotation misrepresented him but there can be no question about the meaning of statements he made after the Korean intervention. Taft complained that Truman had the bad habit to "*assume the innocence* of all the persons mentioned in the State Department." He also declared: "Whether Senator McCarthy has *legal evidence*, whether he has overstated or understated his case, is of lesser importance. The question is whether the Communist influence in the State Department *still exists*." (Italics added.) "This sort of thing," William White could only sadly comment, "was not the Taft one had known."

In domestic affairs the Senator's attacks became sharper and edged closer to the argument that Fair Dealism was a conspiracy of socialists. In foreign affairs, all the matters that were "open to question" in Taft's speech at the time the United States entered the Korean War were now settled and settled against the Administration. The American intervention was "an unnecessary war," an "utterly useless war," a war "begun by President Truman without the slightest authority from Congress or the people." And in explaining the international policy of the Administration the Senator was more and more using phrases that suggested a plot on the part of—to use a 1951 statement of Taft—"men who did not and do not turn their backs on the Alger Hisses."

If the Senator was going far, a large part of the GOP was moving in the same direction. In part this trend represented out-and-out McCarthyism. More of it came from the feeling—to use the phrase current then— that "I don't like some of McCarthy's methods but his goal is good." To the largest extent the development resulted from a fundamental disquietude with foreign and domestic affairs that showed itself in a violent anti-Trumanism, particularly on the issue of Far Eastern policy. The feeling was so extreme that it was willing to hit out almost blindly. Senator H. Alexander Smith, certainly no McCarthyite and not always a Taftite, spoke the attitude in explaining the decisive committee vote he cast against the confirmation of Philip Jessup. Smith said he did not agree with McCarthy's portrayal of Jessup as a pro-Communist. But the real issue was "approval or disapproval of our over-all Far Eastern policy. Dr. Jessup has been identified with those forces . . . responsible for the Far Eastern policy which has led to the present crisis. . . . He participated in the unfortunate events which led to the summary dismissal of General MacArthur. He is the symbol of a group attitude toward Asia. . . ."

At the conclusion of the MacArthur hearings, eight

out of the nine Republicans on the Senate Committee signed a policy statement. The men belonged to no one segment of the party—they included at least one representative from every principal faction—but they united in declaring that the reasons given for MacArthur's dismissal were "utterly inadequate"; in talking darkly about a "pro-Communist State Department group," concerning which "the . . . truth has not yet been revealed"; and in denouncing the management of affairs in the Far East "as the most desolate failure in the history of our foreign policy." As for the Administration's Korean policy of limited warfare in close association with the UN and with allies, the Senators spoke bitterly of a program which worried over the attitude of "certain of our associates" and was based on "no positive plan for achieving a decisive victory."

General Republicans, Taftite Republicans, McCarthyite Republicans, McCarthyite Democrats, and the millions of Americans who fitted none of these categories—in late 1951 and 1952 much of the nation was restlessly, irritably seeking to break through the sense of frustration. People flailed Harry Truman as a caged animal lashes at its bars. The President's Gallup rating sank to a minuscule twenty-six per cent and the personal attacks were so extreme the pro-Truman *New York Post* found itself pleading: "After all, the President of the United States is a member of the human race." Men and women were looking for some bright shining light, some road without endless roadblocks. Captain Henrik Carlsen became a national hero by following a simple forthright code and staying for twelve days on his foundering ship, the *Flying Enterprise*. The mounting religious interest was now reaching the scope of a national phenomenon; even Mickey Spillane turned to the church in early 1952—in his case to the appropriately frenetic doctrine of Jehovah's Witnesses. Before 1952 was done that recipe for swift certainties, *The Power of Positive Thinking*, began a sales career which was to break every best-seller record in modern American history. "The patron saint of Americans today is St. Vitus," said the book's author Dr. Norman Vincent Peale, pastor of the Marble Collegiate Church in New York. "The American people are so keyed up it is impossible to put them to sleep even with a sermon."

In Cleveland Louis B. Seltzer, editor of the *Cleveland Press*, sat down at his typewriter and wrote an editorial:

"What is wrong with us? . . .

"It is in the air we breathe. The things we do. The things we say. Our books. Our papers. Our theater. Our movies. Our radio and television. The way we behave. The interests we have. The values we fix.

"We have everything. We abound with all of the things that make us comfortable. We are, on the average, rich beyond the dreams of the kings of old. . . . Yet . . . something is not there that should be—something we once had. . . .

"Are we our own worst enemies? Should we fear what is happening among us more than what is happening elsewhere? . . .

"No one seems to know what to do to meet it. But everybody worries. . . ."

For days afterward Louis Seltzer's life was a madhouse. Phone calls and letters flooded his office. Strangers stopped him on the street to wring his hand and tell him he sure had hit it right. Forty-one publications throughout the United States reprinted the editorial. Louis Seltzer was not alone in yearning for something that was not there, for something that he was sure had once been there, for an older, simpler America without juvenile delinquents and genteel young men turning into Alger Hisses and five percenters and bewildering doctrines of limited warfare.

Shortly after noon on July 11, 1952, the TV cameras caught the banner of Minnesota waving frantically in Chicago's International Amphitheater. Senator Edward Thye was shouting hoarsely into the microphone: "Mr. Chairman, Mr. Chairman, Minnesota wishes to change—" Great roars went up in the hall, the organ broke into "The Minnesota Rouser," snakedancers started down the aisles. "Minnesota," Thye finally got his words out, "wishes to change its vote to Eisenhower." It was done. After all the efforts of Robert Taft to get the nomination, after all the protestations of Dwight Eisenhower against running for political office, the first ballot had made the General the Republican candidate for the Presidency.

Eisenhower hurried off for a fisherman's vacation near Denver and the country settled back to ponder just what kind of a man had become the GOP standard-bearer. Rarely in American history had so little been known about the views of a major candidate for the Presidency. It was generally agreed that the General was no ecstatic admirer of New Dealism. In fact, while President of Columbia he had gotten off a number of decidedly rightish remarks like "If all that Americans want is security, they can go to prison." On the other hand, it was equally widely assumed that he was much more friendly than Taft to the Half-Century of Revolution in domestic affairs. After all, hadn't liberals pushed Eisenhower for the Democratic nomination in 1948, and was there not a persistent story that he had been offered the 1952 Democratic nomination by no less a Fair Dealer than Harry Truman? As for foreign policy, the General had occasionally made statements such as "If we had been less soft and weak, there might not have been a Korean War." Yet it was unchallengeable fact that all of the most important parts of his career—his leadership during World War II, his period as Army Chief of Staff after V-J, and the NATO command which he resigned to run for the Presidency—had been carried on in intimate association with the Roosevelt-Truman foreign policies.

Eisenhower returned from his fishing trip and was soon talking policy. "The great problem of America today," he said, "is to take that straight road down the middle. . . ." He was for the UN, the General declared. Concerning Korea: "I believe we can point out what appear to all of us, at least from our position, to be the really terrible blunders that led up to the Korean war. But I do not see how these conditions, having occurred and having been created, how you could stay out of the thing, I don't know." In domestic matters he was certain that Americans of all parties approved "social gains" and that the Republicans would administer social legislation more efficiently and honestly than the Democrats had done.

Reporters kept asking about McCarthyism and the attacks on the loyalty of Eisenhower's old superior, General Marshall, by McCarthy and by McCarthy's ally, Senator William Jenner of Indiana. Eisenhower said several times that he would back "all duly nominated Republicans." But he also made a number of statements like "I am not going to support anything that smacks to me of un-Americanism . . . and that includes any kind of thing that looks to me like unjust damaging of reputation." On another occasion the candidate added: "I have no patience with anyone who can find in his [Marshall's] record of service to this country anything to criticize. . . . Maybe he made some mistakes. I do not know about that."

Six weeks after the General was nominated, the nineteen newspapers of the ardently pro-Eisenhower Scripps-Howard chain ran a front-page editorial. "Ike," the editorial declared, "is running like a dry creek." The General's speeches were stamping him "just another me-too candidate" and that would ruin him. Eisenhower was not "coming out swinging"—for example, his comment that he did not know whether Marshall had made mistakes. "If Ike doesn't know, he had better find out. For that's one of the big issues of this campaign. Ask any mother, father or wife of a soldier now in Korea. . . . We still cling to the hope that . . . he will hit hard. If he doesn't, he might as well concede defeat."

Many leading Republican politicians were downcast. Big crowds were turning out for Eisenhower but they seemed more interested in the war hero than the candidate and the General's hazy, fumbling words sent them away unaroused. ("Now he's crossing the 38th platitude again," reporters would sigh.) Senator McCarthy and McCarthyite GOP Senators were taking indirect slaps at Eisenhower. In a number of states Taft men were sulking in their tents. "Until Bob Taft blows the bugle," Indiana's Republican Chairman Cale J. Holder declared, "a lot of us aren't going to fight in the army."

If the General was running like a dry creek, his opponent Adlai Stevenson was rippling along like a spring brook in sparkling sunlight. The country had known little about this one-term Illinois Governor and a good many people were having quite an experience. He would sit on a platform, a smallish man advancing in the hips and retreating at the hairline, so pained by overstatement that when a speaker described him as the "gra-a-a-yate Guv-er-nur" he fussed with his tie and gulped. Then he stood up, cocked his head thoughtfully, started to speak, and electricity came into the hall. "Let's talk sense to the American people," he would say in his taut, clear voice and suddenly people had the feeling that here was a man who had fought out the question within himself and was ready to state his conclusion with no muzziness whatsoever.

Eisenhower went before the American Legion, stumbled through the conventional statements, received ten interruptions of hand-clapping and affectionate cheers when he finished. Adlai Stevenson walked right into the Legionnaires—he kidded them about how he was sure they had been enjoying the many cultural opportunities of New York City. Then the voice took on its special charge. He told the Legion that McCarthy's kind of patriotism was a disgrace and that he was shocked at the attacks on George Marshall. He defined a veteran as a man who owed America something even more than he was owed anything by the nation. The American Legion, citadel of special privilege, hotbed of McCarthyism, loudly cheered Stevenson twenty-five times—especially loudly when he said that the healthy veteran had no claim to favoritism.

And then there was Stevenson on television. "To both the Republican and the Democrat," the well-known TV critic John Crosby wrote in September, "it's now fairly obvious that Gov. Adlai E. Stevenson is a television personality the like of which has not been seen ever before. The man is setting a pace that will not only be almost impossible for succeeding candidates to follow but one that will be pretty hard for Stevenson himself to maintain." The voice would ring like a perfectly cast bell as Stevenson declared: "When an American says he loves his country, he means not only that he loves the New England hills, the prairies glistening in the sun or the wide rising plains, the mountains and the seas. He means that he loves an inner air, an inner light in which freedom lives and in which a man can draw the breath of self-respect." The slightest smile would come and the wit crackled out—a wit that was part Will Rogers, part cocktail lounge. The Republican Party had "been devoid of new ideas for almost 70 years. . . . As to their platform, well, nobody can stand on a bushel of eels." The fact that Eisenhower was accepting so much of the New Deal-Fair Deal record? "I've been tempted to say that I was proud to stand on that record if only . . . the General would move over and make room for me." And the wit that was not merely wit, the cold, stinging indignation: "You can tell the size of a man by the size of the thing that makes him mad, and I hope that regardless of my own political advantage, the matter [of the accusations against Marshall] is not finally resolved by the counsel of those who favor what has been described as the middle-of-the-gutter approach."

Stevenson's platform wizardry was worrying and irritating Republicans. In mid-September the columnist, Stewart Alsop, arrived in Hartford, Connecticut, aboard the Stevenson train. He telephoned his younger brother John, an insurance executive who was head of the Republican Speaker's Bureau in the state, and asked how the campaign was going. When John replied that the situation looked good for the GOP, Stewart brought up the fact that many intelligent and highly educated people who had supported Eisenhower against Taft for the Republican nomination were now switching to Stevenson.

John Alsop bridled. He was a good Republican partisan and he was especially irritated because he knew that what his brother was saying was true. He was also sure, as he recalled later, that "while Stevenson was appealing and appealing strongly to people's minds, Eisenhower, as a man and as a figure, was appealing far more strongly to far more people's emotions." An irascible image of the kind of person who was switching to Stevenson popped into John Alsop's mind—"a large oval head, smooth, faceless, unemotional, but a little bit haughty and condescending."

"Sure," John Alsop remarked on the telephone, "all the eggheads are for Stevenson, but how many eggheads are there?"

To John Alsop, a Yale graduate and anything but an anti-intellectual, the word "egghead" implied no sweeping opprobrium. With the same attitude Stewart Alsop quoted his brother in his syndicated column. Unintentionally the Alsops were adding a new sneer to the American language. Within days the word "egghead" was rapidly spreading, was being applied to Stevenson and the whole group of intellectuals who so ardently supported him, and was taking on bitter connotations. Before long the novelist Louis Bromfield would write that "there has come a wonderful new expression to define a certain shady element of our population. Who conceived the expression, I do not know. . . . It seems to have arisen spontaneously from the people themselves. . . . [It means] a person of intellectual pretensions, often a professor or the protégé of a professor . . . superficial in approach to any problem . . . feminine . . . supercilious . . . surfeited with conceit . . . a doctrinaire supporter of middle-European socialism . . . a self-conscious prig . . . a bleeding heart." If Stevenson won the election, Bromfield concluded, "the eggheads will come back into power and off again we will go on the scenic railway of muddled economics, Socialism, Communism, crookedness and psychopathic instability."

General Eisenhower sat on an Indianapolis platform with the increasingly rabid McCarthyite Senator William Jenner, colored and physically winced as Jenner delivered his diatribe but spoke the words of endorsement for the Senator's reelection. McCarthyite trumpets began to sound for Dwight Eisenhower. Soon the General and Senator Taft had a conference in New York City. The Senator issued a statement saying that any differences between them on matters of foreign or domestic policy were mere "differences of degree," and the Taft men started to go to work.

From the beginning of the campaign the top Republican strategists had more or less agreed that there were three key issues. One day at a conference Senator Karl Mundt, co-chairman of the Speaker's Bureau, lightheartedly referred to the trio of points by the formula K_1C_2 and the phrase was becoming more and more common in GOP strategy letters and conversations. The campaign addresses that were being written

for Eisenhower were also increasingly focusing on
K_1C_2—the Korean War and charges of corruption and
of Communism in the government.

Sharpening up the speeches entirely fitted the General's conception of how the campaign should be
fought. At the early strategy conferences Eisenhower
had expressed few positive opinions. He pointed out
that he was an amateur in this business of politics, that
he preferred for a while to listen and ask questions,
but he did emphasize one consideration. He wanted
to hold his fire at the beginning, to increase it as he
went along, and to finish blazing away. Although
Eisenhower made no reference to previous Republican campaigns, it was assumed by a number of the
men present that he had in mind both the general nature of successful warfare, military or political, and
the specific fact that Thomas Dewey's campaigns
had closed weakly in 1944 and 1948.

The General's speeches were not only acquiring a
more vigorous tone and clearer lines; they were being written with a greater adaptation to the man who
was delivering them. Beginning a Midwestern swing,
Eisenhower answered Stevenson's wit by K_1C_2 interwoven with a let's-not-be-funny theme. "It would be
very, very fine," the General said, "if one could command new and amusing language, witticisms to bring
you a chuckle. Frankly, I have no intention of trying
to do so. The subjects of which we are speaking these
days, my friends, are not those that seem to me to be
amusing. . . . Is it amusing that we have stumbled
into a war in Korea; that we have already lost in casualties 117,000 of our Americans killed and wounded; is
it amusing that that war seems to be no closer to a real
solution than ever; that we have no real plan for stopping it? . . . Is it funny when evidence was discovered that there are Communists in government and we
get the cold comfort of the reply, 'red herring'?" And
what was so uproarious about "the experts in shady
and shoddy government operations . . . coming from

their shadowy haunts" to corrupt the "very operations of democratic government?"

Things were picking up decidedly. The candidate, gathering ease from his successes, fumbled less and less and the famous smile glowed with confidence as well as friendliness. At the whistle stops in Minnesota, Iowa, Nebraska, and Missouri, there was a striking rapport between Eisenhower and the huge crowds that turned out for him. Correspondents who had followed the General in the early days of the campaign could hardly believe they were watching the same man.

Just as the Republican campaign was rolling, on September 18, 1952, the pro-Stevenson newspaper, the *New York Post*, came out with a full-page headline: SECRET NIXON FUND. A "millionaire's club" in California, the *Post* declared, had collected an eighteen-thousand-dollar "slush fund" for the "financial comfort" of the GOP Vice-Presidential candidate, Senator Richard Nixon. The story did not spread widely until the next day but then bedlam broke.

Democratic National Chairman Stephen Mitchell flatly demanded Nixon's resignation. Nixon cried out: "This is another typical smear by the same left wing elements which have fought me ever since I took part in the investigation which led to the conviction of Alger Hiss." The trustee of the fund, the Pasadena lawyer Dana Smith, was explaining away. The arrangement was set up when Nixon was elected to the Senate in 1950, Smith told reporters, and ended when he was nominated for the Vice-Presidency. Seventy-six contributors had put in an average of two hundred and fifty dollars and the largest contribution was a thousand dollars. Smith did all the disbursing of the money and it went exclusively for expenses connected with the Senator's "campaign against Communism and corruption in government. . . . The whole idea of the Nixon fund program was to enable Dick to do a selling job to the American people in behalf of private enterprise and integrity in government."

Everybody was commenting now and the hubbub was hardly pro-Nixon. The powerful Republican newspaper, the *New York Herald Tribune*, said the Senator should offer to withdraw. The independent but pro-Eisenhower *New York Times* editorialized that the contributors "showed poor judgment in making such a gift, and Senator Nixon had shown poor judgment in accepting it." A survey of almost one hundred representative papers, the majority of which were supporting the Republican ticket, showed disapproval of the Vice-Presidential candidate by a ratio of nearly two-to-one. The CIO was hammering hard on Nixon's voting record in the Senate, arguing that he had voted on taxes, housing, and rent control in a way that brought direct financial profit to a number of men among the donors.

Conflicting advice racked the Eisenhower campaign train and the General delayed taking any decisive action. As the days went by, the newspapermen on the train let it be known that they had voted forty-to-two against Nixon and that they believed preparations were under way for a "whitewash." Infuriated, Eisenhower called an off-the-record press conference. Pounding his fist into his palm, he told the newsmen: "I don't care if you fellows are forty-to-two against me, but I'm taking my time on this. Nothing's decided, contrary to your idea that this is all a setup for a whitewash of Nixon. Nixon has got to be as clean as a hound's tooth."

Then, more calmly, the General went on to explain his attitude. He had been enthusiastically for Nixon, he said, because of his age and because he considered him the earnest, upright young man of the type that America needed. He still had faith in his integrity. However, he felt that in a crusade of the kind that he was conducting—a crusade against unethical as well as illegal practices in government—he had to criticize his dearest friend as quickly as his enemy if the friend fell short of the most exacting standards. The whole matter of the fund would be subjected to the most careful scrutiny, Eisenhower concluded.

Nixon, campaigning on the West Coast, was near explosion. He was sure he had done nothing wrong. He was miffed at Eisenhower's failure to give him all-out support and he was staggered by blows like that of the *New York Herald Tribune*. By the time his train pulled into Portland, he was tight-lipped and snappish. Finally, after frantic telephone calls between Eisenhower's train, Nixon's train, and leading GOP figures all over the country, a decision was made. On the evening of September 23 Nixon would go on coast-to-coast radio and television to answer the charges. An offer of commercial sponsorship was considered but quickly dismissed; the Republican National Committee paid the seventy-five-thousand-dollar bill. Most of the day before the telecast Nixon spent alone, filling legal-sized sheets with notes. Later, speaking before an advertising men's luncheon in New York, he recalled September 23 and remarked that "no TV performance takes such careful preparation as an off-the-cuff talk."

An estimated fifty-five million Americans watched or listened to the candidate fighting for his political life. Some of the speech was an argument that none of the eighteen thousand dollars benefited Nixon personally, that it was all used for "this one message, of exposing this Administration, the Communism in it, the corruption in it." Other parts of the talk were straight political argument. But most of the thirty minutes was a story of a family, told in a tone of utter earnestness by an ordinary-looking young man in a none-too-fashionable suit. He grew up in the "modest circumstances" provided by his father's grocery store in East Whittier, California, Nixon said. Then came "the best thing that ever happened to me. I married Pat, who is sitting over here." The war years were not "particularly unusual. . . . I went to the South Pacific. I guess

I'm entitled to a couple of stars . . . but I was just there when the bombs were falling."

"Like most young couples," the Nixons accumulated their possessions and their debts—the 1950 Oldsmobile car, the mortgage on the house, the $4,000 in life insurance plus his GI policy. Like most doting parents, Nixon kept coming back to his two girls, Patricia and Julia, and he told about a gift which a supporter had sent to "our two youngsters. . . . Do you know what it was? It was a little cocker spaniel dog in a crate that he'd sent all the way from Texas, black and white, spotted, and our little girl, Trisha, the six-year-old, named it Checkers. And you know the kids, like all kids, love the dog, and I just want to say this right now that regardless of what they say about it, we're going to keep it." It all wasn't very much, the possessions of the Nixons, the Senator summarized, "but Pat and I have the satisfaction that every dime that we've got is honestly ours. I should say this—that Pat doesn't have a mink coat, but she does have a respectable Republican cloth coat, and I always tell her that she'd look good in anything.

"And now, finally, I know that you wonder whether or not I am going to stay on the Republican ticket or resign. Let me say this—I don't believe that I ought to quit, because I'm not a quitter. And incidentally, Pat's not a quitter. After all, her name was Patricia Ryan and she was born on St. Patrick's Day, and you know the Irish never quit.

"But the decision, my friends, is not mine. . . . Wire and write the Republican National Committee whether you think I should stay on or whether I should get off, and whatever their decision is, I will abide by it.

"But just let me say this last word—regardless of what happens, I'm going to continue this fight. I'm going to campaign up and down America until we drive the crooks and the Communists and those that defend them out of Washington. And remember, folks, Eisenhower is a great man. Believe me. He's a great man. And a vote for Eisenhower is a vote for what's good for America."

Dwight and Mamie Eisenhower watched the telecast sitting in the manager's office at the Cleveland Public Auditorium, where the General was scheduled to speak that night. At the conclusion Mrs. Eisenhower was weeping and the General was obviously trying to control his emotions. Outside in the auditorium Representative George Bender of Ohio was leading wild demonstrations in favor of Nixon.

Eisenhower's press secretary James Hagerty turned to his boss. "General," he said, "you'll have to throw your speech away. Those people out there want to hear about Nixon."

Eisenhower scribbled notes for a new speech and thirty minutes later he was before the crowd. "I have been a warrior and I like courage," the General began. "I have seen many brave men in tough situations. I have never seen any come through in better fashion than Senator Nixon did tonight." But then he added that he needed more than "a single presentation" and that he was asking Nixon to meet him in Wheeling, West Virginia.

Nixon was irritated again. "What more can I explain?" he snapped but he took off for Wheeling. Meanwhile the switchboards of radio and television stations were hopelessly jammed. Where do I send a wire supporting Nixon? the endless voices wanted to know. (Later Nixon said that he had remembered to get into his speech everything he wanted to say except the address of the Republican National Committee.) Wires and letters were addressed to scores of places— to Eisenhower's and Nixon's campaign trains, to Dana Smith, to local Republican committees, to "Richard Nixon" and "Dwight Eisenhower, U.S.A." Western Union officials said that they had never handled as many wires as they did that night. It was a month before the Republican National Committee, using a hundred volunteers, could get the mail opened and sorted. The sentiment was about three hundred and fifty to one in Nixon's favor and enough contributions poured in—mostly in amounts of one dollar or less—to pay sixty thousand dollars of the seventy-five-thousand-dollar cost of the telecast.

As Eisenhower's train moved toward Wheeling, every mention of the Vice-Presidential candidate had the crowds whooping with approval. So many stacks of pro-Nixon telegrams kept being brought aboard that the General pleaded for people to stop wiring. The further the train traveled, the more relaxed Eisenhower became, the more he talked in a folksy vernacular, the more he discussed "Dick Nixon."

The General drove nine miles to the hilltop field at Wheeling and boarded the plane before the Senator could descend. "Boy, am I glad to see you," Eisenhower greeted Nixon.

The Senator had expected to have to seek out Eisenhower in town and he was startled. "You didn't need to come out here," he said.

"Why, you're my boy," Eisenhower replied, putting his arm warmly around Nixon.

The two men talked for six minutes in the plane and then went off to the waiting crowd at Wheeling Stadium. With his first words Eisenhower ended the debate whether Nixon was to continue as the GOP Vice-Presidential candidate. "He is not only completely vindicated as a man of honor but as far as I am concerned he stands higher than ever before."

Democrats cried outrage. Was six minutes of conversation on a plane the careful scrutiny Eisenhower was going to insist upon? Was Nixon's TV speech to settle the matter despite the fact that he had not explained where he got the money for a twenty-thousand-dollar down payment on a home in Washington and another considerable down payment on a house in East Whittier, California? Was this "incredible corn," to use the phrase of the pro-Stevenson *St. Louis Post-Dispatch*, to be accepted as serious political discussion? Even assuming that Nixon had spent none of the money on himself, what about the ethics of taking funds which could easily influence the way a Senator voted? The Stevenson forces cried out and their voices were lost. The whole issue was confused because shortly before Nixon's TV address, the fact was revealed that Stevenson had used money left over from his gubernatorial campaign to augment the salaries of some state employees—a quite different kind of fund, the Democrats insisted, but one which easily sounded the same in the furor. In larger measure the anti-Nixon indignation was swept aside because the Senator had touched a vital nerve.

For two decades Democratic politicians had been benefiting by an emotional identification with the common man as he appeared in the 1930's—the common man worrying over enough food to eat or a decent suit to wear. Nixon, consciously or unconsciously, was identifying himself with the most common American of the 1950's—the man with quite enough food and an entirely respectable suit but worrying over the next step up, a step like Nixon's purchase of an expensive home with a large mortgage hanging over him. And Nixon spoke of this different problem with the same little-man psychology that had been so moving when the little man was worried not about thousands owed to the bank but the week's grocery bill.

Robert Ruark, the Scripps-Howard columnist, caught a good deal of the power of the Nixon performance when he wrote: "Dick Nixon stripped himself naked for all the world to see, and he brought the missus and the kids and the dog and his war record into the act. . . . The sophisticates . . . sneer . . . [but] this came closer to humanizing the Republican party than anything that has happened in my memory. Mr. Thomas Dewey never seemed to share much of the problems of the ordinary Joe. Even the immensely

popular Gen. Eisenhower has not been as you and I.
. . . Bob Taft had a President for a father, and
money of his own. Gen. MacArthur is nearly a deity.
. . . Tuesday night the nation saw a little man,
squirming his way out of a dilemma, and laying bare
his most-private hopes, fears and liabilities. This time
the common man was a Republican, for a change. . . .
Dick Nixon . . . has suddenly placed the burden of
old-style Republican aloofness on the Democrats."

Eisenhower and Nixon—it was now genuinely Eisenhower and Nixon for the Vice-Presidential candidate was drawing big crowds—swung back on their
campaign tours. The pattern of their campaign took
final shape. The gains to ordinary men from the Half-
Century of Revolution in domestic affairs would be
preserved and "extended where wise." But these matters and everything else were to be handled in the
"American style"—without Communism, corruption,
or Korea. Further ways were found of stressing Korea
and Communism. More and more directly Eisenhower accused the Administration of softness toward
Communists in the government. ("We have seen this
sort of thing go on and on until my running mate,
Dick Nixon, grabbed a police whistle and stopped
it.") The General swung into Wisconsin, conferred
with McCarthy, and cut from his speech sentences
praising General Marshall. McCarthy and Nixon went
on TV to associate the danger of Communism with
Stevenson. McCarthy said "Alger—" then stopped and
smirked—"I mean Adlai"—was "an out-and-out pro-
Communist." Nixon declared that the Democratic
candidate had "failed to recognize the threat."

In the Hotel Commodore in New York City, Emmet John Hughes, a *Time-Life* editor, was working
away on speeches for Eisenhower. Hughes had an
idea: The General should promise to go to Korea
when elected. Hughes wrote the idea into a draft of a
speech and Eisenhower liked it. Speaking in Detroit,
the candidate denounced the "false answer . . . that

nothing can be done to speed a secure peace. . . . I shall go to Korea." The crowd liked the idea too. It stood up and cheered in a way few American political meetings have ever done. Democratic strategists did not pretend that this speech, with its implication of a quick end to the war, had not hurt and hurt badly.

Specific developments, spectacular developments— but above and beyond these an undefined and almost indefinable image of the Republican ticket was emerging. Richard Nixon, saying "Gee, this is a great country" and going on talking about "my darling wife Pat . . . my little girls," was helping to create the impression, but fundamentally it was emerging from the figure of the sixty-one-year-old General making his first foray into politics. Dwight Eisenhower was the simple American. He used the phrase *status quo* and quickly apologized: " 'Course, I'm not supposed to be the educated candidate." He was the rugged American. The Democrats were firing "red hot salvos" but he was not disturbed because "I've been shot at by real artillerists." He was the God-fearing American. "The issue always and at bottom is spiritual." He was the American free of bewildering ideology who only wanted it said of his Presidency: " 'He has been fair. He has been my friend.' " Somehow everything he said and did created more and more the image of Dwight Eisenhower of Abilene, Kansas, honest and decent and uncomplicated in a way that America had been before the complexities of social revolution at home and of Communist revolutions abroad.

By eleven p.m. on Election Night it was all over. Eisenhower was on his way to a landslide and to the most genuinely national victory since another candidate, the Franklin Roosevelt of 1936, spoke the mood of another generation. Thirty-nine states were moving into the Republican column, only nine into the Democratic line; more than six million popular votes were separating the two candidates. Eisenhower was the first Republican candidate since 1928 to break the Solid South. He captured large segments of groups that had been Democratic for years—Catholics, organized workers, and young voters. He ran rampant in the areas which most surely characterized the America of 1952, the little white houses of suburbia.

At 11.32 p.m. Adlai Stevenson left the Governor's mansion in Springfield to read his concession statement at Democratic headquarters in the Leland Hotel. He was trying hard to appear jaunty and chipper. His smile was steady; when he arrived at the hotel, he saw a newspaperman he knew and gave him an owlish wink. Stevenson read his concession statement, a generous one, with perfect control and took pains to remind his followers: "It is traditionally American to fight hard before an election. It is equally traditional to close ranks as soon as the people have spoken." Then, suddenly, all the jauntiness was gone. "Someone asked me, as I came in, down on the street, how I felt, and I was reminded of a story that a fellow-townsman of ours used to tell—Abraham Lincoln. They asked him how he felt once after an unsuccessful election. He said he felt like a little boy who had stubbed his toe in the dark. He said that he was too old to cry, but it hurt too much to laugh." In university towns, among writers, wherever men and women had been captivated by the lilt of Adlai Stevenson, people stared at each other blankly and some wept unabashedly. "It's not just that a great man has been defeated," Val Jamison, a professor at the University of Utah, expressed the feeling. "It's that a whole era is ended, is totally repudiated, a whole era of brains and literacy and exciting thinking."

At Republican headquarters in the Hotel Commodore of New York City, the modish gowns and the well-tailored suits swirled around as thousands joined Fred Waring in singing the "Battle Hymn of the Republic," "God Bless America," and "Where Oh Where but in America Can You Sing True Freedom's

Song?" Throughout the country many a member of upper-income America celebrated the end of twenty hateful years.

The jubilant better neighborhoods and the depressed intellectual groups were not alone in their sense of a new era. The day after the election a Harrisburg reporter set out to discover how ordinary Americans were reacting to the election. The first person he talked to was Mrs. Edith Wilson, wife of a mechanic at a Texaco garage. When the reporter put his question to Mrs. Wilson, she paused and shifted her bundles uneasily. Then she said slowly: "I don't want to be silly or anything. But you know it's so big and wonderful—it's like, well, it's like America has come home."

Flare against Communism very high — much McCarthyism

With elect. of Ike, upper-income Amer. was in control

20 yrs. of thinking & actions had come to an end with the elect. of the Repub. Ike

All America had switched Repub — again a unified confident mood predominated among Americans

XI

No Fear
of Conservatism

SHORTLY AFTER the election Dwight Eisenhower landed in Korea, took an intense, worried look at the situation, flew back with his advisers to Guam. There they shifted to the U.S.S. *Helena* and at Wake Island the cruiser paused to take on more aides who had flown from the United States. The *Helena* laid a course for Pearl Harbor, three days away, and the men spent the respite on the Pacific getting acquainted with each other and talking plans.

Eisenhower began one session with a statement of some of his own general ideas. He said that he thought of the office of the Presidency not as Roosevelt and Truman had done but according to an older conception—the Executive as one of three equal branches of the government, who was not to try to do too much leading. It was his profound conviction, he went on, that the 156 million citizens of the United States could best live their lives and improve their lot without controls from above. The government's role in domestic affairs was to assure fair play, not to attempt to direct the national economic life. In only one area did the government have a prime responsibility. By means of its handling of the budget and its credit policies, it should insure a sound and stable dollar. The President-elect repeatedly emphasized his fear of inflation, citing his European experiences to back up his point.

Like Taft, Eisenhower closely connected his economic thinking and his ideas about national defense. American power, he said, rested on two pillars—actual fighting strength and a flourishing industry and agriculture. The United States had to have powerful armed forces, but a prodigal outlay of money on military equipment or tremendous expenditures for other purposes would generate more inflation and thus disastrously weaken the country.

When the talk turned to foreign affairs, the incoming Secretary of State, John Foster Dulles, usually took the lead. Dulles especially stressed one point. All the great wars of modern history, he was sure, were started by national leaders who miscalculated and thought they could get away with something that other nations actually were not willing to tolerate. The North Korean invasion in particular had been undertaken as a result of Acheson's speech concerning America's defense perimeter in Asia. Dulles's implications for the present were unmistakable. The Communist nations should be told the consequences if they did certain things—and the consequences should be serious.

The President-elect, accustomed to the crispness of military briefings, sometimes showed impatience at Dulles's long pauses and somewhat oracular manner. But for the most part Eisenhower listened approvingly. Beneath everything Dulles was saying ran a theme quite congenial to the President-elect. The United States, as Dulles would soon express the attitude in a speech, should operate on the three principles which were "in accord with what used to be the great American traditional foreign policy . . . openness, simplicity, and righteousness." A quest for the traditional, for what they were sure was the sounder, the more American way of doing things—here was the point of view that united Eisenhower and his chief aides.

The President-elect became the President, the attitudes of the Administration began to be spoken out, and millions rejoiced. The Rev. Mr. James Miller of Los Angeles offered up a prayer which began: "Now that virtue has been restored to high places. . . ." The DAR and assorted citizens, having worried for years whether the gold at Fort Knox was safe under the free-spending Democrats, soon managed to get it counted. (When the count of the nation's assets was over and it was found that the United States did have the $30,442,415,581.70 it was supposed to have except for ten dollars which the ex-Treasurer of the United States, Mrs. Georgia Clark, said—some thought Mrs. Clark was being sarcastic—she would send a check to cover.) Of serious import, a large part of the country's businessmen and those with business attitudes, who for twenty long years had felt themselves pushed aside, believed that they and their ideas would now return to their rightful place.

They looked at the new Cabinet and they winced at the Secretary of Labor, who was none other than Martin Durkin, the pro-Stevenson, anti-Taft-Hartley president of the United Association of Journeymen Plumbers and Steamfitters. But for the most part the business world could not have been more pleased. "Eight millionaires and a plumber," "T.R.B." wisecracked in the *New Republic* and the remark, whatever its inaccuracies, did catch the board-of-directors' tone of the group of Presidential advisers. Even before the administration formally began, Charles Wilson, the president of General Motors who was slated to be Secretary of Defense, got off a cardinal point of the businessman's traditional credo before the Senate Armed Forces Committee. For years, Wilson said, he had assumed that "what was good for our country was good for General Motors, and vice versa." The phrase immediately made its way across the United States, usually in the simplified and somewhat distorted form of "what's good for General Motors is good for the country." Democrats cried I-told-you-so. (In his first major speech after the election Stevenson smiled mischievously and remarked: "While the New Dealers have all left Washington to make way for the car dealers, I hasten to say that I, for one, do not believe the story that the general welfare has become a subsidiary of General Motors.") As for Wilson, he was puzzled at the uproar. After all, was he not speaking precisely the feeling of generations of Americans who had labored to build grocery stores or corporations in the firm belief that what was good for their businesses was good for America, the land of business?

Things not only sounded different; they were quite different in fact. From the beginning of Eisenhower's term until Robert Taft's death in July 1953, the Senator from Ohio was an important part of the Administration, advising the President and working closely with him. Before and after Taft's death, the influence of a Taft Republican, George Humphrey, was steadily mounting in the Presidential circle.

Shortly after Humphrey entered the Cabinet as Secretary of the Treasury, a reporter asked whether he had read Ernest Hemingway's *The Old Man and the Sea*. The Secretary replied: "Why would anybody be interested in some old man who was a failure and never amounted to anything anyway?" Humphrey's father, a prosperous lawyer of Saginaw, Michigan, had permitted no one in his home to forget the importance of material success. The mother, when she found it absolutely necessary to use the word, had an unbreakable rule to spell Franklin Roosevelt's name with a small *r*. From boyhood, it was the material, the pecuniary drive, the practical that appealed to George Humphrey. Starting out as a lawyer in Saginaw, he soon realized, as he remarked later, that "in the law business you put your heart and soul into a client. When you finished with his trouble, then you went through it again with the next client. All you could build in the law business was a personal reputation. I was much more interested in building something you could see or touch." In 1918 he turned to the highly touchable and seeable; he went to Cleveland as general counsel for M. A. Hanna and Co., the ore house in which Mark Hanna had been a leading partner. Year after year Humphrey proved his business prowess—pulling the Hanna firm out of a two million dollar deficit, rising to its presidency, expanding it to a giant holding company with subsidiaries in everything from steel-making to plastics and banking. And year after year George Humphrey personally became more the businessman's businessman—a pleasant, vigorous figure, working hard and playing hard, with a mind of impressive clarity, a passion for facts, and an assumption that New Dealism was spending the country into bankruptcy and planning it into chaos.

Secretary of the Treasury Humphrey told President Eisenhower he had only one request. "When anyone talks to you about money, will you ask him if he has seen George?" People saw George and the new Administration hurried toward the Taftite essentials in domestic affairs. The hiring of government exployees was drastically curbed; the number of federal construction projects was cut down. The wage and price controls imposed in the course of the Korean War were abolished. Moves were made toward putting into effect tax, budget, public-resources, and power policies long sought by corporate America. One of the first pieces of legislation urged by the Administration concerned a matter which had become something of a symbol of the clash between New Dealish and pro-business thinking. The Administration called for and Congress passed a bill turning over to state jurisdiction a large part of the tidelands oil.

In March the new order of things was expressed in a form so extreme that it amounted to a caricature. The Secretary of Commerce, the industrialist Sinclair Weeks, had come to Washington anxious, as he expressed it, "to create a 'business climate' in the nation's economy." On March 31 the Department announced the resignation "by request" of Dr. Allen Astin, head of the National Bureau of Standards. When Secretary Weeks testified before the Senate Small Business Committee it became clear that Astin's dismissal was involved with a Bureau of Standards report. The laboratory tests of the Bureau showed results unsatisfactory to Jess Ritchie, the manufacturer of a battery additive.

Secretary Weeks was profoundly dissatisfied with the Bureau, he told the Senate Committee, because of its lack of awareness of "the business point of view." He intended to "get the best brains I can find to examine into the functions and objectives of the Bureau of Standards and re-evaluate them in relation to the American business community." One question the Secretary would raise was whether any product should be subjected to government approval before going on the market. "As a practical man I do not see why a product should be denied an opportunity in the market place." In the ensuing furor Weeks backed down and Astin was re-employed. But a point of view had been pictured, with strokes that a Herblock would not care to improve upon.

In the Department of Agriculture the new Secretary, Ezra Taft Benson, his plain face and plain clothes contrasting incongruously with his huge, glossy office, was working away on a farm program. Benson is a distant blood relative of Robert Taft and ideologically he is a brother. One of the Twelve Apostles, the ruling group of the Mormon Church, he has all of the Mormon's zeal for self-reliance and a commensurate skepticism of federally subsidized agriculture. The President not only agreed with Benson's general attitude; he felt peculiarly close to his Secretary of Agriculture because the two men shared a strong religious bent and a tendency to equate the "spiritual" side of democracy with an individualistic economy. Benson set out to put farm products back in the free market as quickly as possible. In late 1953 his program was emerging—the legislation which was passed by Congress in August 1954. The bill took a decided step toward a free market by replacing rigid price supports with flexible supports. Benson fought hard to provide a price flexibility on all products of between 75 and 90 per cent of parity. Congress decreed that the range should be only 82½ to 90 per cent on the basic commodities—cotton, corn, wheat, rice, peanuts, and tobacco. But in the case of other products, the level of support was at the Secretary's discretion.

Six months after he took office Eisenhower discussed the direction and achievements of his Administration in several South Dakota speeches. The Republicans, he declared, had "instituted what amounts almost to a revolution in the Federal Government as we have known it in our time, trying to make it smaller rather than bigger and finding things it can stop doing instead of seeking new things for it to do." This, he emphasized, was a matter of no small import because "in the last twenty years creeping socialism has been striking in the United States." The fault was not exclusively that of "a few long-haired academic men in Washington." In part it came because some Americans had "not been quick enough to resent socialism if we thought it would benefit us." The next week Eisenhower was pressed at his press conference to give an example of "creeping socialism" and he named TVA. Clarence Manion, chairman of Eisenhower's Commission on Inter-Governmental Relations, promptly advocated the sale of TVA to private utility companies. Did he agree? the President was asked by reporters. Eisenhower replied that his views were well known— he believed in the maximum of free enterprise. But he did not know whether TVA could be sold without bringing about circumstances that would wreck it.

Just as the Administration was getting fully under way headlines reported the physicians' bulletins.

March 4, 1953: STALIN GRAVELY ILL AFTER STROKE. March 5: STALIN SINKING: LEECHES APPLIED. March 6: STALIN DEAD. Within days the new premier, Georgi Malenkov, was making speeches about solving all "troublesome and unresolved questions . . . by peaceful negotiations." With a rush of hope the American public asked: Did the end of the tough old dictator mean the end of the Korean War?

During his postelection trip to Korea, Eisenhower had become convinced that continuation of the stalemate was intolerable. The one major remaining issue between the UN and the Communist negotiators was whether the more than 22,000 North Korean and Chinese prisoners of the UN who said they did not want to go home would be forced to return. Nothing had seemed to be able to break this deadlock, including a proposal made to the UN by India in November, 1952. Prisoners unwilling to be repatriated, New Delhi urged, should be supervised by a commission made up of Poland and Czechoslovakia, both Communist, and Sweden and Switzerland, both neutral, and a fifth nation to be named. The mildest comment any Communist leader made about the plan at the time was Andrei Vishinsky's "unacceptable, unsuitable, unbelievable." Eisenhower agreed with Dulles that the Communists should be told that the new American policy was: Peace or else. The Administration would continue to negotiate sincerely. But if the stalemate went on, the United States would fight to win, and this meant air attacks beyond the Yalu and the tactical use of atomic arms. The Secretary of State undertook to see to it that the Chinese thoroughly understood the American position. He explained it personally to Prime Minister Nehru of India—a man with decidedly good communication lines to Peiping.

In 1956 Dulles expressed his belief that the American threats broke the deadlock in the truce negotiations. Other experts have argued that the prime difference was the willingness of the new Soviet regime to permit an armistice. Indian spokesmen have pointed to their proposal, maintaining that it provided a sensible solution which the Communists ultimately recognized as sensible. Whatever the reason or reasons, things happened in early 1953.

On February 22 the UN commander, General Mark Clark, had written the Communists another in a long series of letters urging that something be done about exchanging sick and wounded prisoners. He did not receive a reply until March 28 but he was startled at its contents. The Communists were not only ready to arrange such an exchange; they wanted to discuss "the smooth settlement of the entire question of prisoners of war." Truce negotiations which had been given up since the fall were resumed, the sick and the wounded were exchanged, and the conferences moved toward peace. By June 17 a settlement seemed close.

But the postwar remained the postwar, endlessly productive of jarring news. That June 17 the Associated Press carried eighteen special bulletins in the day period, sixteen in the night report, and for one twenty minute period news came in so fast that nothing was put on the trunk wire except flashes. East Berlin, restive after Stalin's death, broke into open revolt. Supreme Court Justice William Douglas stayed the execution of the convicted atom spies, the Rosenbergs. Near Tokyo a C-124 crashed in the worst air tragedy up to that time, killing 129 soldiers and airmen. And 78-year-old Syngman Rhee, determined that there should be no truce except one which united Korea under him, capped all the bulletins with an act of utter defiance.

At 2 a.m., June 18, Dulles was awakened by the ringing of a telephone in the bedroom of his Washington home. An officer at the State Department was calling to say that Rhee's soldiers were cutting through the wire compounds and freeing thousands of North Korean and Chinese prisoners. Dulles listened quietly, grunting an occasional "yow" and trying to shake off the sleep. As he reached over to switch on the light, he broke through the heaviness and realized that the United States was close to major fighting, perhaps on the verge of a nuclear World War III. Wouldn't the Communists now walk out of the peace conference, bringing into effect the drastic measures which he and Eisenhower had agreed upon? "This is as critical as June, 1950," the Secretary believed.

Dulles picked up his direct phone to the White House and had the President awakened. Both men were ready to go ahead. The bombing targets beyond the Yalu had already been carefully picked so as to limit them to areas of indisputable military importance.

But the Communists really wanted a truce. Their representatives stormed and they sulked but they went right on negotiating. Soon the final papers were ready. The military demarcation line was fixed near the 38th parallel. (South Korea gained 2,350 square miles of North Korean territory and North Korea added 850 square miles south of the 38th parallel.) The forced repatriation issue was settled approximately along the lines of the Indian proposal. During the months of bitter negotiations each side had made important concessions. The UN had not gained acceptance of an inspection system trustworthy enough to make sure that preparations for another attack did not go ahead in North Korea. The Communists, although they won face-saving amendments to the original Indian proposal, were denied forced repatriation.

Promptly at 10 a.m. on Monday, July 28 (it was 9 p.m. Sunday, July 27 in Washington) the two senior negotiators entered the little truce building at Panmunjom—the mild-mannered General William K. Harrison, tieless and without decorations, and the bristling North Korean, General Nam Il, sweltering in a heavy tunic sagging with gold medals. Aides carried back and forth nine copies of the main documents (three each in English, Chinese, and Korean) and the two men sat at separate tables, silently writing their signatures. By orders of Syngman Rhee, no South Korean signed. When Harrison and Nam Il had finished, they rose and departed without a handshake or a word.

After thirty-seven months and two days the war that was never officially a war, which had cost America alone 25,000 dead, 115,000 other casualties, and twenty-two billion dollars, was over. The UN and the U.S. had stopped aggression; they had neither won nor lost the war. They had managed to arrange a truce; the truce was as flimsy as the bitterness of Syngman Rhee or the plans of the Communists might make it. They had established emphatically before the world that Communist advances could be resisted. They had not necessarily contributed to anti-Communist feeling in pivotal Asia.

Along the front lines UN soldiers heard the news broadcast in nine languages, smiled and yelled a bit but mostly stood around talking quietly. Once in a while somebody would grin and say something like: "Don't forget where you put your gun. You'll need it next week." General Mark Clark told reporters: "I cannot find it in me to exult at this hour." Foreign correspondent Dwight Martin cabled back that many top U.S. military men in Korea were perfectly aware of the arguments that freedom had been defended and aggression repelled but took little joy in the truce. "They all seem concerned," he added, "that some day they will be called on to explain why they signed the present armistice. Several I've talked to specifically think in terms of investigating committees demanding to know whether it is a fact that they sold out Korea. They frankly admit that complex justifications and explanations, currently acceptable, may look pretty lame in a year or so."

The evening of the armistice President Eisenhower appeared on television solemn-faced. He spoke of his relief that the killing had been stopped but he quickly added that what had been gained was "an armistice on a single battleground, not peace in the world. We may not now relax our guard nor cease our quest." Here and there in the United States celebrations started up and quickly petered out. In Philadelphia a soldier who had already managed quite an evening tried to keep things going. He went up to a man standing on the corner. "Wonerful, ishn't it? Jus' plain dern wonerful."

The man hailed his cab and paused for a moment. "I don't know whether it's wonderful, son. But anyhow it's over."

The removal of the specific pressures of the Korean War permitted the Administration to develop more rapidly its general defense and foreign policies. In part they sprang from a strategic calculation—that there was no longer any one year in which the danger of war was greatest but that policies must be laid down to take care of a number of years, any one of which might be critical. But more basically the change came from an impatience at the Democrats' dependence on the policy of containment, with its huge year-after-year expenditures for armament and for economic aid to other countries, its tremendous concern for the opinion of allies, and its assumption of the necessity for adjustment to a world-wide social revolution that would probably go on for decades. The Republican policies were heavily influenced by the Taftite insistence on economy and the Taftite skepticism that talk of adjusting to a world social revolution was just so much more global New Dealism.

The basic decisions were made in late 1953 and summarized in a speech which Secretary of State Dulles delivered before the Council on Foreign Relations on January 12, 1954. The Administration, the Secretary said, was aiming for "a maximum deterrent" of aggression at "a bearable cost." To achieve this, it was going to de-emphasize "local defense" and rely more on "the deterrent of massive retaliatory power . . . a great capacity to retaliate, instantly, by means and at times of our own choosing." Instant retaliation by means and at times of America's own choosing—the United States was not going to be too concerned about the attitude of allies. Less dependence on local defense —the United States was going to cut down expensive ground forces and rely more on air power and atomic weapons.

In line with the policy of massive retaliation the Administration took what Admiral Arthur Radford, chairman of the Joint Chiefs of Staff, called a "New Look" at the defense budget. It trimmed $2,300,000,-000 in expenditures and $5,247,000,000 in defense-spending authority from the Truman proposals for the fiscal year 1954. At the same time the Administration was taking a new and skeptical look at the whole policy of economic aid abroad. A raft of statements came from officials which gave credence to the report that Eisenhower would propose cutting off all economic aid by June 30, 1956.

The new defense and foreign policies, particularly the massive retaliation speech, provoked strong and sustained opposition. Adlai Stevenson, dropping his banter, solemnly charged that the Administration was putting dollars before defense and threatening the unity of the Western world. Within the Administration itself General Matthew Ridgway, a member of the Joint Chiefs of Staff, fought the whole trend so hard that he brought about some amendments to the plans for cutting the ground forces. But for the most part the Administration stood its ground and with a way of arguing that emphasized the heart of its policies.

At the heart was restlessness, the restlessness of generations of Americans at having to deal with a strange and unruly world, a restlessness enormously magnified by the exasperations and fears of the post-World War II period. The massive retaliation speech was essentially another declaration of peace-or-else; it probably marked, as the strongly pro-Eisenhower historian

Merlo Pusey has commented, "the zenith of the cold war." A dozen speeches implied that the United States was not willing to settle for containing Communism. We were going to be "positive," the President said. He had not given up his policy of "liberation," Dulles added. Cantankerous allies as well as Communists were not to be dallied with indefinitely. The French, the Secretary of State made plain, could bring about "an agonizing reappraisal of basic United States policy" if they did not do as America wanted and join the European Defense Community. And always there was the traditional American assumption that only a few evil leaders stood in the way of a world-wide acceptance of American values and hence of peace.

"What we need to do," Dulles declared, "is to re-capture the kind of crusading spirit of the early days of the Republic when we were certain that we had something better than anyone else and we knew the rest of the world needed it and wanted it and that we were going to carry it around the world."

On Capitol Hill Senator Joseph McCarthy was asked his judgment of the new Administration and he smiled loftily. The Administration's record on anti-Communism, he said, was "fair."

Circumstances were hardly such as to curb the arrogance of Joseph McCarthy. The Republican capture of the Senate in 1952 had made him for the first time the chairman of his own committee—the powerful Committee on Government Operations—and he also headed its formidable subcommittee, the Permanent Subcommittee on Investigations. With a handful of exceptions the whole Senate treated him with respect or at least with care. He seemed to have proved what a politician respects most—an awesome ability to affect votes. He himself had been re-elected in 1952 by a majority of more than 140,000. No less than eight of the men in the Senate—six who had been elected in 1952—were thought to owe their seats largely to his campaigning. Around the country his name had an increasing potency. A belligerent if small pro-McCarthy faction was making itself heard even among the group which had shown the most solid bloc resistance to him, the intellectuals of the United States.

Probably most important of all, the man in the White House had a conception of his role which very specifically ruled out openly battling McCarthy. Eisenhower not only wanted to respect the Constitutional division between the Executive and legislative divisions. He was keenly aware that he was the head of a divided party and anxious to unite it along the lines of his own thinking. Whatever the President's own tendencies toward the right, his views were quite different from those of the right-wingers, who for the most part were bitter anti-New Dealers, all-out isolationists with respect to Europe, all-out interventionists with respect to Asia, and enthusiasts for the kind of anti-Communism represented by McCarthy. These men followed the President reluctantly when they followed him at all and Eisenhower wanted to do nothing to increase the friction. It was the President's "passion," his aide C. D. Jackson remarked, "not to offend anyone in Congress" and this attitude soon permeated most of his subordinates.

Month after month McCarthy went to further extremes and month after month the Administration sidestepped, looked the other way, or actually followed his bidding. At the beginning of the Administration McCarthy declared that he believed there were still Communists in the State Department and that Dulles could go a long way toward rooting them out by naming a good security officer. The Secretary named a good security officer—Scott McLeod, widely assumed to be a McCarthy disciple. March 1953 and the Senator announced that he had negotiated with Greek shipowners to stop trading at Soviet and satellite ports. Director of Mutual Security Harold Stassen angrily pointed out that this was a flagrant Senatorial interference with the functions of the Executive Branch and that by negotiating with a small group "you are in effect undermining and are harmful to our objective" of stopping the general trade with the Communists. Immediately a mollifying statement came from Frank Nash, Assistant Secretary of Defense for international affairs, and Secretary of State Dulles and McCarthy got together for a congenial lunch. At his press conference, the President did the final smoothing over by suggesting that both McCarthy and Stassen had gone a bit far. The Senator had probably made a "mistake" and the Director of Mutual Security probably meant "infringement" rather than "undermining."

All the while McCarthy was stepping up his campaign against the State Department's overseas information program. The country began to hear about the two 27-year-olds, Roy Cohn, the Subcommittee's chief counsel, and G. David Schine, an unpaid Subcommittee consultant. They left on an eighteen-day whirl through western Europe to ferret out "subversion" in the overseas program. Seventeen hours in Bonn, twenty hours in Berlin, nineteen hours in Frankfurt —these and a sprinkling of other stops and McCarthy was proclaiming "appalling infiltration." The State Department reacted dutifully. It asked for resignations —including those of men like Theodore Kaghan who had probably dabbled with radicalism in the late 1930's and who now was known through central Europe as one of the most effective organizers of anti-Communist propaganda. (When the Subcommittee made its charges Leopold Figl, the ultraconservative former Chancellor of Austria, wrote Kaghan: "What goes on? After all, April Fool's day has long passed by. . . .") The State Department also issued a new directive banning from American information activities all "books, music, paintings, and the like . . . of any Communists, fellow travelers, *et cetera*" and ordering that "librarians should at once remove all books and other material by Communists, fellow travelers, *et cetera*, from their shelves and withdraw any that may be in circulation."

Many librarians, taking no chance on having a work by an *et cetera* on their shelves, removed the books of authors like Bert Andrews, chief of the Washington bureau of the Republican *New York Herald Tribune;* Walter White, head of the anti-Communist National Association for the Advancement of Colored People; Richard Lauterbach, former European correspondent of *Time;* Clarence Streit, chief figure in the strongly democratic movement for a federal union of the North Atlantic democracies; and Foster Rhea Dulles, a decidedly anti-Communist professor at Ohio State and cousin of the Secretary of State. Some librarians stored the books they removed; others burned them.

At the height of the book purge, on June 14, President Eisenhower went to Dartmouth to receive an honorary degree. Among those sharing honors with him were his friend John J. McCloy, Judge Joseph M. Proskauer of New York, and Lester B. Pearson, Canadian Secretary of State for External Affairs. The President overheard these three discussing with horror the book burnings and joined in the conversation. When he rose to make his extemporaneous remarks, Eisenhower said: "Don't join the book burners. Don't think you are going to conceal faults by concealing evidence that they ever existed. Don't be afraid to go in your library and read every book as long as any document does not offend our own ideas of decency. That should be the only censorship.

"How will we defeat communism unless we know what it is? What it teaches—why does it have such an appeal for men? . . . We have got to fight it with something better. Not try to conceal the thinking of our own people. They are part of America and even if they think ideas that are contrary to ours they have a right to have them, a right to record them and a right to have them in places where they are accessible to others. It is unquestioned or it is not America."

Anti-McCarthy opinion in the United States was jubilant. At last the President was taking a stand; now the Senator would have the whole prestige and power of the Administration thrown against him. Many papers were like the *Baltimore Sun* in calling the Dartmouth remarks an "important turning point."

The day after the speech Secretary Dulles met his regular press conference and reporters quickly got around to the book purge. Yes, books had been burned, Dulles said, but after all they were only a small number of titles among the more than two million volumes in the libraries.

But didn't the President's speech indicate a new policy? the newsmen asked.

No, just the use of more sense in applying the directive, the Secretary of State replied. As the reporters pressed on, Dulles abruptly changed the subject.

On June 17 Eisenhower met the press for the first time since his Dartmouth speech. He was asked if he intended the remarks to be "critical of a school of thought represented by Senator McCarthy." The President replied that he must refuse to talk personalities. The speech was not a stand in favor of using government money to propagate Communist beliefs. He was against book burning, which to him meant a suppression of ideas.

No, he had not ordered any directives canceled, although he had asked Dulles to see him about the problem. He really didn't know much about the whole matter.

A newsman asked about the "controversial" but non-Communist books. The President replied that if they were on the shelves of libraries in this country, it was all right to have them in our libraries abroad, generally speaking. Then Eisenhower added that if the State Department was burning a book which was an open appeal to everybody in a foreign country to be a Communist, then he would say that the book falls outside the limits in which he was speaking. The State

Department could do as it pleased to get rid of such books.

For two weeks reporters harried Eisenhower for clarification. At one press conference Raymond Brandt, chief Washington correspondent for the *St. Louis Post-Dispatch*, questioned the President sharply and at length. Eisenhower was having trouble keeping his temper as he answered.

Brandt: "Do you and Secretary Dulles hope to get a clear directive [about overseas library policy] eventually?"

The President: Well, certainly.

Brandt: "Is that possible?"

The President: Certainly, he hoped that it was.

Brandt: "Is it possible?"

The President: It should be; yes, it should be. There was no question as to where he stood. Now, he thought we could make it clear so that any reasonable person could understand exactly what was meant.

Brandt: "I think there was some confusion between your Dartmouth speech and your press conference speech in which you said it was perfectly all right for the State Department to burn books or do as they pleased with them."

By now the President was glowering. He snapped back that he didn't believe he said that. He said that the Government would be foolish to promulgate and help to support the distribution of a book that openly advocated its own destruction by force.

Brandt: "One of the writers was Dashiell Hammett, who writes detective stories. So far as I know—and I have read several of them—I don't see anything Communistic about them, but they were thrown out by the libraries. . . ."

Eisenhower smiled and his composure returned. He thought someone got frightened, he said. He didn't know why they should—he wouldn't. He would tell them that—he wouldn't. And there the discussion ended.

McCarthy rampaged on. With the opening of 1954 he and his staff concentrated increasingly on the Department of the Army and a number of top Army officials tried hard to work with them. In January the Senator began to hammer on the case of Major Irving Peress, a New York dental officer. Peress had been permitted to receive his regularly due promotion and granted an honorable discharge after he had refused to sign an Army loyalty certificate and after he had refused, on the grounds of possible self-incrimination, to answer a number of questions at a Subcommittee hearing. In a letter to McCarthy, Secretary of the Army Robert Stevens acknowledged that the Peress case had been mishandled and stated that if he found the promotion had been anything but routine he would discipline the officers involved. He also ordered that in the future Reserve officers who refused to sign a loyalty certificate were to be given an other than honorable discharge.

Unappeased, the Senator summoned Peress and a group of Army officials, including Brigadier General Ralph Zwicker, to a Subcommittee hearing. At one point, when the hearing was in executive session, McCarthy demanded that Zwicker answer questions concerning the processing of the Peress case and Zwicker replied that such information was inviolate under a Presidential order. The Senator was furious. According to Zwicker, McCarthy shouted at the General: "You are a disgrace to the uniform. You're shielding Communist conspirators. You are going to be put on public display next Tuesday. You're not fit to be an officer. You're ignorant."

Zwicker was a highly esteemed officer who was obviously simply following orders. The Army seethed with resentment. Secretary Stevens heatedly accused McCarthy of humiliating Zwicker and of undermining Army morale, and ordered two officers not to appear before the Senator's Subcommittee. McCarthy promptly replied that Stevens was an "awful dupe" and summoned the Secretary himself to testify. Stevens decided to go and prepared a strong statement which he intended to read at the hearing. But the statement was never read. Instead Stevens met with McCarthy and other members of the Subcommittee and accepted a "Memorandum of Agreement." When the memorandum was released few commentators, pro- or anti-McCarthy, interpreted it as anything but complete and abject surrender on the part of the Secretary of the Army.

That afternoon the White House was filled with glum discussions of ways to do something about the Stevens debacle. In the Capitol a reporter passed by the hearings room of the Subcommittee, noticed the door open, and looked in. He saw McCarthy and Roy Cohn sitting at the end of the table and "laughing so hard," the newsman remembered, "that the room seemed to shake."

During the Administration efforts to counteract the Memorandum of Agreement, photographers snapped the President out on the White House lawn practicing his putting. He was taking the respite, as was his habit, to calm his boiling temper. But to many serious observers the symbolism was perfect for the trend of American affairs in the winter of 1953-4.

An amiable, well-intentioned President was taking his model from leadership of pre-F. D. R. days. Government was "teamwork." You got together a team, primarily of executives from corporations, and put them to work on their specialties. You struck up cordial relations with Congress. Then the President presided over the ensuing co-operation much like a constitutional monarch and the nation moved gently, sensibly toward sound, economical, thoroughly American ways.

All the while men and women with programs of rancor worked away. In both houses of Congress and throughout the country the right wing of the

Republican Party was making a bold bid for power. Word kept coming from the Senate that the Bricker Amendment, the isolationist's dream, might well pass. Movements were building to strip away the substance of New Deal domestic legislation that had long been considered inviolate. Informed pro-Eisenhower observers wondered aloud whether the smiling General had not lost control of his party and of the nation. In December 1953, Walter Lippmann proclaimed a "crisis," brought about by the "abdication of the powers of the Executive and the usurpation of Congress."

McCarthyism was permeating every state and every occupation, sometimes ridiculous, sometimes frightening, sometimes bordering on the incredible. Five distinguished ex-diplomats warned that the assaults on the State Department were having "sinister results. . . . A premium has been put upon reporting and upon recommendations which are ambiguously stated or so cautiously set forth as to be deceiving. . . . The ultimate result is a threat to national security." The major drama publisher, Samuel French, announced a playwriting contest in which one of the conditions was that the sponsor "reserves the right at any time to declare ineligible any author who is, or becomes publicly involved, in a scholastic, literary, political, or moral controversy." The crackdown on scientists and teachers had reached the point where Albert Einstein was advising his correspondents to resort to the "way of non-cooperation in the sense of Gandhi's"—a refusal to testify before any Congressional committee about personal beliefs and a willingness to go to jail as a result.

In Indiana Mrs. Thomas J. White, a member of the State Textbook Commission, charged that "there is a Communist directive in education now to stress the story of Robin Hood. They want to stress it because he robbed the rich and gave it to the poor. That's the Communist line. It's just a smearing of law and order." Governor George Craig declined comment and State

Superintendent of Education Wilbur Young announced that he would reread *Robin Hood* to consider the merits of Mrs. White's charge. The 1953 Sheriff of Nottingham, England, William Cox, was more definite. "Why, Robin Hood was no Communist," he said.

Paul Hoffman, chairman of the board of the Studebaker-Packard Corporation, was taken aback when he finished a speech on freedom at a large southwestern university. A student came up to him and asked: "Do you think there ought to be any study of communism in a school such as this?"

"Yes," Hoffman said, "I think we ought to teach what communism *is*, so that the new and most important generation of Americans can know exactly why it is such a menace to our way of life."

"I think so, too," the student said, "but it's dangerous to say that around here now."

In Washington Martin Merson, an ex-Dixie Cup executive who gave up his plans for a business of his own in the flush of his pro-Eisenhower enthusiasm, tried to function as an official of the United States Information Administration. When the McCarthyite thrusts undermined the whole organization, Merson assumed that there must be something he could do to save the agency. He helped arrange a dinner meeting with Senator McCarthy, Cohn, Schine, and George Sokolsky, a pro-McCarthy columnist, and later they were joined by others. McCarthy was relaxed, jovial, and a bit puzzled why Merson was so exercised.

Finally something brought a real reaction from McCarthy and his group. Cohn mentioned the composer Aaron Copland, whose music was used in the overseas information programs. Sokolsky argued that the music should not be blacklisted and Cohn felt strongly that it should be banned. "As I sat quietly listening to the Copland colloquy," Merson remembered later, "I was suddenly struck by the ludicrousness of the whole evening's performance. Cohn, Schine, Mc-

Carthy, Sokolsky, and for that matter the rest of us, meeting to discuss the manners and morals of our times. By whose appointment? By what right?" The question was asked by many people. The answer was lost somewhere in the miasma of the winter of 1953-4.

On February 6, 1954, the President and 7,500 Republican leaders gathered at a Lincoln Day box supper in Uline Arena in the Capital. Herbert Hoover made a surprise appearance and was given a tremendous ovation. Everybody munched his box of fried chicken and joined in singing "God Bless America" and Eisenhower made a little speech in which he included the term "conservative." He paused, then added firmly: "And don't be afraid to use the word." The crowd cheered loudly.

In the winter of 1953-4, for the first time in twenty years, the term "conservative" was being used in the United States widely and without embarrassment. With the exultant thrust of the right-wing Republicans and with the way the Eisenhower Administration reacted, some Americans worried that the word would be not simply conservative but reactionary.

Ike Admin brought complete change - sought to keep small

Ike took stand vs McCarthy in that we should be aware of what Commism is, & how it threatens us.

Conservatism present

XII

The Eisenhower
Equilibrium

At first the war scares kept right on coming. The Korean truce was hardly signed when the civil war in Indochina, which had been dragging on since 1946, erupted into a major Communist assault on Dien Bien Phu. A number of high Administration figures, including Vice-President Nixon and Secretary of State Dulles, let it be known that the United States might well send troops. Dien Bien Phu fell, an armistice was signed (giving the Communists 60,000 square miles containing a population of 14,000,000), and Indochina quieted. Six months more and the Chinese Communists seized Yikiang, north of Formosa, and talked loudly of invading Quemoy, Matsu, and Formosa itself. President Eisenhower asked Congress for broad authority to use American armed forces in the area and, with the country expecting a Chinese thrust any day, the Senate passed the resolution by the sweeping majority of 85 to 3.

Over everything, more than ever, hung the knowledge that another major war could be a war of oblivion. On March 1, 1954 American scientists set off the first explosion of an H-bomb and the scientists themselves were surprised at the range of its ability to injure.

Radioactive ash fell on a Japanese fishing boat eighty miles away and twenty-three fishermen were hospitalized for burns. A chill went through the United States. Scores of cities reported that automobile windshields were suddenly pock-marked as if by some exhalation from the H-bomb. The scientific explanation was normal erosion—plus mass jitters.

Yet during all the fears of 1954 and 1955 a quite different feeling was growing in the United States. Cautiously, incredulously, Americans were asking: Was not the danger of World War III definitely receding? For one thing, whatever the threats to peace, armies were no longer fighting each other. With the signing of the Indochinese truce on July 20, 1954, no shooting war existed anywhere on the globe for the first time since the Japanese invaded Manchuria twenty-three years before. The failure of the Chinese Communists to carry out their threats continued the fact of actual peace. For another thing, strange and hopeful events were happening in the Soviet Union. The post-Stalin Russian leaders were not only continuing their conciliatory language. On occasion they were acting in a way which strongly suggested that the bear could change his habits.

Early in 1955 Premier Georgi Malenkov resigned with the explanation of "insufficient experience . . . I see clearly my guilt" and went right on staying alive while the premiership was taken over by Nikolai Bulganin and Nikita Khrushchev emerged as the power in the Communist Party organization. On the international scene, the Soviet government did things which had the authentic ring of a desire to soften the East-West clash. In June 1955 Americans really rubbed their eyes. Russian fliers shot down a United States plane over the Bering Strait and the Soviet government quickly expressed its regrets and offered to pay half the cost of the plane.

Probably most important of all, the feeling was growing in America that science had made large-scale war so terrifying that no nation would start one. 1954-5 was the period when it became clear that both the United States and the Soviet Union had an effective H-bomb and that both were far along in the development of intercontinental missiles. President Eisenhower expressed the spreading American attitude when he said: "We have arrived at the point. . . [where] there is just no real alternative to peace."

In the new climate of expectations of peace the United States naturally relaxed and sought to go back to its customary ways. But just what was normal for 1954-5? To what extent could one apply the pre-F.D.R. conception of America as a nation determining by itself its role in the world, zestfully individualistic, cherishing Home and Mother, delighting in a free economy and all the values that went with it?

Certainly the tug toward the traditional was powerful in American thinking. Every area of living showed the trend. Most of the college girls were telling the pollsters they wanted babies, not careers. The vogue among men was to stay home at night and do-it-yourself (insurance statisticians said more than 600,000 men a year were cutting their fingers with saws, setting themselves afire with spray paints, or shocking themselves with electrical tools). The intellectuals were showing greater and greater interest in a "new conservatism." And Dwight Eisenhower, who more than any President since William McKinley liked to deliver little homilies on Home and Mother, held on to his enormous popularity—in part, observers agreed, because of his emphasis on traditional values.

Yet if the trend was unmistakable, it was no plainer than certain counter facts. One of the assumptions of old-style America had been the acceptance of a society in which great differences in economic and social standing existed. The United States of 1954-5 was not only a product of the Half-Century of Revolution in domestic affairs; the revolution was not only continuing; the pressures for still more economic and social gains were strong and sustained. By 1955 the inflation had definitely slackened. The Republicans said their policies had brought about the change; the Democrats declared it came from long-term programs and the end of the Korean War. Whatever the cause, the result was a girding of all lower- and middle-income groups to see to it that the altered situation brought no wage cuts or other obstacles in the way of a continually rising standard of living.

Citizens of lower social status kept pressing hard for opportunities to improve their standing in the community. Those of less esteemed nationality and religious backgrounds had never been so persistent. Negro leaders battled untiringly. On May 17, 1954 they won the critically important Supreme Court decision declaring that no child could be barred from a public school simply because of his color. Without a pause, the National Association for the Advancement of Colored People threw tremendous energies into efforts to get the decision speedily enforced and to remove Jim Crow from further parts of American life.

Partly because of the techniques that had been used to bring the social upsweep, partly for a dozen other reasons, millions of Americans now found themselves in a position where the genuine attitudes of individualism were not so much wrong as irrelevant. The average industrial worker belonged to a union and the average farmer was deeply involved in at least one occupational organization. The typical clerical worker was employed by a corporation or a business with more than two hundred employees, and the typical executive was not the owner but an employed manager of the business. A web of relationships bound most Americans in with state and federal governments. The very manner of living was having its effects. The unquestionable trend was toward a home in a suburb— the mushrooming miles of middle-class and worker's suburbs—where the prime virtue was adjustment to *trend of 54-5*

what the neighbors thought and did. Under the circumstances the ~~urge~~ *public* was not so much for individualism as it was for getting oneself into the most profitable and comfortable relationship with some larger group or organization.

Particular developments in the United States were making large numbers fearsome of facing society by themselves and deeply concerned with keeping and extending special governmental and nongovernmental protections. In the existing state of the American economy and of the world market, farming was simply not profitable without a subsidy. The decades-old urbanization of the nation had brought a huge segment of the population to the complexities and the anonymity of city living. The relative number of women had been steadily mounting and many of them were in a vulnerable economic position; in 1954 a female headed about one in ten households. The population was growing older, bringing all the fears and uncertainties of age. In 1900, one person in seven was forty-five to sixty-four; by the early 1950's the ratio had changed to one in five and one in every twelve persons was sixty-five or over. The white, Protestant, "Anglo-Saxon" had long felt especially secure in the United States. But now year after year a smaller percentage of Americans were white, Protestant, and born of parentage which traced back to "Anglo-Saxon" lands.

Whether in a special category or not, the American of 1954-5 was likely to be a man who could not forget the crash of 1929. No matter the rampant boom, no matter the fact that during all the years since the beginning of World War II most families had been prospering; the edginess about a possible depression continued. Any dip in the economy, any flutter of the stock market brought wide concern. The very quieting of the international scene had many Americans asking: Wouldn't a peaceful situation and the cutting down of defense expenditures bring the crash? "Depression psychosis," the economist John Galbraith called it. Whether it was psychosis or good sense, the apprehensions about depression brought an added element into the national response to any governmental talk or action that smacked of the 1920's.

As for Home and Mother, attitudes were inevitably adjusting somewhat to the facts. In a thousand ways, little and big, the general reactions of the American had been growing less sentimental. Family living itself had been undergoing important changes. There was not only the possibility that mother was the head of the household; there was the decidedly better chance that she was out working (women were making up about 21,000,000 out of a total working force of roughly 64,000,000). Scores of other developments in the home, decidedly unsettling of the old ways in themselves, were dwarfed by the television revolution. By 1954-5 it had gone so far that for many Americans home was close to meaning the place where the TV set was located.

In 1954 the Water Commissioner of Toledo, puzzled why water consumption rose so startlingly during certain three-minute periods, checked and rechecked his charts, theorized and retheorized, finally hit on the answer: Toledo was flushing the toilets during the commercials. That same year the "TV dinner" was born—the turkey, sweet potatoes, and peas pre-cooked in a compartmented tray—and the family did not have to talk to each other even during supper. The offerings of TV were hardly dominated by lavender and lace. The plunging necklines had plunged to a point where only an abyss could provoke comment. More people were murdered on TV in 1954, one dour commentator estimated, than the United States lost in Korea. And Lucille Ball of *I Love Lucy*, redefining the decorous, proceeded to give a week-by-week viewing of most of her pregnancy period, including Desi Arnaz's sympathetic morning sickness.

If the American scene itself was sharply untraditional, the feelings of world peace which were settling over the nation were still more unconventional. They lacked the fundamental of the usual American conception because they did not permit the country to forget about the world. The Soviet leaders might be cooing, but Communism in and outside Russia was obviously as much of a reality as ever and constantly threatening to increase in strength. In fact, the apparent Soviet swing away from attempts to advance Bolshevism by wars was merely being replaced by an intensified drive to extend Communism by internal subversion and by political, diplomatic, and economic techniques. If this was peace, it was plainly no 1865 or 1919 or even 1945 but a peace that constantly had to be worked at.

A strong urge toward the traditional amid situations that were inescapably new—here was the general pattern of the America that was relaxing in 1954-5. Such a nation could find its normality only along some wavering, in-between path.

Ever since the beginning of the 1952 campaign, Dwight Eisenhower had frequently used the term "middle-of-the-road" in describing his approach to public affairs. His Administration up to the winter of 1953-4, with its restrained Executive leadership, its toleration of extreme right-wing Republicans, its tendency toward the past in domestic and foreign policies, had certainly moved down the right side of the middle. But even in the most conservative days of 1953-4, other elements were present in Eisenhower's thinking.

All the while that he was emphasizing that the Executive should respect Congress and pointing to Roosevelt and Truman as men who had tried to lead too much, the President liked to repeat some remarks made by his old friend, General George Patton. One day Patton was discussing leadership and his eye fell on a plate of spaghetti. Leadership was like trying to get a piece of spaghetti across a table, Patton said. Push it and you would only break it. But get a bit in front of the piece of spaghetti, pull it gently, and you would get it across the table intact. Dwight Eisenhower, however much he was a leader who wanted to keep the Republican Party intact, nevertheless was quite conscious of the importance of getting out ahead a bit and pulling gently.

The President's attitude toward specific domestic and foreign problems also had its varying aspects. He was, as he frequently remarked, "basically conservative." But it was just as true to say that he was—and more so than any President in recent American history—generally non-ideological. Eisenhower tended to look for an *ad hoc* solution to a given situation and was willing to listen sympathetically to quite contrasting points of view. If he was inclined to believe that a successful businessman had thereby proved his sagacity, he deeply admired his younger brother Milton ("Milt inherited all the brains in the family"), whose mind had been shaped by years of high New Deal and Fair Deal positions.

Any policy in any field had to stand the test of the President's persistent tendency to react less along the lines of doctrine than according to the human aspects of the problem. The journalist Stewart Alsop has recalled an incident of the 1952 campaign. At first Eisenhower was strongly inclined to make a major issue of what seemed to him the excessively pro-labor attitude of Truman in dealing with a serious steel strike. Before committing himself, he asked to be briefed on the facts and some of his labor advisers explained the demands of the union in terms of what the benefits meant to the men's families in a period of rising prices. Eisenhower's reaction was, "Why maybe they ought to have had more than that," and the steel strike never became an important campaign issue.

Around the President were a group of men who were also "basically conservative," most of them more so than Eisenhower, but they had their own flexibility. All of the principal aides had spent their mature careers learning to operate within a New Deal-Fair Deal society. A number of them had served in specific functions for a Democratic Administration. This was particularly true of Eisenhower's chief adviser on foreign affairs, Secretary of State Dulles, who had worked with the State Department during most of the post-World War II period and who played a part in bringing about the highly untraditional decision to intervene in Korea. The two most influential advisers in domestic and defense matters, Secretary of the Treasury George Humphrey and Secretary of Defense Charles Wilson, were decidedly not businessmen of the 1920's type. They were part of the new, more adaptable managerial class.

In 1948 Wilson, wearied by the struggles between General Motors and the United Automobile Workers, had invented the famous "escalator clause" (tying wages to the cost of living) which labor liked so much and which was important in preserving industrial peace in the following years. In 1947 Humphrey demonstrated a similar flexibility. Facing a coal strike, he and Benjamin Fairless of United States Steel met with John L. Lewis for private talks and brought about a settlement largely on Lewis's terms. Many industrialists and a large section of Congress were indignant but Humphrey defended the move on pragmatic grounds, including the statement that Lewis's demands were largely reasonable. Discussing these episodes, the astute journalist Robert Coughlan has commented that "Wilson and Humphrey . . . have about as much resemblance to the Republican Big Businessman of the Coolidge-Hoover era as the Indian elephant has to the hairy mammoth—the general outline is the same, but there are vital differences in detail. . . . These two performances were neither 'conservative' nor 'liberal.' They were, however, practical."

Practical men, headed by an essentially non-ideological President, trying to govern a nation with conflicting urges—after the winter of 1953-4 the Administration moved increasingly from the severe conservatism of its early phase. The shift was evident in many ways, but it was clearest of all in the fact that Eisenhower was departing somewhat from his pre-F.D.R. conception of the Presidency.

He talked less and less about offending no one in Congress, left fewer major decisions to subordinates, spoke out more frequently on public issues. He was giving the appearance at press conferences that he no longer merely tolerated them but intended to use them to press forward his purposes. Only occasionally did he still remark that he just didn't know about the matter under discussion. No one quite said it but a dozen newsmen now came close to applying to this President Bert Andrews's remark about Harry Truman after the election of 1946: Dwight Eisenhower is becoming President of the United States.

The most immediate problem facing an Executive who was genuinely trying to lead was the rampant right-wing of the Republican Party, particularly one Joseph McCarthy. A relaxing America was stirring against the extremities of the Senator from Wisconsin. As Secretary of the Army Stevens apparently yielded to McCarthy on February 24, 1954, feelings were at white heat throughout the country. Within the next ten days Adlai Stevenson bluntly called the Republican Party "half McCarthy and half Eisenhower." The Republican Senator from Vermont, Ralph Flanders, took the floor of the Senate with anger and scorn. "He dons his warpaint," the elderly Vermonter said. "He goes into his war dance. He emits his warwhoops. He goes forth to battle and proudly returns with the scalp of a pink Army dentist. We may assume that this represents the depth and seriousness of Communist penetration at this time." That night Edward R. Murrow used his CBS documentary TV show, "See It Now," for a film-clip program which was potently

anti-McCarthy. CBS stations reported a flood of applauding calls (15-1 against the Senator in San Francisco and New York, 2-1 against him in Chicago).

From the day of the Memorandum of Agreement the
Administration moved against McCarthy, sometimes
indirectly but steadily. Secretary Stevens countered
the Memorandum with a strong statement and the
President made plain that he backed his Secretary "one
hundred percent." On March 11, 1954 the Army attacked with the charge that Senator McCarthy, Roy
Cohn, and Francis Carr, the Subcommittee staff director, had sought, separately and collectively, by im-
proper means, to obtain preferential treatment in the
Army for G. David Schine, the Subcommittee consultant who was now a private in the Army. McCarthy
and "associates" promptly replied with forty-six
charges against the Army, of which the key one was
that Secretary Stevens and John Adams, the department counselor, had tried to stop the Subcommittee's exposure of alleged Communists at Fort Monmouth and that they used Private Schine as a "hostage"
to this end. Four more days and the Subcommittee
voted to investigate the Army-McCarthy clash, with
TV cameras in the room and with McCarthy tempo-
rarily replaced by the next ranking Republican, Senator Karl Mundt of South Dakota. Once again a TV
spectacle would transfix the country and once again
television would have a major part in shaping opinion
on a critical national issue.

Shortly after 10 a.m. on April 22, 1954 the red lights
in the cameras went on amid the florid Corinthian col-
umns and the brocaded curtains of the large Senate
Caucus Room. Senator Mundt tapped his big pipe,
leaned forward, and delivered a little speech about
how everything was going to be done with "dignity,
fairness, and thoroughness." The ranking Democrat,
John McClellan, said a few words to the same effect.

"Thank you very much, Senator McClellan," Chairman Mundt declared. "Our counsel, Mr. Jenkins, will now call the first witness." Ray Jenkins opened his mouth but the words came from down along the table. "A point of order, Mr. Chairman," McCarthy was saying. "May I raise a point of order?"

For thirty-six days and more than 2,000,000 words of testimony the hearings went on. A thousand impressions were driven into the public mind—Senator Mundt, roly-poly and pliable and so torn between his McCarthyite sympathies and the fact that he was supposed to be an impartial chairman that someone thought to call him the "tormented mushroom"; the Subcommittee's special counsel, Ray Jenkins, the homicide lawyer from Tellico Plains, Tennessee, chin stuck forward, intoning away with his questions; Senator John McClellan of Arkansas, the real terror of the Subcommittee, cadaverous and saturnine and pursuing everyone with a rasping logic; Robert Stevens, earnest and decent but having to pour out his, the Secretary of War's, pathetic attempts to mollify the friends of buck private G. David Schine; Roy Cohn, leaning over to make a point to McCarthy with a mouth that seemed perpetually pouting, obviously tremendously attached to Schine, obviously tremendously attached to Roy Cohn; Cohn and Schine, endlessly Cohn and Schine. But with each passing day one impression was having an increasingly potent effect on the millions at their TV sets. It was Joseph McCarthy, full-life, acting precisely like Joseph McCarthy.

"Point of order, point of order, Mr. Chairman," the Senator would interrupt in his scowling, sneering way until the children of the United States were imitating him on the streets. He repaid loyalty, like that of bumbling Senator Henry Dworshak of Idaho, by riding contemptuously over what the supporter was trying to say. He seized the floor from opponents by physical force, repeating in his strong, singsong voice until the opponent wearily gave way. McCarthy flung smears and constantly accused others of smearing; his aides tried to use a cropped photograph and he cried deceit at the Army; he sidetracked, blatantly sidetracked, and demanded the end of "diversionary tactics." Day after day he was still Joe McCarthy of the boyhood fights, ceaselessly, recklessly swinging for the knock-out.

The more reckless McCarthy became, the more strongly the Administration opposed him. In mid-May the President threw the Constitution of the United States at him. McCarthy became involved in demands that were flagrant violations of the rights of the Executive and from the White House came a blunt statement of those rights, which "cannot be usurped by any individual who may seek to set himself above the laws of our land." No one, not even the President of the United States, not even a President of his own party, was immune to the Senator's standard weapon, the charge of softness toward Communism. McCarthy's answer to Eisenhower was to talk once again of "the evidence of treason that has been growing over the past twenty—" Then he paused and added darkly: "twenty-one years."

The hearings ground on. The changing national mood, the Presidential opposition, and the appearance McCarthy was making on TV were costing the Senator heavily in public support. But he was still not a ruined man. The evidence was certainly not giving either side a clear-cut victory in the issues immediately at stake. Had the McCarthy group sought preferential treatment for Schine? Clearly they had. Had the Army tried to stop McCarthy's investigation at Fort Monmouth? Equally clearly it had—though it was emphasizing that it was anxious to get "that type" of hearing ended because it demoralized the Army. Other charges and countercharges were tangled in a maze of conflicting testimony. Throughout the country a good many pro-McCarthy or anti-anti-McCarthy people were wavering but they were only wavering. The Senator could have emerged from the hearings partially intact if he had now made some moves to present himself as a reasonable, responsible person. But Joseph McCarthy was not interested in being partially intact. He went on looking for the hay-maker and the right man was present to see to it that when the Senator swung his wildest, he swung himself flat on his face.

The chief Army counsel, Joseph Welch, was a sen-ior partner of the eminent Boston law firm of Hale and Dorr and he had a well-deserved reputation as an infi-nitely shrewd trial lawyer. But friends emphasized more Welch's innate sense of human decency and his gift of ironic laughter. They associated him with his spacious colonial home in Walpole, where he puttered around studying his thermometers (there were twelve in the house), spending a day fishing or an evening in a game of carom or cribbage, delighting more than anything else in kindly, bantering talk about the cos-mos. Mrs. Welch had a favorite story about the whim-sicality of the man. She liked to tell how she had urged him to take up gardening, which he loathed, and he countered that he would garden if she would drink beer, which she detested. So on weekends the two would alternately garden in the broiling sun and stop for a beer in the shade, both grinning through their periods of suffering.

At the hearings Welch sat questioning away, his long, drooping face quizzical, his questions softly spo-ken and deftly insidious, dropping a damaging little jest and looking utterly surprised when people laughed. The sessions were only eight days old when the Army counsel drew blood. Welch was driving hard at a photograph which the McCarthy forces had produced, cropped to show only Stevens and Schine together although the original photograph contained two other men. The Army counsel brought out that the original had hung on Schine's wall and he ques-tioned James Juliana, a Subcommittee employee who had arranged the cropping, as to why he had not brought the whole picture.

JULIANA: "I wasn't asked for it. . . ."

WELCH: ". . . You were asked for something different from the thing that hung on Schine's wall?"

JULIANA: "I never knew what hung on Schine's wall. . . ."

WELCH: "Did you think this came from a pixie? Where did you think this picture that I hold in my hand came from?"

JULIANA: "I had no idea."

There was a stir of voices and McCarthy interrupted. "Will counsel for my benefit define—I think he might be an expert on that—what a pixie is?"

Welch's face was beatific. "Yes. I should say, Mr. Senator, that a pixie is a close relative of a fairy. Shall I proceed, sir? Have I enlightened you?"

The spectators roared. Roy Cohn's pouting lips hardened into angry lines. The Senator glowered.

In the world of Joseph McCarthy nothing was more alien than the deft, and the Senator's feelings about Welch steadily mounted. He denied the Army counsel, or was wary of giving him, what he considered the ordinary camaraderie. McCarthy would walk up to friends and opponents alike, hand extended and the other hand grasping an arm, but he moved a wide circle around Joseph Welch. He first-named almost everybody—Secretary Stevens was "Bob" and the obviously hostile Senator Stuart Symington was "Stu." Welch was "Mr. Welch" or "the counsel."

Eight days before the hearings ended, on June 9, the Army counsel led Roy Cohn through a mocking, destructive cross-examination and McCarthy sat fuming. Now Welch was pressing Cohn as to why, if subversion was so serious at Fort Monmouth, he had not come crying alarm to Secretary Stevens. When Welch went ahead along this line, McCarthy began to grin broadly.

The Army counsel got in another dig at Cohn: "May I add my small voice, sir, and say whenever you know about a subversive or a Communist or a spy, please hurry. Will you remember these words?"

McCarthy broke in, bashed his way to attention. "In view of Mr. Welch's request that the information be given once we know of anyone who might be performing any work for the Communist Party, I think we should tell him that he has in his law firm a young man named Fisher whom he recommended, incidentally, to do work on this committee, who has been for a number of years a member of an organization which was named, oh, years and years ago, as the legal bulwark of the Communist Party. . . ."

The Senator was grinning ever more broadly, pausing now and then to lick his lips and savor his words. Roy Cohn sat in the witness chair, his legs dangling apart, the blood drained from his face, and once his lips seemed to be forming the words "Stop, stop." McCarthy went on: "Knowing that, Mr. Welch, I just felt that I had a duty to respond to your urgent request. . . . I have hesitated bringing that up, but I have been rather bored with your phony requests to Mr. Cohn here that he personally get every Communist out of government before sundown. . . .

"I am not asking you at this time to explain why you tried to foist him on this committee. Whether you knew he was a member of that Communist organization or not, I don't know. I assume you did not, Mr. Welch, because I get the impression that, while you are quite an actor, you play for a laugh, I don't think you have any conception of the danger of the Communist Party. I don't think you yourself would ever knowingly aid the Communist cause. I think you are unknowingly aiding it when you try to burlesque this hearing in which we are trying to bring out the facts, however."

Welch was staring at McCarthy with the look of a man who was watching the unbelievable. The puck was gone; his face was white with anger. "Senator McCarthy," Welch began, "I did not know—"

McCarthy turned away contemptuously and talked to Juliana. Twice the Army counsel demanded his attention and the Senator talked to Juliana in a still louder voice, telling him to get a newspaper clipping about Fisher so that it could be put in the record.

Welch plunged ahead. "You won't need anything in the record when I have finished telling you this.

"Until this moment, Senator, I think I never really gauged your cruelty or your recklessness. Fred Fisher is a young man who went to the Harvard Law School and came into my firm and is starting what looks to be a brilliant career with us.

"When I decided to work for this committee I asked Jim St. Clair . . . to be my first assistant. I said to Jim, 'Pick somebody in the firm who works under you that you would like.' He chose Fred Fisher and they came down on an afternoon plane. That night, when we had taken a little stab at trying to see what the case was about, Fred Fisher and Jim St. Clair and I went to dinner together. I then said to these two young men, 'Boys, I don't know anything about you except that I have always liked you, but if there is anything funny in the life of either one of you that would hurt anybody in this case you speak up quick.'

"Fred Fisher said, 'Mr. Welch, when I was in law school and for a period of months after, I belonged to the Lawyers Guild.' . . . I said, 'Fred, I just don't think I am going to ask you to work on the case. If I do, one of these days that will come out and go over national television and it will just hurt like the dickens.'

"So Senator, I asked him to go back to Boston.

"Little did I dream you could be so reckless and so cruel as to do an injury to that lad. It is true that he is still with Hale & Dorr. It is true that he will continue to be with Hale & Dorr. It is, I regret to say, equally true that I fear he shall always bear a scar needlessly inflicted by you. If it were in my power to forgive you for your reckless cruelty, I would do so. I like to think I am a gentle man, but your forgiveness will have to come from someone other than me."

The Senate Caucus Room was hushed. McCarthy fumbled with some papers, began saying that Welch had no right to speak of cruelty because he had "been baiting Mr. Cohn here for hours."

Welch cut off McCarthy. "Senator, may we not drop this? We know he belonged to the Lawyers Guild, and Mr. Cohn nods his head at me." Cohn was quite plainly nodding.

WELCH: "I did you, I think, no personal injury, Mr. Cohn."

COHN: "No, sir."

WELCH: "I meant to do you no personal injury, and if I did, I beg your pardon."

Cohn nodded again. The Army counsel turned back to McCarthy and his emotion was so great that on the TV screens his eyes seemed to be filling with tears. "Let us not assassinate this lad further, Senator. You have done enough. Have you no sense of decency, sir, at long last? Have you left no sense of decency?"

McCarthy tried to ask the Army counsel a question about Fisher. Welch cut him off again. He had recovered his composure now and his voice was cold with scorn. "Mr. McCarthy, I will not discuss this with you further. You have sat within 6 feet of me, and could have asked me about Fred Fisher. You have brought it out. If there is a God in heaven, it will do neither you nor your cause any good. I will not discuss it further. I will not ask Mr. Cohn any more questions. You, Mr. Chairman, may, if you will, call the next witness."

For a long few seconds the hush in the room continued. One of the few rules Chairman Mundt had tried hard to enforce was the one against demonstrations and six policemen were present to assist him. But suddenly the room shook with applause. For the first time in the memory of Washington observers, press photographers laid aside their cameras to join in the ovation for Welch. Chairman Mundt made no effort to interfere and instead soon called for a five-minute recess.

Joseph McCarthy sat slouched in his chair, breathing heavily. Spectators and reporters avoided him. Finally he found someone to talk to. He spread out his hands in a gesture of puzzlement and asked: "What did I do wrong?"

Joseph McCarthy would never know. And that June day, 1954, millions at their TV sets learned once and for all that Joseph McCarthy would never know.

The children stopped saying "Point of order, point of order." The housewives went back to *I Love Lucy*. A different subject was filling conversations. Agricultural prices were dropping, the textile and auto industries were laying off workers, general unemployment was mounting (by mid-1954 the government figures put it over 2,000,000). Everywhere in the United States there was talk of depression.

November 1954 was not far away and GOP political leaders shuddered at the thought of a Republican Administration having to face the polls during a decline in the economy. They were keenly aware that the success in 1952 had been much more an Eisenhower than a Republican victory and they did not ignore the association in so many people's minds between Republicanism and the depression of 1929. The elections of 1954 came, the Democrats did take both houses of Congress, and the point went on having its effects in high GOP circles. It was a continuing prod to an Administration which was not indisposed for other reasons to move from the conservatism of its early period.

The domestic policies that emerged in 1954 and 1955 represented no sharp break. The Administration kept its businessman tone. Just before the elections of 1954, Secretary of Defense Wilson was at it again with his observation, in discussing unemployment, that "I've always liked bird dogs better than kennel-fed dogs myself—you know one who'll get out and hunt for food rather than sit on his fanny and yell." As late as May 1956 another high Administration official, a deputy assistant to the President, Howard Pyle, was apologizing for his "off-hand comment" that the "right to suffer [by unemployment] is one of the joys of a free economy." Particularly in its policies toward government finance, power, and public resources the Administration continued the lines of its first period to such an extent that the New Dealish had tart words. Which was the more serious corruption? they demanded to know. Mink coats and deep-freezers or disposals of the national forests and utility contracts which could mean millions for a few corporations? And Administration figures were still capable of providing caricatures of the conservative leeriness of welfare expenditures by the federal government. When the Salk polio vaccine was announced on April 12, 1955, the problem arose as to how poor families were to get the protection without having to go through the humiliation of declaring that they could not pay for it. A bill was presented in Congress to have the federal government provide free vaccine for all children. Mrs. Oveta Culp Hobby, Secretary of Health, Education and Welfare, was horrified. The bill was "socialized medicine"—by "the back door."

Yet the shift, however restrained, was on. In late 1954 a White House adviser remarked: "The President's changed, George Humphrey's changed—we've all changed since we came here." Eisenhower was seeing more and more of Dr. Arthur Burns, a Columbia economist and now chairman of the Council of Economic Advisers, who believed that "it is no longer a matter of serious controversy whether the Government should play a positive role in helping to maintain a high level of economic activity. What we debate nowadays is not the need for controlling business cycles, but rather the nature of governmental action, its timing and its extent." Humphrey, who had taken Taftite steps to raise interest rates, was encouraging measures that would bring them down. "The first moves," he explained in his pragmatic way, "were to stop price rises and inventory inflation. Then, finding we had credit a little tight, we turned around and loosened it."

In April 1954 Secretary of Agriculture Benson cut the price support of butter from 90 to 75 per cent of parity. The dairy industry was furious but Benson, probably the most dogged free-enterprise man in the Cabinet, indicated he would stand firm. The Secretary of Agriculture was soon summoned to the White House. "Ezra," the President said, "I think maybe we went a mite too far this time." Eisenhower pulled a pad of paper toward him and drew a base and a summit line. He pointed to the bottom line. "This is where we are." Then he tapped the upper line. "And this is where we eventually want to arrive. But we'll have to go more slowly with our changes—like this." The pencil zig-zagged up the length of the sheet. "This is the way we'll have to go—first this way, then that. But we'll always be headed here"—*here* meaning an agriculture more responsive to the play of market forces.

The threatened depression did not come but the Administration shift continued. The trend is summarized by a comparison of the President's 1953, 1954, and 1955 State-of-the-Union messages. The 1953 document had an unmistakable Taftite tone. By 1955 the nature of the address had changed to one which the *New York Times* correctly characterized as a call "for limited extension of measures along the lines of the New Deal." The new direction was plain in the highway, school, slum-clearance, medical insurance, and widened social security bills sent to Congress. They were decidedly un-New Dealish in the amounts of money called for, some of the methods proposed, and the extent to which the Administration pressed for their passage. But they were also decidedly non-Taftian in their assumption that the federal government had to assume responsibility for broad social needs. So far as amount of expenditure was concerned, the programs would raise federal spending in these categories to an annual level four billion dollars higher than it had been under Truman.

Throughout the shift of his Administration, Eisenhower was feeling his way toward some general statement of the domestic aims of his Presidency. He no longer emphasized "conservatism" alone. He tried "dynamic conservatism," "progressive, dynamic conservatism," "progressive moderation," "moderate progressivism," "positive and progressive." But more and more he adopted a formula along the lines of the one he expressed in December 1954. The Administration, Eisenhower remarked then, "must be liberal when it was talking about the relationship between the Government and the individual, conservative when talking about the national economy and the individual's pocketbook."

Adlai Stevenson met a Chicago press conference and said: "I have never been sure what progressive moderation means, or was it conservative progressivism? [Laughter] I have forgotten, and I am not sure what dynamic moderation or moderate dynamism means. I am not even sure what it means when one says that he is a conservative in fiscal affairs and a liberal in human affairs. I assume what it means is that you will strongly recommend the building of a great many schools to accommodate the needs of our children, but not provide the money. [Laughter]" Unquestionably there was something ludicrously muddled about the Administration's efforts to describe itself in its new direction, but the very confusion bespoke the essence of where it was going. Conservative in economic matters and liberal in human affairs—the social gains of the New Deal and the Fair Deal were to be preserved, some extensions would be advocated but for the most part not vigorously pressed, and the whole was to be set within a severe budget consciousness.

The most striking fact about the Eisenhower domestic policies, in their earlier or later phase, was the same characteristic that had marked the programs of the Truman years—action on the home front was usually much less significant than action abroad.

In the all-important foreign field, the Administration was paralleling its domestic shift. It held to the main lines of the New Look defense policy. But it went along with an increasing number of amendments to it. It was noticeable, too, that the Administration was defending the policy less and less in terms of budget-balancing and more by that totally non-ideological argument—the world situation and the development of new weapons dictated a shift in the American defense. As time went on, the question arose just how new the New Look was. How much was it a reversion to Taftism and how much simply another instance of the immemorial American habit—practiced after every war and decidedly practiced by the Truman Administration—of slashing defense expenditures when the guns were quiet?

Still more change from the early Eisenhower days was evident in the attitude toward economic aid and technical assistance. The talk within the Administration of ending all such expenditures died down. The smallness of the appropriations asked for by the President continued to distress deeply men of a Point Four persuasion. Chester Bowles, Ambassador to India during the Truman Administration, cried out: "Let it not be said by future historians that in the second decade after World War II freedom throughout the world died of a balanced budget." But a degree of economic aid continued, with the Administration fighting off right-wing attempts to cut severely the amount or add hamstringing restrictions. Meanwhile Eisenhower was putting into effect something of an atomic age Point Four—his plan for the United States to join in spreading the peaceful uses of atomic energy by giving knowledge and by selling atomic reactors at half price.

The change in the Administration's policy toward the world was most marked in the most important aspect, the matter of general attitude. The basic question was the same as it had been throughout the post—World War II period: To what extent was the United States going to break with its deeply felt tradition of the quick, final solution, brought about largely by the United States alone? The specific debate was now less over the word "containment" than the word "coexistence," with all its implications of a long, slow process of adjustment during which the continued power of Communism would be assumed and the world would stay thoroughly entangled.

Any favorable mention of coexistence brought from McCarthy-type sentiment cries of treason. To many Americans of less extreme views, the idea was dangerous nonsense. In particular Senator William Knowland, the Republican leader in the Senate, was arguing forcibly that coexistence was a "Trojan horse" that would lull America into a sense of false security, to be followed by disaster. The United States, Knowland solemnly warned, must take "every possible step"—often the Senator sounded as if this included war—to throw back Communism or in time it would find itself overwhelmed. "The civilizations that flourished and died in the past had opportunities for a limited period of time to change the course of history. Sooner or later, however, they passed 'the point of no return,' and the decisions were no longer theirs to make."

1954-5 saw Secretary Dulles move appreciably toward the coexistence position. His speeches became a good deal less impatient and bellicose. He dropped any emphasis on liberation and instead gave most of his enormous energies to building the Southeast Asia Treaty Organization—a NATO-type defense organization which certainly assumed a long, hard pull. Of still greater importance, President Eisenhower, who had never entirely shared his Secretary's belligerence, was more and more determining the general outlines and the tone of the country's foreign policy.

With each passing month the President increased his emphasis on the importance of the slow processes of conciliation and adjustment in world affairs. In July 1954 UN headquarters were filled with talk that Red China was about to be admitted. Senator Knowland, speaking for a considerable body of opinion in the United States, was bitter. America, he declared, should make plain that it would leave the UN the day Red China entered. As for himself, if the UN made the move he would resign his Republican leadership in the Senate to lead an agitation to take the United States out of the world organization. What did President Eisenhower think? reporters wanted to know. He did not believe that Red China would be admitted, Eisenhower replied. But if the UN should make this mistake, the attitude of the American government would have to be decided on the basis of how it could best advance the cause of peace. But what about Knowland's insistence on American withdrawal? the newsmen pressed. The President said he had not yet reached any such decision. No, he hadn't.

In November 1954 Red China announced that it had sentenced as spies thirteen Americans, eleven of them fliers who had fought in the Korean War. It was not only obvious that the charges against the fliers were fraudulent; Red China had clearly violated the Korean armistice agreement by not repatriating the airmen. A good many Americans besides William Knowland were furious, and the Senator demanded that the Chinese should be handed an ultimatum: Release the fliers or the United States would impose a naval blockade.

Eisenhower made plain to his press conference that he believed a blockade meant war and he was against imposing one. The President went further. He delivered a little fifteen-minute speech which he permitted the reporters to quote directly. A President, Eisenhower said, "experiences exactly the same resentment, the same anger, the same kind of sense of frustration almost, when things like this occur, as other Americans, and his impulse is to lash out. . . . In many ways the easy course for a President, for the Administration, is to adopt a truculent, publicly bold, almost insulting attitude." But the easy course had one terrible flaw—it led toward war. The sensible path was the hard way and "the hard way is to have the courage to be patient, tirelessly to seek out every single avenue open to us in the hope finally of leading the other side to a little better understanding of the honesty of our intentions. . . ."

The courage to be patient, the slow, hard way, using every possible avenue—a climax of coexistence was near and Eisenhower did not stand in its way. During all the bitternesses over foreign affairs in the postwar, one image in particular had inflamed the critics of the Roosevelt-Truman policies. It was their picture of the President of the United States sitting in Big Four conferences, joking and tossing off Martinis with the Soviet leaders, signing secret agreements that sold more millions down the river to Communism. As the summer of 1955 came on, the pressure for a Big Four conference steadily mounted. The Russians were calling for one; a good deal of world opinion agreed; in the Democratic-controlled Congress, Senator Walter George of Georgia, chairman of the powerful Senate Foreign Relations Committee, was pressing hard. President Eisenhower moved warily. He attempted to make certain that the time and the conditions were propitious for American purposes and he announced firmly that there would be no secret agreements— probably no agreements at all but merely exploratory talks. Then, on July 18, 1955, he joined the leaders of Britain, France, and the Soviet Union at a Big Four conference in Geneva.

The Russians tried hard to tell the world that they were men of peace. Party chief Nikita Khrushchev grinned endlessly for the photographers and said: "Things are different now." Premier Nikolai Bulganin went around in an open car beaming at everybody and waving his gray fedora. Foreign Minister Vyacheslav Molotov, he of the eternal *nyets* in the UN, got to talking of the photograph of him on a recent American visit wearing a ten-gallon hat. He'd like people to think of him, the Foreign Minister said to reporters, "as something more than a man who says no." The hat didn't fit, Molotov added, "but it's more important to have good publicity than to have a hat that fits."

If the Russians were friendly, Dwight Eisenhower was coexistence incarnate. He opened the conference with a moving appeal for "a new spirit. . . . No doubt there are among our nations philosophical convictions which are in many respects irreconcilable. Nothing that we can say or do here will change that fact. However, it is not always necessary that people should think alike and believe alike before they can work together." The President overlooked no amenity. Eisenhower, Bulganin later recalled delightedly, "opened the Martini road." When the President learned that the daughter of his World War II colleague, Soviet Marshal Georgi Zhukov, was about to be married, he promptly sent to Moscow gifts of a desk pen inscribed "From the President of the United States" and a portable American radio. And then as the conference neared its end, with many observers declaring that it was really getting nowhere, the President rose from his seat, began reading his formal paper prepared by the State Department, put it aside. He took off his glasses, laid them on the table, continued extemporaneously.

"Gentlemen," he said, "I have been searching my heart and mind for something that I could say here that could convince everyone of the great sincerity of the United States in approaching this problem of disarmament." Eisenhower turned and directly faced the Russians. "I should address myself for a moment principally to the delegates from the Soviet Union, because our two great countries admittedly possess new and terrible weapons in quantities which do give rise in other parts of the world, or reciprocally, to the fears and dangers of surprise attack."

The translations of the President's words were not yet coming through but his face alone, cocked to the side in earnestness and gravity, told that he was speaking important words. The usual bustle of the conference room quieted. "I propose, therefore," Eisenhower went on, "that we take a practical step, that we begin an arrangement very quickly, as between ourselves—immediately. These steps would include: to give each other a complete blueprint of our military establishment. . . . Next, to provide within our countries facilities for aerial photography to the other country." Firmly Eisenhower added: "What I propose, I assure you, would be but a beginning."

The Russians were sitting bolt upright. In the United States experts broke into puzzled discussion. How practical was the plan? Why should the Soviet exchange something it had, knowledge of the American military establishment, for something the United States might well not have and very much wanted—information about the Russian facilities? What was the essence of the Eisenhower foreign policy anyhow, with its wariness toward the world on the one hand and on the other hand its invitation to fly Soviet planes over America? The President found no phrase to express his program in international affairs, at least nothing as simple as his conservative-liberal description of his domestic policies. Perhaps it was because the emerging program for abroad, with its restraints on defense money, its hesitancies about large-scale economic aid, and its acceptance of coexistence, was— even more confusingly than the domestic policy—a blend of conservatism and of New Dealism. Perhaps it was because the Eisenhower foreign policy, in a very real sense, was Robert Taft in many of its tactics and Dean Acheson in its larger strategy.

When the President's plane, the *Columbine III*, neared the Washington airport, a summer shower was spattering the Capital. Vice-President Richard Nixon issued an instruction to the officials going out to the airport. No umbrellas, the Vice-President said, because people might be reminded of Prime Minister Neville Chamberlain coming back with his umbrella from the Munich appeasement of Hitler. Nixon need hardly have been concerned. By the summer of 1955 Eisenhower's in-between concept of the President's role, his conservative-liberal domestic policies, his mixed attitudes in foreign affairs, his warm but unaggressive personality, were sweeping him to a political potency unapproached since the heyday of Franklin Roosevelt.

The right wing of the Republican Party lay at his feet, powerless if not shattered. Senator Knowland was issuing no more calls for ultimatums and he was making it very plain that he was for Eisenhower first and last. To the farthest right there were only occasional yawps breaking the still of the cemetery. Senator McCarthy was now duly censured by the Senate of the United States and by a vote of 67 to 22. Flailing away at the descending oblivion, he summoned a press conference and "apologized" for having supported Eisenhower in 1952. The President smiled and the nation yawned.

Harry Truman was stirring restlessly. Where were

the give-'em-hell assaults? Why were there so few calls for "real" liberalism? The head of the Democratic Party, Adlai Stevenson, would soon answer: "We must take care lest we confuse moderation with mediocrity, lest we settle for half answers to hard problems. . . . [But] I agree that it is time for catching our breath; I agree that moderation is the spirit of the times."

Moderation, middle-of-the-road—the phrases were filling the country until Charles Comiskey, vice-president of the Chicago White Sox, could say with a straight face: "Henceforth, we'll do our trading in moderation, we'll be middle-of-the-roaders." In every part of America, in every part of American living, people were working out the clashes created by a decade of turbulent change with a thousand conscious and unconscious compromises. If women were saying they wanted babies, not careers, they were also making sure that the phone number of a baby sitter was at hand. If the intellectuals were discussing a "new conservatism," the new conservatism, for the most part, was heavily streaked with the old liberalism. The trend was emphasized by the reports from the oncoming generation. The pollsters polled, the magazines questioned away, and in Los Angeles a UCLA coed summarized the findings in a few words. What, in general, did she want out of living? "Why, a good sensible life." The coed added quickly: "But, you know, of course not too darned sensible."

Somehow, amid all the bitter disagreements of the post–World War II period, the United States had felt its way to a genuinely national mood. It was not the kind of arrival that could be announced in ringing tones. It contained, in fact, a determination not to be too sure where you were or where you ought to go. It was nothing more or less than the decision on the part of a people who were so in-between in so many of their attitudes to go on cautiously, hopefully maintaining equilibrium. In the murky way of history, another era in the life of the United States was closing. The ten years from the end of World War II in the summer of 1945 to the Geneva Summit Conference in the summer of 1955 were over—and over not only in a chronological sense.

Some astute observers have found little good in the decade, only a muddled descent of American civilization. The "Dismal Decade," the "Years of Neuroses," the "Age of the Vacuum Tube," they have called the period. They see in it the culmination of deeply disturbing trends in the national life, and picture the end-product as a country dominated by a banal mass culture, a worship of the material, the gaudy, the violent, and the mediocre.

Certainly such portrayals cannot be airily waved aside. After all, the America of 1955 was a country where Altman's in New York City had quite a run on mink-handled openers for beer cans and a women's shop in Beverly Hills, California sent out charge plates made of fourteen-carat gold; where the disc jockeys took off "O, Happy Day" only to put on "If a Hottentot taught a tot to talk ere the tot could totter"; where the stock-market craze reached the point that millions of shares of blatantly wildcat uranium ventures were snapped up; where a major crime was committed every fifteen seconds; where approximately one hundred million dollars a year—or just about four times the expenditures on public libraries —were paid out for comic books; where the most popular of all its citizens, Dwight Eisenhower, defined an intellectual as "a man who takes more words than is necessary to say more than he knows."

Yet there is another way of viewing the decade, a way with a quite different emphasis. The ten years from 1945 to 1955 were a decade of high importance in American history, a Crucial Decade. When World War II ended, the Half-Century of Revolution in domestic affairs had reached a critical state. It had gone far enough to influence profoundly American living and to pile up a strong and bitter opposition. During the years immediately after V-J Day, the problem of international affairs reached a similar critical juncture. The emergence of the world-wide Communist threat brought changes in American foreign policy fully as revolutionary as the trends which had been developing on the domestic scene, and these jolting breaks with tradition also provoked potent resistance. Intermingling with the mounting storm, taking strength from it and giving strength to it, was the surge of McCarthyism which, in essence, amounted to an exasperated urge to club everything back into a simpler, more comfortable pattern. At the height of the drive for the traditional, during the tensions of the goadingly untraditional Korean War, two fateful questions were emerging. Would the United States continue, through extensions of the welfare state and of welfare capitalism and a variety of other techniques, the Half-Century of Revolution in domestic affairs? Would it continue moving along the new international path marked by the attitudes clustering around the concepts of containment and coexistence? What is crucial about the Crucial Decade is that during the years from 1945 to 1955 the American people faced these questions and they answered them.

Whatever the swings from Democrats to Republicans, McCarthyism to moderation, intellectualish New Dealers to practical-minded businessmen, there was a basic continuity in the era. Gradually, with many a contrary movement and sidewise venture, a greater and greater percentage of the population decided that the Half-Century of Revolution in domestic affairs was here to stay and that it should be forwarded. Still more gradually, and with much more bridling, an increasing percentage came to the conclusion that the traditional idea of a quick, total solution to international problems, executed largely by the United States alone, simply would not do. The coming of a general attitude of equilibrium in the summer of 1955 was accompanied by the arrival of a broad consensus in

the thinking of Americans about the basic public issues of the day. Most of them had come to agree on
continuing social change at home, if not so much, so
swiftly, and on a shift in their attitude toward the
world, if not so sharply, so expensively.

The continuity of the period also expressed itself in
political terms. In a very real sense, the Truman and
the early Eisenhower years blended into one development. It was the Truman Administration that began
codifying New Dealism in domestic affairs—slowing
down its pace, pushing its attitude only in areas of outstanding need. (It is easy to overlook the fact that as
early as 1949 Truman was describing his domestic
policy as the "middle-course" and defining the phrase
in a way that Eisenhower would not have found too
hard to accept.) Meanwhile the Truman years were
also bringing the departures in foreign policy. The
Eisenhower Administration, whatever its modifications, continued the codification in domestic affairs
and accepted and extended the breakaways in the foreign field. Moreover, it was bringing the Republican
Party, a large part of which had been talking for
twenty years as if it would do everything drastically
differently, into line with the long-running policies
and thus changing them from partisan to national programs. The consensus on fundamental public issues that
was reached in the summer of 1955 was so genuine a
consensus because it developed slowly and survived
the test of savage political warfare.

From the perspective of future years the arrival at
this consensus may well be considered one of the most
important facts in all the American story. Over the
centuries more than one powerful nation has, out of
meanness and shortsightedness, tried to walk against
a great tide of human aspirations and been swallowed
ignominiously. The two problems Americans faced
during the years 1945-55 were actually parts of one
such tide—a world-wide struggle of poor people or
men of lower status to achieve more income and more

of a sense of human dignity. Inside the United States the surge took the form of the demands for the Half-Century of Revolution. Around the world it appeared as the stirrings of underdeveloped colonial lands under Communist, partially Communist, or non-Communist impetus. On occasion during the exasperating, frightening years after World War II, the American people came close to saying that they had enough of aspirations, foreign or domestic. But they never quite said it and in time they managed to say something quite different.

As the Crucial Decade closed in the summer of 1955, the American people could face the onrushing years and the onrushing crises with one solid fact to buttress them. Whatever their addiction to chrome, comic books, and comic-book politics, whatever their yearning for the prepackaged, one-minute solution to everything, they had not, however sorely tempted, committed the supreme foolishness of trying to defy history.

Ike attitude + policies of gov gradually changed

Amer attitude: "Middle-of-the-road"

XIII

More of the Same

THREE WEEKS after the Geneva Summit Conference, on August 14, 1955, President Eisenhower left Washington for a long vacation at the Denver home of his mother-in-law, Mrs. John S. Doud. In the mornings the President would do a quick run-through of official tasks; most afternoons he was off to the golf course or to the sparkling Rocky Mountain trout streams. On the afternoon of Friday, September 23, he played twenty-seven holes of golf and then spent a quiet evening with Mrs. Eisenhower and Mrs. Doud. In the middle of the night he was awakened by a pain in his chest and his physician, Major General Howard Snyder, hurried to his bedside. Shortly after 2 p.m. on Saturday, Acting Press Secretary Murray Snyder made the announcement: Dwight Eisenhower had suffered a heart attack and had just been taken to Fitzsimons Army Hospital.

The nation gasped, then fidgeted uneasily. Suddenly fervid Republicans realized to what extent their hopes for victory in 1956 rested on this one sixty-four-year-old human being. Suddenly ardent Democrats, who had developed a hatred for Richard Nixon such as had never before been visited on a mere Vice-President, recognized how close they might be to having Nixon in the White House. And suddenly too millions of Americans, who were neither particularly Democratic nor Republican, became aware just how much their troubled transition from old ways of thinking in public affairs had been eased by its association with this amiable national hero who made all the innovations seem so common sense, so American.

The President pulled through the first critical days in the oxygen tent. A few more weeks and he appeared out of any immediate danger. Five months after the attack, Eisenhower's physician, the distinguished heart specialist Dr. Paul Dudley White, assured the nation: "The President has made a good recovery. . . . Medically the chances are that the President should be able to carry on an active life satisfactorily for another five to ten years." People settled back again, as they wanted so much to do. The Crucial Decade was over, its decisions made; now let the details be worked out with as little fuss as possible.

The Presidential election of 1956 seemed hardly a contest. Adlai Stevenson, the lilt gone from his voice, ran with all the zest and decisiveness of a man taking the final steps to the gas chamber. The landslide re-election of Eisenhower was accompanied by a victory of the Democrats in the Congressional race. They held their majority in the Senate and increased it in the House—for the first time since 1848 a Presidential candidate had won without giving control of at least one branch of Congress to his party. Even this situation scarcely ruffled the scene. Since World War II, different parties had controlled the White House and at least one branch of Congress for almost one-third of the time; Americans were growing accustomed to split authority in Washington. What's more, the atmosphere of consensus had so affected the parties that one had to find the distinctions between them largely in matters of degree, of emphasis, of nuance. People were smiling understandingly at the story about the political writer who was hard pressed at a dinner party to answer the question, What *really* is the difference between a Republican and a Democrat nowadays? He tried, tried again, and was embarrassed by his own pronouncements. Finally he said: "A Republican, why a Republican when he makes a highball takes a jigger and measures out the whisky. A Democrat, a Democrat just pours."

Before and after the election, from 1955 on through 1957, the decisions of the Crucial Decade were executed in both domestic and foreign affairs. The Half-Century of Revolution at home inched ahead. For the most part the Eisenhower Administration, always budget-wary, held back on large-scale federal expenditures; for the most part, the Democratic majorities in Congress were less reluctant. Everything was compromise, adjustment, but some bills became law. Many Democrats in the House and Senate wanted a considerably liberalized social-security system; Eisenhower, fewer extensions. They agreed on legislation adding somewhat to the categories of people eligible. After a similar hassle, 70,000 more low-rent public-housing units were authorized. A thirty-three-billion-dollar proposal for highway building pleased the President and conservative Congressmen because of defense and general considerations, and delighted New Dealish Representatives and Senators because it would serve as economic pump-priming in the event of a recession. The debate was over where the money was to come from and finally all sides settled for a user's tax. Eisenhower successfully vetoed a Democratic bill to return to high, rigid price supports for agricultural products but accepted a billion-dollar "soil bank" plan, which smacked of Henry Wallace's Triple A by paying farmers to take land out of production.

In the most sensitive area of economic and social legislation, rights for Negroes, the disagreeing went on across party lines in Congress as well as between Congress and the Administration. The unreconstructable Dixiecrat Presidential candidate of 1948, now Democratic Senator Strom Thurmond of South Carolina, set a new filibuster record of twenty-four hours and eighteen minutes trying to talk away any civil-rights legislation. But a bill reached the statute books, the first such legislation in eighty-two years, and it established a Federal Civil Rights Commission with the kind of functions which in time could undermine the power of the Thurmonds in Southern life.

Outside the field of legislation, the social upsweep continued. In 1956, almost without notice, the United States hurried by a milestone comparable in significance to the disappearance of the American frontier in the 1890's. The government issued figures indicating that the number employed in the worker's job of producing things was now less than the number making their livings from largely middle-class occupations. More than half the population had reached or was just about to reach the cherished status of the white collar. Other signs of the social upsurge were less statistical, more satisfying. Ivy League colleges were scouting the secondary schools to enroll able students regardless of family background. More miles of suburbia were stretching out, inhabited not only by the $25,000-a-year old-stock American but by the automobile worker, the man who ran the pharmacy in the city, the children of immigrants. Month after month, in one area of life after another, Negroes scored more "firsts." 1957 brought a later-day Jackie Robinson story. For centuries tennis had been a decidedly upper-class sport. On July 6, 1957, Althea Gibson, daughter of the Harlem streets, curtsied before the Queen of England, murmured "at last, at last," and received the Wimbledon trophy.

Of most basic importance in the Negro's advance, the 1954 Supreme Court decision ordering the desegregation of schools was chipping away at the ancient crust of custom. When the fall term opened in September 1957, desegregation troubles were plentiful. Alabama, Georgia, Mississippi, and South Carolina refused to budge; Virginia was talking "massive resistance." The Border State of Arkansas so brazenly defied the Supreme Court that President Eisenhower ordered federal troops into Little Rock. Yet most seasoned observers agreed with Harry S. Ashmore, the moderate editor of the Arkansas *Gazette*, whose editorials said in a dozen different ways: Here in Little Rock, and throughout the United States, it's only a matter of time.

From abroad the scare headlines kept coming. The Chinese Communist leaders would make threatening noises, subside, start up again. The Hungarians, long restless under their Russian rulers, erupted into street fighting and the Soviet, sending huge tanks clanking over the bodies of men armed only with rifles or sticks, reminded the United States that Communists, coexisting or not, could be utterly ruthless. All the while the turbulent Middle East was made more turbulent by the rabid nationalism of Egypt's new leader, Gamal Ábdel Nasser.

In 1956 Nasser was busy making deals with the Soviet Union for guns, bombers, and tanks. Many of the guns went into the hands of Egyptian commandoes for hit-and-run raids on Israeli territory, and it was hardly a secret that Nasser yearned to find the right opportunity to launch a full-scale attack against the Jewish state. The United States, trying to turn Egyptian nationalism to the amelioration of Egyptian poverty, offered to help finance a gigantic dam at Aswan on the Nile, which would irrigate some 2,000,000 acres of land and increase the arable territory of the country by more than thirty per cent. Nasser liked the idea of American dollars for an Aswan Dam; he also cuddled closer and closer to the Soviet Union. In July 1956, Secretary of State John Foster Dulles abruptly canceled the American offer of financial aid. Nasser exploded. In the course of a three-hour tirade, he announced that he was "nationalizing" the largely British and French-owned Suez Canal and that the Aswan Dam would be built from the profits of the Canal. The Canal, he stormed, "belongs to Egypt

. . . and it will be run by Egyptians! Egyptians! Egyptians!" What's more, Egypt was mobilizing. "We will defend our freedom to the last drop of our blood."

In Israel, political leaders had their own theory about the reason for the Egyptian mobilization. Our only choice now, one of them remarked, is whether "to wait and be wiped off the map and then be eulogized and mourned by our friends, or to attack, to survive, and then explain to our friends." On October 29, 1956, Israeli troops attacked and slashed across the Sinai Peninsula in triumph. (Later 6,000 Egyptian prisoners were exchanged for four Israelis.) The British and French, equally anxious to get rid of Nasser, joined the assault with air and naval units. From the Kremlin came a rapid-fire of statements. The Soviet Union would not let Egypt stand alone against "imperialist aggression"; Russian "volunteers" were eager to intervene. Inferentially, the Soviet threatened to bombard Britain and France with nuclear missiles if the invasion were not halted. In Washington, responsible men talked nervously about the coming of World War III.

Alarms, missile-rattling, intimations of nuclear doomsday—but somehow it all settled down. The United States, working with the UN, threw its full weight behind restoring peace in the Middle East. Under this pressure and the pressure of the Soviet threats, Israel, Britain, and France backed down. The Middle Eastern crisis even produced a promising new UN technique. To keep Egypt and Israel from each other's throats, the international organization set up a "United Nations Emergency Force" consisting of 2,600 troops from Colombia, Denmark, India, Norway, and Sweden. Shortly after 9 p.m. on March 7, 1957, advance battalions of Danes and Norwegians, riding in jeeps and trucks flying the blue-and-white flag of the UN, went splashing through the ancient mud of Gaza—history's first international task force to keep the peace.

Even the most pessimistic Americans were heartened by the Soviet political shake-up that came in July 1957.

Out went the tough old Bolshevik, First Deputy Premier Vyacheslav Molotov, and the Stalin protégé, Deputy Premier Georgi Malenkov—Molotov all the way out to Outer Mongolia, where he was to serve as "Ambassador," and Malenkov to remote Kazakhstan, where he would manage a hydroelectric plant. Bulganin was still Premier, Khrushchev still First Secretary of the Communist Party. But in describing state occasions, *Pravda* now started listing Khrushchev first —roly-poly, wisecracking, gladhanding Nikita Khrushchev, whom most observers said was a strong advocate of seeking an understanding with the West.

As 1957 drew to a close and the first period after the Crucial Decade ended, the United States ambled down its middle road, worried now and then, even having its frenetic moments, but usually happily absorbed in private affairs. The decisions made during the Crucial Decade seemed to be doing their job and they seemed enough. The great waves of prosperity kept rolling in, overwhelming any concerns about the world. In 1957 the government could issue figures establishing that, despite the slowly continuing inflation, most Americans were enjoying more real income than ever before. The signs were everywhere, in the way people lived, played, risked their money. In 1954 the New York Stock Exchange had ordered a public-opinion poll, which found that only twenty-three per cent of the population knew what a stock was and only ten per cent were even considering putting a penny in the market. Now, one in nine adults owned stock—in some cities, Berkeley, Hartford, Pasadena, St. Petersburg, and Wilmington, for example—one in every five people, babies included, were receiving dividends. Vacation time brought migrations bigger than the original march across the continent. In the summer of 1957 well over half the population, some 90,000,000, was going somewhere and spending about two and a half billion dollars to do it

Middle-class Americans found money for whisky-flavored toothpaste; glass poles that were guaranteed to frustrate suburban woodpeckers; and radar-type fishing rods that sent out an electric wave to locate the fish and report back where it was. Everyone who served the rampant middle classes was lifting his sights. The new Montgomery Ward catalogue had two pages of "live listings"; you could get a Great Dane pup for $120 or a Shetland pony for $300. At drive-in restaurants in the Southwest, the girl in the cute uniform rushed out, placed a portable air conditioner around you as you ordered your hot-dog.

People who couldn't purchase things rented them—the booming rental business now included a secretary from the Kelly Girl Service, garden tools, silverware, cocktail glasses, and zircons. People who couldn't buy things or rent them got them by credit. Men who understood the America of 1957 were building the Diner's Club into a multi-million-dollar operation and launching a new national habit that reached a temporary climax when a Duluth businessman proudly exhibited to photographers his fifty-eight credit cards, each readied for instant use in a special accordion-type wallet. Department stores were not lagging behind. They were advertising their programs whereby a housewife could remain indefinitely in debt up to a certain sum, say $500. And if it was all too much bother, firms were springing up that called themselves "debt counselors." For a fee, they took your check each month, gave you a living allowance, parceled out the remainder to your creditors.

The form of prosperity most enjoyable to Americans, prosperity which permitted exhibiting each new step up the social ladder, kept offering its fresh delights. Was a new dress no longer enough to impress the neighbors? Millions of American women (an estimated one in three) had the money to go to a beauty shop and have their hair tinted practically any color it was not—Golden Apricot, Sparkling Sherry, Fire Silver, or Champagne Beige. Could anyone go off to a vacation of lying on the beach? The magazines said "the influentials" were turning to skin-diving and the sales of web feet were up by more than a quarter of a million. Did the crummiest homes in town have TV these days? Hi-fi sets were roaring in and, to make sure the neighbors knew you had one, they were being played so loud that a professor of psychology announced a new neurosis, "audiophilia," turning up the sound until it "reaches the level of physical pain."

The automobile, traditional yardstick of status in America, was swept into rococo phases. Yearly the American cars grew longer, wider, cushier, more gadgety, and with bigger, shinier fins. If you wanted to be sniffish about chrome, the pint-sized foreign cars were coming in—only 56,000 imported in 1955, more than 200,000 in 1957. General Motors stirred to take care of those who couldn't find a sufficiently expensive car. It announced for $13,074 the Cadillac Eldorado Brougham, which offered on its dashboard a tissue box, vanity case, lipstick, and four gold-finished drinking cups. Those who wanted to assert status above all status-seeking could turn to the ultimate in inverted snobbery: the plain black Ford station wagon.

For the most part, intellectuals were glum, warning. They kept insisting that the decisions made in the Crucial Decade were not enough in either foreign or domestic affairs. They added that the very roads Americans had chosen brought their own great dangers. A nation dedicated to lifting endlessly the standard of living and to a long-time coexistence with a powerful enemy could easily turn into a militarized, overfat, numb civilization, increasingly oblivious to the value that had stoked American progress—individualism. Among such critics, the phrase of the immediate post-Crucial Decade years undoubtedly was "organization man," taken from the title of the 1956 volume by William H. Whyte, Jr., a part-descriptive, part-satirical, and all hortatory analysis of the civilization that was emerging in the United States. The dissidents went on reading and writing their books; encouraging the few rebels of the oncoming generation such as youthful Jules Feiffer, whose sad, fragile humor reflected his feeling that the new America made real satire impossible—"satire doesn't stand a chance against reality any more"; huddling together with the talismans of their unhappiness, like the mimeographed sheets that were passed around with waspish glee in intellectual circles.

On the sheets were the anonymous words of some newspaperman in Washington. Fed up with President Eisenhower's middle-of-the-roadism and his muddled way of expressing it, the reporter rewrote the "Gettysburg Address" as Eisenhower would have delivered it: "I haven't checked these figures, but 87 years ago, I think it was, a number of individuals organized a governmental setup here in this country, I believe it covered certain eastern areas, with this idea they were following up, based on a sort of national independence arrangement. . . .

"Well, now of course we are dealing with this big difference of opinion, civil disturbance you might say, although I don't like to appear to take sides or name any individuals. . . . Here we are, you might put it that way, all together at the scene. . . . We want to pay our tribute to those loved ones, those departed individuals who made the supreme sacrifice here on the basis of their opinions about how this setup ought to be handled. It is absolutely in order and 100 per cent OK to do this.

"But if you look at the overall picture of this, we can't pay any tribute—we can't sanctify this area—we can't hallow, according to whatever individual creeds or faiths or sort of religious outlooks are involved, like I said about this particular area. It was those individuals themselves, including the enlisted men—very brave individuals—who have given this religious character to the area. The way I see it, the rest of the world will not remember any statements issued here, but it will never forget how these men put their shoulders to the wheel and carried this idea down the fairway. . . .

"We have to make up our minds right here and now, as I see it, they didn't put out all that blood, perspiration and—well, that they didn't just make a dry run here, that all of us, under God, that is, the God of our choice, shall beef up this idea about freedom and liberty and those kind of arrangements, and that government of all individuals, by all individuals and for the individuals shall not pass out of the world picture."

The intellectuals satirized and gloomed and warned, and the general public did not listen. The general public, if it was harking to anything except the incessant wheels of upper mobility, was responding to the voice of religion. The increased interest noticeable soon after World War II now burst into a full-scale revival. Some of the new attention to religion was undoubtedly a sincere turning to the rigors and consolations of faith; knowledgeable and hardheaded religious leaders could point to incontrovertible facts. But a good deal of it was certainly a false religiosity, compounded of social aspirations and a fervid desire to avoid thinking. In 1956 the Reverend Dr. John Sutherland Bonnell, minister of the Fifth Avenue Presbyterian Church in New York City, began running a highly successful ad. "FOR A SPIRITUAL LIFT IN A BUSY DAY," the ad said, "DIAL-A-PRAYER. CIrcle 6-4200. One minute of inspiration in prayer." The bookstores were offering *Go with God* or *The Power of Prayer on Plants* or *Pray Your Weight Away*, while the juke boxes joined in with "I've Got Religion," "Big Fellow in the Sky," and "The Fellow Upstairs." *Modern Screen* magazine ran a series called "How the Stars Found Faith," in which Jane Russell announced: "I love God. And when you get to know Him, you find He's a Livin' Doll."

Week after week Billy Graham, a sincere Fundamentalist evangelist who was now organized into a tremendous operation with the efficiency and impersonality of a Dewey campaign, went around saving more cities, not to speak of the Los Angeles hoodlum Mickey Cohen. Shortly after Cohen declared his conversion, it seems, he got together with W. C. Jones, a member of the governing board of the Billy Graham Crusade. Brother Cohen and Brother Jones prayed together over breakfast, then Cohen addressed a meeting of the Los Angeles Union Rescue Mission at which five men made decisions for Christ. "After that," Jones recalled, "I was convinced that Michael—I always called him Michael in those days—was converted," and after that Michael, who said he needed "a little stake" for his new life as a Christian, borrowed about $5,000 from the Graham organization which he never repaid. "I don't begrudge him the money," Jones added sadly. "But I've now come to the conclusion he wasn't sincere when he said he was following Billy Graham." The Crusade rolled on, on to its climactic New York meeting in 1957, where a $1,300,000 budget had taken care of everything, including special climate studies to predict when to schedule outdoor meetings and special surveys of the habits of strap-hangers to learn the most effective placement for subway ads.

In Minnesota, a wholesale groceryman listened to a re-broadcast of Billy Graham's opening sermon at Madison Square Garden, drove off with a friend for some fishing. In ten minutes his new radar-type rod had produced an eight-pound trout. He put the fish in his ice container, opened a beer, and settled back for a bit of heavy thinking. "You know," he said to his friend, "those Russians talk and talk and bluster. But with God and with good old American knowhow"—he tapped his glistening rod—"with those on our side, I just can't get bothered."

XIV

*The Middle Road
Grows Bumpy*

THE UNITED STATES read the headlines on Saturday morning, October 5, 1957. The Soviet news agency, Tass, announced: "The first artificial earth satellite in the world has now been created. This first satellite was successfully launched in the U.S.S.R. . . . Artificial earth satellites will pave the way for space travel and it seems that the present generation will witness how the freed and conscious labor of the people of the new socialist society turns even the most daring of man's dreams into reality."

Americans took another astonished gulp of coffee, read on eagerly. The Tass dispatch was not reticent. The satellite was twenty-two inches in diameter, weighed 184.3 pounds, was whirling about the earth at a maximum height of 560 miles and at a speed of 18,000 miles an hour, circling the globe once every hour and thirty-five minutes. Inside were two radio transmitters that continually beeped scientific information to earth. The Russians called the satellite a "sputnik," meaning an object that was traveling with a traveler—that is, an object that was traveling with the earth which in turn was traveling through space. By nightfall of this strange Saturday, the most eerie day since Harry Truman announced the atomic bomb in far-off 1945, the word "sputnik" had a firm place in the American language.

The reactions came in a caterwaul of disagreement. Here and there Americans pooh-poohed, including Rear Admiral Rawson Bennett, Chief of the Office of Naval Research, who wanted to know why all the fuss over a "hunk of iron almost anybody could launch." Leading Democrats cried shame. "If this now known Soviet superiority," Senator Stuart Symington, of the Armed Services Committee, said for them, "develops into supremacy, the position of the free world will be critical." Yet "for fiscal reasons this Government . . . continues to cut back and slow down its own missile program." Symington demanded an investigation by the Senate Armed Services Committee. "Only in this way can the American people learn the truth. Putting it mildly, they have not been getting the truth." "The launching," added Senator Henry M. Jackson, chairman of the military applications panel of the Joint Congressional Committee on Atomic Energy, was "a devastating blow to the prestige of the United States as the leader in the scientific and technical world." It corroborated, Jackson said, the Soviet claim of the previous August that it had launched an intercontinental ballistic missile and had developed an effective missile-propulsion system.

Republicans varied in their emphases but most took the line which President Eisenhower expressed through his press secretary. The satellite, said James Hagerty calmly, was "of great scientific interest."

But what about its defense and security aspects? reporters pressed.

He was staying with its "scientific interest," Hagerty replied. His manner became still more nonchalant. The sputnik "did not come as a surprise." Besides, "we never thought of our program as one which was in a race with the Soviet's." Other Administration statements had the same unruffled tone. The United States had decided to separate its military-missile and its space-missile programs and to emphasize the former. Hence the Soviet success in getting a satellite up first.

It soon became clear that many scientists engaged in government research had opposed this separation. A number now spoke out, not only arguing against continuation of the separation, but maintaining that their progress on both programs had been slowed by interservice rivalries and by the Administration's insistence on holding down costs. Almost all scientists agreed that the launching of the sputnik proved that the Russians were well ahead of the United States in building and controlling rockets. After all, they pointed out, the United States in its most optimistic planning had expected to launch a satellite of only 21.5 pounds—seven times lighter than the sputnik. Dr. Joseph Kaplan, chairman of the American program for the International Geophysical Year, spoke the general scientific estimate of the Russian achievement. It was nothing less than "tremendous." Dr. Kaplan added: "If they can launch one that heavy, they can put up much heavier ones."

Just twenty-nine days later, on November 3, the Soviet put up a whale of a lot heavier one—Sputnik II, weighing 1,120.29 pounds and orbiting as much as 1,056 miles away. About half its weight was a labyrinth of scientific instruments reporting back to earth. Sputnik II also contained the sure harbinger of a coming Russian attempt to put a man into space. In a hermetically sealed, air-conditioned compartment was a live dog of the laika breed, with instruments strapped to the animal's chest which broadcasted its reactions to space conditions.

In Washington, people had a new story. It was about the reporter who called up the U.S. Space Agency and asked how the American program was going. The girl in the office replied: "Sir, are you calling *for* information or *with* information?" Throughout the United States a sense of alarm, exasperation, humilia-

tion, and confusion mounted. Sputniks I and II dramatized as nothing else could have done that the chief
thing on which Americans had depended for their
national security and for victory in a competitive
coexistence with Communism—the supremacy of
American technical know-how—had been bluntly
challenged.

At the White House James Hagerty was no longer
issuing casual statements. The President moved up a
speech scheduled to be delivered on November 13.
Four days after Sputnik II, on November 7, he
made the address and it included an announcement
of the appointment of James R. Killian, Jr., president
of the Massachusetts Institute of Technology, as Special Assistant to the President for Science and Technology "to have the active responsibility for helping
me to follow through on the scientific improvement
of our defense." The next day Secretary of Defense
Neil H. McElroy revised a long-standing Administration policy. Heretofore the American satellite program
had been under the charge of the Navy, with all
other branches concentrating on long-range ballistic
missiles. Now McElroy ordered the Army, which had
a well-tested Jupiter-C rocket, to take over on satellites and to get an artificial moon into orbit.

The Defense Department was soon issuing press
releases: on December 4 the United States would put
a satellite into orbit at Cape Canaveral, Florida. Tens
of thousands of spectators and hundreds of reporters
gathered. The countdown started at 5:30 a.m. and was
stopped; a fuel valve was not working. Another countdown, another halt because of mechanical failure. In
early afternoon the announcement came that the
launching would be delayed forty-eight hours, until
December 6. The foreign press broke into loud hee-
haws. "Flopnik," "Stay-putnick," "Kaputnik," British
papers labeled the American satellite. The Ameri-
canized Japanese press wrote about "Sputternick."
The Communist East German papers took the Ger-

man word for "late," *spaet*, and sneered "Spaetnik." In Washington, people passed around another wry wisecrack: "The American satellite ought to be called Civil Servant. It won't work and you can't fire it."

At Cape Canaveral, December 6 came in a startlingly beautiful day. The thousands gathered again, buzzed expectantly as the reports said all was going well. Precisely on schedule, at 11:45 a.m. the satellite blasted off, its orange blaze seething against the blue of the sky. Seconds later the orange turned into a dingy brown-black smoke. The satellite had started up, exploded, crashed back burning on its pad. This time a comment came from the First Secretary of the Communist Party of the Soviet Union. Nikita Khrushchev was playful, condescending. The Soviet sputniks were "lonely." They were "waiting for American satellites to join them in space." Then the cold, crunching truth: "Who wants to overtake whom in science? The United States would like to overtake the Soviet Union."

More frantic weeks, in Washington and at Cape Canaveral. On January 31, 1958, President Eisenhower was vacationing in Augusta. At about 5:30 p.m. Hagerty began going back and forth between the press room and the President's cottage, giving Eisenhower the latest word from Cape Canaveral. After dinner, he brought the President firm news. The satellite would definitely be fired that night; the blast-off would come at 10:48 p.m. A direct telephone line was connected from Eisenhower's cottage to Dr. J. Wallace Joyce at the National Science Foundation in Washington. Dr. Joyce received word that the satellite had been launched faultlessly. He waited seven minutes, giving it time to reach a height permitting it to go into orbit. He waited another 114 minutes while his instruments told him that it was making a first swing around the earth. Then Dr. Joyce put the call through to Atlanta. "It's in orbit," the scientist said. The Eisenhower smile had never been more radiant. "That's wonderful, simply wonderful," the President replied.

The whole United States heaved a sigh of relief. But for a considerable part of the population the old, post-Crucial Decade days of assurance were gone. The American satellite, the Explorer, weighed only 30.8 pounds; whirling proudly in space, it nevertheless was a conspicuous symbol that the United States was second best in a field that could prove decisive. Under the circumstances the unending crises abroad took on a greatly heightened power to worry and to frighten.

About three months after the Explorer went into orbit, on March 27, 1958, Khrushchev became clear-cut boss of the Soviet Union, and four days later his government issued an ambiguous but decidedly trouble-brewing statement that it intended to suspend nuclear tests while reserving the right to resume them if the United States and Britain did not follow suit. By the summer of 1958, the Middle East was again in such turmoil that American Marines were ordered into Lebanon. Fall brought more threats from the Chinese Reds about the islands lying off Formosa, Quemoy and Matsu. On November 27, 1958, Khrushchev delivered what sounded like an ultimatum on the delicate subject of Berlin. Within six months, he said, West Berlin must be "free," which was standard Communist language for putting West Berlin in a situation where it would end up Communist-controlled. Spring 1959, and the most remote region of the world rang an alarm bell. Chinese Communists were cracking down on the Tibetans, sending the Dalai Lama fleeing to India.

"When are we going to land on the moon?" a Muscovite asked Khrushchev. The Soviet leader slapped his thigh and laughed. "Why should we go there? We're doing all right here on earth." Scores of respected American commentators were pointing out that the Soviet was doing fine in impressing, cajoling, and pressuring nations here on earth. In a number of "neutral" countries both pro-Communism and anti-Americanism, whether pro-Communist or not, seemed to be increasing. Americans had to watch the process going on just ninety miles south of Florida. On January 1, 1959, Fidel Castro's bearded revolutionaries took over Cuba. Within months some Communist infiltration of the government was plain. A few more months and most of Cuba's institutions were marked by a bitter and systematized anti-Americanism. The press of the United States was filled with dispatches like the description of the new educational process in the Havana schools:

The teacher of the third-grade class asks: "What did José Marti do?"

The eight-year-old boy answers: "José Marti freed Cuba from the Spaniards."

"And what did Fidel Castro do?"

"Fidel freed Cuba from the United States, which seized all our land."

"Correct," the teacher says. She turns to a girl student: "What happened on February 15, 1898?"

"The United States blew up the *Maine* so they could intervene in Cuba."

The Portland *Oregonian* spoke a national mood when it commented in connection with the Castro movement: "All this sort of thing was bad enough when we were first learning about the Communist menace. It is downright terrifying with those sputniks staring down at us."

The new apprehension in the United States ranged beyond events in foreign countries, particularly to the area most sensitized by the Soviet sputnik success—the American attitude toward learning in general and toward science in particular. The Soviet schools, Americans were being told, were tough, purposeful, heavily emphasizing science in every year from the fourth grade up, ruthlessly ready to separate the mediocre from the outstanding students and to push the latter. And the schools of the United States? "I will tell you about the American schools," a Nobel Prize physicist said to a New York City group. "This is the way they decide how to teach. People who know what they are talking about say, 'We should teach that the world is round, not square.' The superintendent, one eye on the mommas of the Parent-Teachers-Association, the other eye on the Chamber of Commerce, the labor unions, the Croatian-American Society, and what-have-you, says, 'I will find out how many voters in this town think that the world is round and how many think that it is square.' "

Five months after Sputnik I, *Life* began a series of articles which summarized and prodded the growing national concern. "Crisis in Education," the series was called. For years, *Life* said, "most critics of U.S. education have suffered the curse of Cassandra—always to tell the truth, seldom to be listened to." Now the sputniks had brought "a recognized crisis" and its "salient points" were:

"The schools have been overcrowded for years. . . .

"Most teachers are grossly underpaid (some are not worth what they get). A great many . . . have to work without help, understanding or proper tools.

"In their eagerness to be all things to all children, schools have gone wild with elective courses. They build up the bodies with in-school lunches and let the minds shift for themselves.

"Where there are young minds of great promise, there are rarely the means to advance them. The nation's stupid children get far better care than the bright. The geniuses of the next decade are even now being allowed to slip back into mediocrity.

"There is no general agreement on what the schools should teach. A quarter century has been wasted with the squabbling over whether to make a child well adjusted or teach him something.

"Most appalling, the standards of education are shockingly low."

Shockingly low—in the post-sputnik era, Americans were reading harsh words about their schools and, beyond their schools, about their whole way of life. Intellectuals said it, now more vigorously than ever.

Democrats and dissident Republicans said it, worriedly, angrily. Quite different people were also speaking up. Mrs. Clare Boothe Luce, high Republican and so often a spokesman of American self-satisfaction, now declared: The beep of the Russian sputniks is an "outer-space raspberry to a decade of American pretensions that the American way of life is a gilt-edge guarantee of our national superiority."

In the week that Sputnik I went up, a band blared "When the Saints Go Marching In" and 1,753 delegates of the International Brotherhood of Teamsters marched into the Miami Beach Auditorium. Fat President David Beck bellowed for an hour a sentiment no one could deny—"God never created me in the crucible of infallibility"—and was retired to a $50,000-a-year pension and indictments for wholesale fleecing. Up went the roars for Jimmy Hoffa, the abundantly exposed prime target of Senator John McClellan's Labor Rackets Committee. A Chicago Teamster, Thomas Haggerty, tried to run against Hoffa on moral grounds and the delegates had a wonderful time. "We got a new slogan," they said with roars of rib-poking laughter. "Haggerty for integrity, Hoffa for President." When Hoffa was duly named President of the nation's largest union, some Teamsters could not contain their pride. "Jimmy," they chanted over and over again, "is the greatest little bastard who ever put on shoes." Many another American wondered what was happening to the simplest, the most basic conceptions of morality in the United States.

They were getting none too comforting answers. The McClellan Committee went on revealing sleazy union practices, often condoned by the rank-and-file members and often connived in by management. The House Subcommittee on Legislative Oversight, headed by Representative Oren Harris of Arkansas, reported that Bernard Goldfine, a businessman with decided needs for connections in Washington, had paid the cost of a vicuna coat and of hotel stays for none other than the chief assistant to the President of the United States, Sherman Adams. Still protesting that he had "done no wrong," Adams had to be forced off the national scene by Republican politicians worried about the coming Congressional election. American politics, Republican or Democratic, continued to produce peculiarly disconcerting incidents. In 1958 a federal grand jury indicted for income-tax evasion the Reverend Mr. Adam Clayton Powell, Jr., minister of the Abyssinian Baptist Church, a Democratic Congressman rhapsodically popular in Harlem, and one of the most vigorous spokesmen of the upcoming Negro minority (the jury disagreed and returned no verdict). At the same time the mass media were picking up a book by Professor Philip E. Jacob of the University of Pennsylvania, who had surveyed the American colleges and concluded that cheating "is so widespread as to challenge the well-nigh universal claim of students that they value honesty as a moral virtue. Frequent cheating is admitted by 40% or more at a large number of colleges, often with no apology or sense of wrongdoing." And all the while, the clouds were gathering around the one folk hero who had emerged in post-Crucial Decade America.

Week after week during late 1956 and 1957 Charles Van Doren had been seen on the NBC program *Twenty-One*. On the TV screen he appeared lanky, pleasant, smooth in dress and manner but never slick, confident but with an engaging way of understating himself. The long, hard questions would come at him and his eyes would roll up, squeeze shut, his forehead furrow and perspire, his teeth gnaw at his lower lip. Breathing heavily, he seemed to coax information out of some corner of his mind by talking to himself in a kind of stream-of-consciousness. Like a good American, he fought hard, taking advantage of every rule. ("Let's skip that part, please, and come back to it.") Like a good American, he won with no crowing. And, like a good American, he kept on winning, downing corporation lawyers or ex-college presidents with equal ease on questions ranging from naming the four islands of the Balearic Islands to explaining the process of photosynthesis to naming the three baseball players who each amassed more than 3,500 hits. Charles Van Doren was "the new All-American boy," the magazines declared, and to millions he was that indeed—a crew-cut, gray-flannel image to an America yearning for the crew-cut, gray-flannel life.

After Van Doren finally lost and NBC made him a $50,000-a-year commentator on Dave Garroway's *Today* show, the arrival of the sputniks soon gave him an even more solid place as a folk hero. Was he not the son of America's most famous intellectual family? Had he not won his celebrity on an egghead program and continued to teach the youth at Columbia for $4,400 a year despite his large NBC salary? Of the letters that continued to pour in to Van Doren, one in four was written by a parent or teacher telling him that he was an idol for the young who counteracted Elvis Presley, that he had taken the curse off studying, that he had proved an egghead could be as glamorous as Gary Cooper or Mickey Mantle. "I am damned happy about these letters," said Charles Van Doren.

From the beginning of the big-money TV quizzes, some people had been unhappy. They argued that the programs were giving the public the dangerously distorted idea that learning consisted of knowing petty, disconnected facts for a fat fee. Others were skeptical about the reality of the contests; they insisted that at least some of the shows must be fixed. Evidence emerged that some of the minor shows were in fact fixed; the New York County Grand Jury became interested. Most unhappy of all was a chunky, bristle-haired, abundantly articulate young man, Herbert M. Stempel, a C.C.N.Y. student who had won $49,500 on *Twenty-One* before losing to Van Doren.

Stempel had problems. His big winnings had been tossed away. His psychiatrist bills were mounting. Worst of all of Stempel's problems was his ego. He kept saying to friends that the producers of *Twenty-One*, Daniel Enright and Albert Freedman, had made him muff questions to which he knew the answers ("I was forced to say that Gothic architecture originated in Germany when I know damn well it was France"). Enright had instructed him in unnatural grimaces and gestures, insisting that he "think violently" in the isolation booth ("I call it the Dan Enright school of acting"). Then, because "we've reached a plateau, we need a new face," Enright ordered him to "take a dive" to Charles Van Doren, "a guy that had a fancy name, Ivy League education, parents all his life, and I had the opposite. . . . All of this [fame and money of Van Doren] should have been coming to me." The more Stempel thought about what had happened, the more his psyche bothered him. He was especially upset one night "when I took my wife to the theater . . . and I overheard somebody saying, 'That's the guy who was beaten by Van Doren.' It hurt me egotistically." In April 1958 Stempel massaged his bruised ego by talking to District Attorney Frank Hogan and to the New York *World-Telegram and Sun*. His story amounted to the charge that *Twenty-One*, including Van Doren's participation, was rigged.

Reporters hurried to Van Doren's smartly redecorated Greenwich Village home. The All-American boy was "sad" and "shocked" at such talk. Of course he had played "honestly. . . . At no time was I coached or tutored."

The Grand Jury finished its investigation and Judge Mitchell Schweitzer impounded the record on the ground that it contained allegations that could seriously hurt people who had not had an opportunity to reply. Stories leaked from the Grand Jury; more ex-contestants were talking. The reporters went back to Van Doren again. This time the All-American boy showed a proper American indignation. "It is an insult," he said, "to keep asking me these questions."

"Well," a reporter pressed, "is it absolutely true that you have never been coached in any way?"

"Hell, no!"

The leaks, the rumors went on. A new Grand Jury convened. District Attorney Hogan was calling people in, including Van Doren. Under oath he flatly denied any part in rigging. On October 6, 1959, Representative Oren Harris's Special Subcommittee on Legislative Oversight (in this case oversight over the Federal Communications Commission) began closed hearings on the quiz shows. Van Doren telegraphed to the Committee a categorical statement that he had not been "assisted in any form." He was "available" to the Committee any time it might like to question him.

A few more days of testimony and the Committee decided it would very much like to question him. It sent Van Doren a telegram inviting him to appear voluntarily; the telegram was not answered. The Committee issued a formal subpoena for his appearance. The process-server could not find him.

Six days went by. On October 14 Van Doren appeared at the Hotel Roosevelt in New York City, was handed the subpoena, and walked into a jammed press conference. Smiling but showing strain, he read a prepared statement. He had not been evading the subpoena. He had been "distressed" by the rush of events, asked for a week's leave of absence from Columbia, and went with his wife to New England "to gather my thoughts . . . in the October beauty of the region." He did not know he was being sought until yesterday.

Reporters closed in with questions. How could he have failed to know about the subpoena when it was the big news in the newspapers and on radio and TV? When was he going to tell the real story? Van Doren paled, clutched the rostrum until his knuckles showed white. He would say no more. He respected the

United States Congress too much to answer questions until he reached the "appropriate forum," the Harris Committee.

On November 2 Van Doren made his way into the House Caucus Room, a pale, tense young man in an Oxford-gray suit and a dark-figured tie. The huge, high-ceilinged chamber was jammed and standees flowed into the corridor; 120 reporters and seventeen photographers scrambled for vantage points. Van Doren eased himself uncomfortably into the witness chair, asked for some water. A hush fell over the room as he began to read a prepared statement in a low, taut voice: "I would give almost anything I have to reverse the course of my life in the last three years. . . . I have learned a lot in those three years, especially in the last three weeks. . . . I've learned a lot about good and evil. They are not always what they appear to be. I was involved, deeply involved, in a deception."

Van Doren's voice steadied as he became accustomed to the still of the room. He was reading calmly now, with none of the gestures that millions had associated with him. He had not been gradually lured into the deception; the faking started "with my first actual appearance on 'Twenty-One.' I was asked by Freedman to come to his apartment. He took me into his bedroom where we could talk alone. He told me that Herbert Stempel . . . was unpopular, and was defeating opponents right and left to the detriment of the program. He asked me if, as a favor to him, I would agree to make an arrangement. . . . Freedman guaranteed me $1,000 if I would appear for one night. I will not bore this committee by describing the intense moral struggle that went on inside me. . . . The fact is that I unfortunately agreed, after some time, to his proposal."

Van Doren had not faked occasionally; everything was rigged. "I met him [Freedman] next at his office, where he explained how the program would be controlled. He told me the questions I was to be asked, and then asked if I could answer them. Many of them I could. But he was dissatisfied with my answers. They were not 'entertaining' enough. He instructed me how to answer the questions: to pause before certain of the answers, to skip certain parts and return to them, to hesitate and build up suspense, and so forth. On this first occasion and on several subsequent ones he gave me a script to memorize, and before the program he took back the script and rehearsed me in my part. This was the general method which he used through my fourteen weeks on *Twenty-One*."

Van Doren was fully aware of the dishonesty of what he was doing. He was "deeply troubled" but "the show ballooned beyond my wildest expectations. . . . I became a celebrity. I received thousands of letters and dozens of requests to make speeches, appear in movies, and so forth. . . . I was winning more money than I had ever had or even dreamed of having. I was able to convince myself that I could make up for it after it was over."

As the weeks went by, he grew "terribly uncomfortable. . . . Frankly, I was very much afraid." He told Freedman of his fears and asked "several times" to be released from the program. Freedman explained that Van Doren would have to leave by being defeated in "a dramatic manner." Van Doren went on performing on *Twenty-One*. An attractive blonde attorney, Mrs. Vivienne Nearing, appeared on the program as an opponent of Van Doren; Freedman apparently liked her performance. She played a series of dramatic tie games and then Freedman "told me that . . . I would be defeated by her. I thanked him."

When the revelations began to close in on Van Doren, he was "horror-struck. . . . I simply ran away. . . . Most of all, I was running from myself." After he was served the subpoena, he "spent the rest of the week trying hopelessly to seek a way out. . . . There was one way out which I had, of course, often considered, and that was simply to tell the truth." But "emotionally" he did not find this a "possible" solution.

Van Doren's voice was tensing up again. He looked up from his manuscript, glanced nervously at the crowd. In the end, he said, "it was a small thing that tipped the scales. A letter came to me . . . from a woman, a complete stranger, who had seen me on the Garroway show and who said she admired my work there. She told me that the only way I could ever live with myself, and make up for what I had done—of course, she, too, did not know exactly what that was —was to admit it, clearly, openly, truly. Suddenly I knew she was right. . . ."

His voice calmed again. "In the morning I telephoned my attorney and told him my decision. He had been very worried about my health and, perhaps, my sanity, and he was happy that I had found courage at last. He said 'God bless you.'" Charles Van Doren laid aside his manuscript, turned to his lawyer, and smiled.

Rarely, in the long history of public confessions, had anyone revealed an episode of more thoroughgoing fraudulence. Van Doren had knowingly entered into a total deception and received huge returns for it, in money and in non-pecuniary returns. Then, when the charges came, he had lied to his family, his lawyer, the Grand Jury, the reporters, and a Congressional Committee. In his appearance before the Committee, he had lied, or at least not told the whole truth, even in the course of confessing that he had lied. The woman who liked Van Doren on the Garroway show may have influenced him finally to tell the truth; he could hardly have been uninfluenced by the fact that his appearance at the Congressional hearing was the last possible moment when he could avoid a perjury charge. He stated that he had asked producer Albert Freedman to let him off the show but that Freedman refused. He did not explain why he did not simply

leave the program or, if he preferred to be extra polite, just miss a question he was not supposed to miss.

As Van Doren finished his statement, the room was
in dead silence. Chairman Oren Harris spoke first. He
wanted to "compliment" Van Doren on his statement.
Other Congressmen or Committee officials hastened to
"commend" him for his "soul-searching" statements,
his "fortitude," his "forthrightness." Congressman
Peter F. Mack, Jr., Democrat of Illinois, expressed the
hope that NBC would not fire Van Doren; Representative William E. Springer, Republican of Illinois, that
Columbia University would not act "prematurely."
The crowd applauded at each remark.

Representative Steven B. Derounian, Republican of
Nassau County, New York, was a little restless at all
this. "I don't think," he said coldly, "an adult of your
intelligence ought to be commended for telling the
truth." There was no applause.

Chairman Harris ended the brief proceedings. He
had some further thoughts that anybody who "tells
the whole truth in a matter that is so important to the
American people and the public interest is to be
highly complimented. . . ." He turned to Van Doren,
smiled benignly. "I think you have a great future
ahead of you. . . . I think I could end this session by
saying what your attorney did say to you the other
day; that is, 'God bless you.' "

Five hours after the Committee adjourned, Columbia University announced it was accepting Van Doren's "resignation"; the next morning NBC fired him
without circumlocution. Newspaper editors competed
with the pulpits in their sermons on the state of American morality. The networks fell over each other trying to show that each was fumigating the fastest until the actor Walter Slezak moaned: "Everybody in
TV is so suspicious that if you say 'Oh, my God' on
television, they think you're being paid off by the
Holy Father." CBS, the wags added, was about to
move *Church of the Air* to prime evening time.

But the general public showed no such reaction; its tone was like that of Chairman Harris and most of his Committee. Letters flooded into NBC; they were 5 to 1 against the firing of Van Doren. At Columbia a large group of students held a rally to protest his dismissal. Several colleges hinted they would like to employ him, including his alma mater, St. John's, which prided itself on a special emphasis on the values of Western Civilization. In Hollywood, the well-known producer Mervyn LeRoy said he was offering Van Doren an acting position—as a prosecutor in a movie. The "punishment" had gone too far; besides, "it's time someone gave him a job that would pay a living wage." Newspapers and magazines, checking the general reaction, found a majority of Americans fully supporting Van Doren. One responsible journal declared that three out of four were saying that "most people" would have done what Van Doren did for the money and the fame.

At the end of 1959, *Look* magazine sent out a team of twelve experienced reporters to question all kinds of Americans about their general moral attitudes. Editor William Attwood, summarizing the findings, said that they were capsuled by the remark of a young woman in Pennsylvania: "Who am I to say what's right and wrong?" For most Americans, "moral relativism" had replaced moral certitudes and brought in its wake moral lassitude and confusion. Out of the confusion, Attwood continued, "a new American code of ethics seems to be evolving. Its terms are seldom stated in so many words, but it adds up to this: Whatever you do is all right if it's legal or if you disapprove of the law. It's all right if it doesn't hurt anybody. And it's all right if it's part of accepted business practice."

The essential fact behind the new code was the group, "that is, you no longer refrain from doing something because you couldn't live with yourself— you refrain from doing something because you couldn't live with your neighbors." In most group codes, some cheating was tolerated—even approved and demanded. A *Look* reporter had found an extreme and ironic case of group morality in Colorado, where a man who did *not* chisel on his income tax boasted that he did in order to be well regarded by his friends. "So it would seem that your changing code of ethics is creating a fifth American freedom—the freedom to chisel."

In or outside group morality, Attwood was sure, "moral indignation is out of fashion. It isn't smart to get mad. Nor are people concerned with making moral judgments unless they are discussing clearly criminal behavior. The thing to be these days is cool, sophisticated—and tolerant of wrongdoing. . . ."

A cool abstention from indignation, a "group" morality that put relatively few restraints on the individual, scandal after scandal culminating in the Van Doren episode and even more in the public reaction to it—ever since the Kefauver Hearings of 1950 thoughtful Americans had been increasingly concerned about the trend of American attitudes toward right and wrong. Now John Steinbeck wrote a passionate letter to his friend, Adlai Stevenson. "If I wanted to destroy a nation," the novelist declared, "I would give it too much and I would have it on its knees, miserable, greedy, and sick. . . . [In rich America] a creeping, all pervading, nerve-gas of immorality starts in the nursery and does not stop before it reaches the highest offices, both corporate and governmental. . . . On all levels American society is rigged. . . . I am troubled by the cynical immorality of my country. It cannot survive on this basis."

The Steinbeck letter was printed, reprinted, re-reprinted, endlessly discussed. And as people discussed it, they read that eight Chicago policemen were under arrest for serving as lookouts while their burglar friends looted businesses and that you could pay New York agencies to take your college exam or to write your Ph.D. dissertation.

Three days after the Van Doren testimony, reporters brought up the quiz scandals at the White House press conference. President Eisenhower said he was "astounded and almost dismayed," stated that he did not believe that such things meant "America has forgotten her own moral standards," and dropped the matter.

During 1959 and 1960, the President was pushing little on the home scene. He had never really been inclined to strong action in the domestic area. Now he was an old man, moving in the shadow of his heart attack, hankering for the surcease of the golf course. As he said of himself, he was holding to the middle road but growing "more conservative," and in modern America, conservatism in home affairs has meant largely inactivity, particularly inactivity in using Presidential prestige, federal powers, or public money to bring about social and economic change. The Congressional elections of 1958 confirmed Eisenhower's natural tendency. The returns, as the gagsters said, made even Alf Landon look good. The Democrats swept everything, electing more Congressmen and getting control of more State Houses than at any time since the F.D.R. landslide of 1936. President Eisenhower was bewildered, hurt—and wary. He saw the incoming Congress as a band of Treasury marauders and braced for a crusade of inactivity in the realm of spending.

Endlessly the President talked economy, balanced budget, cutting down the national debt. (If he were to tell his grandson a bedtime story, Eisenhower remarked without a smile, even it would make the point: "I am not supporting you—you are supporting me.") The President's economy-mindedness was successful enough in arousing public opinion so that the Democratic Rayburn-Johnson team in Congress, which had its own reservations about spending, led a House and a Senate which did not push very hard. A labor-reform bill, including a "bill of rights" for rank-and-file members, became law; so, too, did another civil-rights measure, providing for federal-court-appointed "referees" who were to help give Negroes the vote in the South. The admission of Hawaii rounded out the fifty states of the Union. Beyond that, the internal life of the United States was left untouched by important new legislation.

The President was the less inclined to push domestic action because, with each passing day, his heart and his mind were concentrated more on foreign affairs. During his Administrations, Eisenhower's conception of his role in history gradually changed. He had prided himself on ending the Korean War and of having taken some of the acrimony out of the American political atmosphere; restoring and maintaining fiscal "prudence" were always on his mind. But increasingly he saw for himself one overarching historic mission, to further a "just and lasting peace." He had run for re-election in 1956, he told friends, because "I want to advance our chances for world peace, if only by a little, maybe only a few feet." In 1958 he stated to a press conference: "There is no place on this earth to which I would not travel, there is no chore I would not undertake, if I had any faintest hope that, by so doing, I would promote the general cause of world peace." Eisenhower's sense of mission in world affairs became still more compelling after the death of the strong-minded Secretary of State John Foster Dulles in May 1959, when the President tended to concentrate foreign policy in his own hands.

The situation looked propitious. Despite the continuing crises in American-Soviet relations, Khrushchev appeared genuinely to wish an end to the Cold War, or at least an armistice. The prevailing theory in Washington was that the Soviet leader personally was a man of peace and that his people were pressing for consumer's goods, thus making him the more willing to reach a *détente* which would permit him to shift the Soviet economy from its overwhelming emphasis on armaments.

Genuine improvement in the relations between the Soviet and the United States would be especially furthered by some settlement of the recurrent Berlin crisis and by steps toward disarmament, particularly steps toward an international agreement for the ending of nuclear tests and for the control of existing nuclear weapons. Khrushchev had a standard proposition to settle these or almost any difficulties: Call a summit meeting. President Eisenhower was leery. He had been none too happy with the Geneva Conference of 1955, which offered a magnificent occasion for Soviet propaganda and produced no solid results. But pressures were building for another meeting of the Big Four. In the United States a large number of thoughtful and influential people were saying that such a conference could produce a real breakthrough in the world deadlock. Some of America's allies, especially the Macmillan government of Britain, agreed. Khrushchev was constantly stepping up his own pressure for a summit meeting. He went barnstorming around the world presenting the Soviet as the true friend of peace because it was ready and eager for such a conference. Ever more openly he used the Berlin situation. Something had to be done soon to "free" West Berlin or the Soviet would move, he declared in increasingly blunt ways, and the only way to get something done was a summit meeting.

Meanwhile a number of things, little and big, made it seem that this time a summit conference could produce real results. A flurry of exchanges between Soviet and American scientists, students, athletes, and politicians went off well. In July 1959 Vice-President Richard Nixon flew into Moscow, was greeted pleasantly along the streets, spent a cordial night at Khrushchev's cream-colored *dacha* twenty miles from Moscow. The two men visited the United States National Exhibition set up in Moscow and wandered into the kitchen of a model house. There, amid the glistening gadgets, the Vice-President of the United States and the Premier of the Soviet Union got themselves into a curiously heartening donnybrook.

Khrushchev: "You Americans think that the Russian people will be astonished to see these things. The fact is that all our new houses have this kind of equipment."

Nixon: "We do not claim to astonish the Russian people. We hope to show our diversity and our right to choose. We do not want to have decisions made at the top by one government official that all houses should be built the same way."

The Premier made some vagrant remarks about washing machines, but the Vice-President pushed the argument. "Is it not far better to be talking about washing machines than machines of war, like rockets? Isn't this the kind of competition you want?"

Khrushchev's voice rose angrily. "Yes, this is the kind of competition we want. But your generals say they are so powerful they can destroy us. We can also show you something so that you will know the Russian spirit."

Nixon's face tightened. "You are strong and we are strong. In some ways you are stronger, but in other ways we might be stronger. We are both so strong, not only in weapons but also in will and spirit, that neither should ever put the other in a position where he faces in effect an ultimatum."

The scores of officials, reporters, and security guards in the kitchen crowded closer, tense and wide-eyed, as Nixon went on with his obvious reference to Khrushchev's threats about Berlin. "I hope the Prime Minister has understood all the implications of what I said. What I mean is that the moment we place either one of these powerful nations, through an ultimatum, in a position where it has no choice but to accept dictation or fight, then you are playing with the most destructive force in the world."

The muscles in Khrushchev's face tightened. He wagged a stubby finger near Nixon's face. "We too are giants. If you want to threaten, we will answer threat with threat."

Nixon bent close to the Premier and tapped his lapel. "We never engage in threats."

Khrushchev: "You wanted indirectly to threaten me. But we have means at our disposal that can have very bad consequences."

Nixon: "We have too."

Khrushchev's tone became friendlier. "We want peace with all other nations, especially America."

Nixon relaxed too. "We also want peace," he said. He mentioned Russian Foreign Minister Andrei Gromyko, "who looks like me but is better looking." "Only outwardly," Khrushchev replied with a grin. Soon the Vice-President of the United States and the Premier of the Soviet Union wandered out of the kitchen, talking with pleasant casualness.

The Gallup Poll rating for Nixon shot up—and so did the percentage in the United States favoring a summit meeting. The kitchen hassle, projected into millions of American living rooms by TV, seemed heated, but it also presented Nikita Khrushchev, wagging a high-spirited finger, giving and taking blows, joshing his own foreign minister, as a very human human being, one you could do business with. The next step came soon. On August 3, 1959, President Eisenhower and Premier Khrushchev announced reciprocal visits, to be opened by the Premier's arrival in America on September 15.

Nineteen hours before Khrushchev's arrival, Soviet scientists hit the moon with a 858.4-pound missile complete with metal pennants bearing the Communist sickle and hammer—hit it just eighty-four seconds later than they predicted and just about where they had anticipated (near, of all places, the "Sea of Tranquillity"). The Premier swept into Washington in his big white jet and presented a model of the lunik to

President Eisenhower, who took it with cool politeness. The whole receptions in Washington and New York were cool and polite and the atmosphere was not improved by some of Khrushchev's heavy-handed remarks. To an especially unsmiling Allen Dulles, director of the American Central Intelligence Agency, the Premier said: "I believe we get the same reports —and probably from the same people."

Khrushchev took off for California and the goodwill trip almost ended. "Disneyland" was removed from his itinerary because the police were worried about his safety in the labyrinth of gewgaws. Khrushchev glowered, snarled at the reporters. "Just imagine, I, a Premier, a Soviet representative . . . told that I could not go. . . . Why not? . . . Do you have rocket-launching pads there? . . . Or have gangsters taken hold of the place?" Hollywood, forgetting that atheistic Bolsheviks can also have a puritanical streak, proudly showed the Premier the shooting of a dance scene for *Can-Can*. The Premier let it be loudly known that he thought the dance was "immoral," fit only for the "insatiable." Besides, "a person's face is more beautiful than his backside."

That night, at a dinner in the Ambassador Hotel in Los Angeles, Mayor Norris Poulson tried a bit of grandstanding for the home folks. Recalling the celebrated remark by Khrushchev that "we shall bury you," the Mayor struck his best Patrick Henry stance and declaimed: "You shall not bury us. . . . If challenged, we shall fight to the death." The Premier, dark-faced, hurried through his prepared text, then turned coldly to Poulson. He had already made clear to the United States, Khrushchev said, what he meant by the remark—he meant that the inevitabilities of history would bring about a Communist world. "I trust that even mayors read the newspapers." More tongue-lashing of Poulson and then Khrushchev pounded the rostrum and his voice rose to a yell. "It is a question of war or peace between our countries, a question of the life or death of the people. . . . If you think the cold war is profitable to you, then go ahead." As for himself, "I can go, and I don't know when, if ever, another Russian Soviet Premier Minister will visit your country."

San Francisco was San Francisco. The city had on its fall charm, the crowds were friendly. Khrushchev relaxed, rolled unannounced into a union meeting, swapping his felt hat for a worker's white cap, toured an IBM plant and jovially lined up for lunch in the company cafeteria. From then on the Premier was all smiles, pleasant quips, and good fellowship. In Des Moines he exuberantly downed his first hot-dog. In the corn fields near Coon Rapids, Iowa, he roared with laughter as a farmer shied fodder at newsmen who were crowding and shoving. In Pittsburgh he fingered a machine tool admiringly and startled reporters by saying: "We can learn much from you." The American crowds, responding to Khrushchev's new mood, gave him warmer and warmer receptions.

The height of the cordiality came at the climax of the visit, the leisurely period which President Eisenhower and Premier Khrushchev spent at Camp David. For three days the two leaders ate their meals together, ambled along the winding gravel paths, talked freely and fully. As Khrushchev was taken to the airport for the flight home, he was beaming. The President and he, the Premier said, had agreed that all disputes "should be settled not by force but by peaceful means —by negotiation." Khrushchev added firmly: "Let us have more and more use for the short American word O.K." At his next press conference, Eisenhower appeared equally pleased by the results of the visit and mentioned a specific consequence of great importance. The conversations at Camp David had "removed many of the objections that I have heretofore held to a Big Four meeting." Reporters knew what the President meant. By now the news was out that at Camp David Eisenhower had refused to go to the summit under Khrushchev's ultimatum about Berlin, and the Premier had agreed to remove it.

With a Big Four meeting so obviously approaching, Eisenhower decided to play what so many Administration men considered the American ace card—his own world prestige and world popularity—to bring as much neutral opinion as possible behind the West and to iron out differences among the Western allies. On December 3 he began a 22,000-mile, eleven-nation swing that took him along the southern tier of Europe and Asia, then back to a meeting of the Western allies in Paris. Through one ancient capital after another the President went, Rome and Ankara and Teheran and Athens, armed with his smile, a slogan ("peace and friendship—in freedom"), and a promise delivered in scores of different forms: "We want to help other peoples to raise their standards of living." By car and bicycle, on foot, by camelback, and in bullock carts, millions crowded into the cities along his route and gave him a reception of enormous warmth.

The welcome in India staggered the President and had him shaking his head in incredulity. Twilight was falling as Eisenhower and Prime Minister Nehru began the drive from the airport to New Delhi. Thousands of bonfires and thousands of lanterns swung high by hollow-eyed Hindu functionaries lit the way. An estimated million and a half Indians of every class— disease-scaled peasants, trim little civil servants, fierce-looking Sikhs, bare-bottomed children, old men smoking their hookahs, lovely women clad in rich saris —a million and a half human beings jammed the road, cheering, stomping, shrieking. Some of the enthusiasm had an eerie undertone. People had walked with their children ten or twelve miles to see the figure they were sure was the reincarnation of Vishnu, the "protector" in the Hindu trinity. "Did he not send us wheat when we needed it and build us dams?" explained seventy-year-old Kanthi from a village eleven miles south of New Delhi. "Could he not destroy the world by a mere wish but never uses his power except as a shield against evil?"

The police were helpless to clear a path for the President's big black Cadillac. Worried, Prime Minister Nehru got out of the car, entered an escorting jeep, and rode along shouting for the people to make way. His voice was lost in the din. Nehru climbed back in the car and, chin in hand, gazed stoically ahead while the Cadillac inched along. Once the caravan reached New Delhi, the enthusiasm was even wilder. WELCOME PRINCE OF PEACE, the endless signs screamed. Flowers by the pound flew at Eisenhower until he was standing foot deep in them and the Secret Service men were panting from batting down the clumps of blossoms. In the closing hour of Eisenhower's visit, Prime Minister Nehru told the President: "As you go, you take a piece of our heart." Newsmen with decades of experience agreed that at no time, anywhere, had they seen so rhapsodic a reception of a public figure.

On to more capitals, more cheers, and then to Paris for the meeting with the leaders of England, France, and West Germany. Here the President ran into problems that were anything but flower-laden. In particular, President Charles de Gaulle of France wanted to get some things straight about NATO and Algeria before he mounted any summit. Eisenhower and Macmillan wheedled and smoothed, agreed to disagree on this or that until more staff work was done, and the four men were ready: the invitation was to go out to Khrushchev for a summit meeting in May 1960.

Never, in all the ups and downs of opinion since the beginning of the East-West clash, had the world shared such optimism. From the Kremlin, from Western capitals, from the centers of neutralism came agreement with British Prime Minister Macmillan's statement: "At this wondrous moment we seem on the threshold of genuine, practical steps toward peace." In the United States, the *Bulletin of Atomic Scientists*, which had been talking nuclear doom since 1945, reset the ominous clock that regularly appeared on its cover. The hands of the clock had stood at two minutes to twelve. Now they were moved back to seven minutes to twelve.

Just eleven days before the summit meeting, on May 5, 1960, Prime Minister Khrushchev came near the end of his three-and-a-half-hour address to the Supreme Soviet. He paused, glowered, then went on: "I am duty bound to report to you on the aggressive acts . . . by the United States of America." On May 1 the Soviet Union had shot down over Russian territory a plane on a mission of "aggressive provocation aimed at wrecking the Summit Conference." Eisenhower, the Premier declared, seemed to want peace but was surrounded by "imperialists" and "militarists."

The rest came in trip-hammer blows of news:

May 5. The U.S. National Aeronautics and Space Administration states that a high-flying U-2, the plane used by Americans for weather observation, is missing on a flight in Turkey after the pilot reported oxygen trouble. It suggests that the plane strayed over Soviet territory.

May 6. Lincoln White, State Department press officer, agreeing that the plane in question is a weather one, adds: "There was absolutely no—N—O—no deliberate attempt to violate the Soviet air space, and there has never been." When asked by newsmen to identify the missing pilot, White begs off, saying that the pilot's mother is suffering a serious heart condition and should not be shocked.

The efforts of the State Department and the NASA are not co-ordinated. NASA releases the name of the "weather pilot," Francis G. Powers, and thus gives Khrushchev the final detail he needs to catch the United States in a bald lie.

May 7. Khrushchev springs his trap. He announces

that the Soviet had captured Powers "alive and kicking," that he had been shot down near the industrial city of Sverdlovsk, some 1,300 miles inside Russia, and that the pilot had confessed to being on a spy flight which began in Pakistan and was to end in Norway. Triumphantly the Premier displays the equipment allegedly found in the plane, including a poison needle with which the spy was to commit suicide if caught and pictures of Soviet airfields developed from Powers's camera.

The State Department admits that the flight was one of "surveillance." It states that such flights had gone on for four years, ever since the Soviet rejected the American "open skies" proposal made at the Geneva Summit Conference of 1955. In all of his statements, Khrushchev seemed to be exonerating Eisenhower of any blame. The State Department goes along with this by saying that "the authorities" had not authorized "any such flights as described by Mr. Khrushchev."

May 8. Dismay throughout the Western world over the timing of the flight, the trapping of the United States in a lie, and the statement which implied that the President of the United States did not know that something so important as spying on the Soviet Union eleven days before a summit meeting was being carried on by his own subordinates.

May 9. The Eisenhower Administration reverses itself. Secretary of State Christian Herter declares that the President had authorized the general program of spying though not specific missions. Herter adds a sentence which unmistakably implies that the United States intends to continue the intelligence flights over the Soviet: "The United States has not and does not shirk this responsibility."

May 10-14. The Eisenhower Administration continues to leave the impression that it will continue the spy missions. President Eisenhower speaks of them in the present tense—as a "distasteful but vital necessity." White House Press Secretary James Hagerty categorically knocks down a story by James Reston of the *New York Times* that the President has ordered a suspension of the flights.

May 15. The Big Four arrive in Paris. De Gaulle, Macmillan, and Khrushchev confer and the Russian lays down his terms for participating in the summit conference: (1) a cessation of the flights; (2) an American apology for "past acts of aggression"; and (3) punishment of "those responsible." Informed of these terms, Eisenhower states that the flights have already been stopped but the other terms will never be accepted by the United States.

May 16. The summit meeting opens, without a single exchange of pleasantries or a single handshake. At the first opportunity, Khrushchev takes the floor, curt, rude, and defiant. He repeats his three-point demands, accuses President Eisenhower of "treachery" and a "bandit" policy. He startles his listeners by the statement that the U-2 incident "deeply involves" the "internal politics" of the Soviet and by the suggestion that the summit be postponed for six to eight months in the hope that "another United States government will understand the futility of pursuing aggressive policies." Khrushchev has one more insult for the President of the United States. "Conditions have now arisen which make us unable to welcome the President with the proper warmth which the Soviet people display toward fond guests." The invitation for the reciprocal Eisenhower visit to Russia is therefore canceled.

President Eisenhower sits tight-lipped and grim. In carefully controlled words, he repeats that the overflights are ended but that the Khrushchev "ultimatum" is utterly unacceptable to the United States. The President returns to the American Embassy and explodes. "He was not just angry," an aide recalls. "He was absolutely furious."

May 16 and 17. De Gaulle and Macmillan make last-

ditch efforts to save the conference. At 3 p.m. on
May 17, the Big Three assemble for the first business session. Khrushchev is not present; he is off visit-
ing the French countryside, chopping wood and
joking with the peasants. An aide telephones to ask
whether Eisenhower is ready to apologize for the
flights and to punish those responsible. At 5 p.m. on
May 17 the summit meeting that never started ends.
May 18. Khrushchev summons a press conference in
the Palais de Chaillot and for two and a half hours
delivers himself of a public spleen unprecedented
even in the annals of Cold War diplomacy. Pounding the table, sneering, shouting, he calls the actions
of the United States "thief-like," "piratical," and
"cowardly," and denounces Eisenhower as a "fishy"
friend. American "aggressors," he storms, should
be treated the way that he as a boy handled cats that
stole cream or broke into pigeon lofts. "We would
catch such a cat by the tail and bang its head against
the wall, and that was the only way it could be
taught some sense." He threatens "devastating"
rocket blows at any nation used as a base for
American espionage flights and announces that the
Soviet will take action about Berlin by signing a
treaty with Communist East Germany—just *when*
is "our business."

What did it all mean—the sudden transition of the
exuberant apostle of coexistence to a snarling, rocket-
rattling exponent of Cold War? Responsible observers
in the Western capitals agreed that the U-2 incident
was not the primary cause of the Premier's shift; it was
more of a pretext. They believed that in the weeks
immediately preceding the summit gathering, firm
statements by American State Department officials
had made it clear that the Soviet was not going to get
from the summit what it most wanted—concessions
concerning Berlin. At the same time Khrushchev was
under increasingly heavy pressure from the Chinese
Communist leaders and from a faction in the Kremlin,

both of which groups were Stalinist in tendency, had never agreed with Khrushchev's coexistence policies, and had been asking more and more sharply: What are you gaining by the friendship line? Expecting to win nothing important from the meeting, having positive reasons not to participate in it, the Premier had snatched at the U-2 episode as an excuse to blow up the conference—and to get in some tirading that would sound good in Moscow and Peiping.

Most commentators added that the American handling of the U-2 incident had been unwise. Permitting a flight so close to the time of the Paris meeting gave hostages to Khrushchev. The confusion in Washington at receipt of the news bewildered and frightened friendly and neutral nations. The American admission that the U-2 flight was a spy mission, and that such missions had been going on for four years, made a mockery of Khrushchev's repeated assurances to his people that the Soviet was invulnerable and made it essential, if he was to maintain his stature at home, to talk tough. The action of President Eisenhower in taking personal responsibility for the flight hardly made it politically expedient for Khrushchev to sit down in friendly conference with him.

Khrushchev arrived at the Paris airport and got in a warning to Foreign Minister Gromyko, who was about to fly to a UN meeting in New York: "Be careful of those imperialists. Be careful to cover your back. Don't expose your back to them." Then he climbed in his own plane, headed for East Germany, and abruptly changed his tone. There would be no swift move about West Berlin, he told a disappointed Communist crowd. The existing situation would be preserved "until the heads of government meeting which, it is hoped, will take place in six or eight months." A few weeks later the Premier took the occasion of a Bucharest Communist assemblage to rap "left-wing opportunists" among the Red leaders, to declare that the only sensible course was coexistence and negotiation, and to describe the "present deterioration" in East-West relations as a "passing phase." On the other hand, Moscow radio was back to its old ways, competing with Peiping in hurling slurs at the United States. And, ever more truculently, the Soviet pushed its campaign to get rid of the American bases which ringed it.

What did it all mean in the long run? Was the world back to the furies and the dangers of full-scale Cold War or, as Khrushchev said, only passing through an unfortunate phase? The answer was hardly clear, but one fact was eminently plain. Any assumption of an easy coexistence, of steady progress toward peace through hot-dog munching guests and flower-strewn visits and genial get-togethers at the summit, of an American-Soviet relationship which would permit the United States the luxury of complacency and bungling —any such assumption simply would not hold.

Epilogue

SHORTLY AFTER the Administration bungling in handling the U-2 incident, the Gallup Poll asked Americans its periodic question about whether they approved of the way the President was carrying out his job. The answer was a thumping 68 percent approval—a near all-time high in the phenomenal record of Eisenhower popularity. But at the same time, one segment of American opinion was disturbed as it had not been since the first emergence of the seriousness of the East-West clash in 1947.

This division in American attitudes, present throughout the Crucial Decade and the immediate post-Crucial Decade years, had widened and deepened with each jarring event after Sputnik I went up in 1957. In part the split was partisan. Naturally the opposition Democrats did the most worrying, and this tendency was increased by the fact that so large a part of the long-dissident intellectual class was Democratic. But partisanship was not the whole story, and probably not the most important part of it. Some leading Republican commentators, like Walter Lippmann, were among the most forceful spokesmen of the criticism. The generally pro-Eisenhower publications, *Life* and the *New York Times*, were joining in. Two weeks after the summit debacle, one of the country's most prominent Republican political figures, Governor Nelson Rockefeller of New York, spoke out his disquietude with basic trends in American political leadership and in American society. It was noticeable too that Rockefeller's statement was

drafted by Emmet John Hughes, a long-time aide of
the President who had now broken not only with
Eisenhower but with Eisenhowerism as a way of
thinking.

Except for a few shrill voices on the far right, none
of the critics were quarreling with the two great decisions of the Crucial Decade. They assumed that the
New Deal and the Fair Deal were here to stay and that
social changes within the pattern of the Half-Century
of Revolution would and should go ahead. They also
assumed that the only sensible foreign policy was coexistence with world Communism and patient efforts
to work out specific agreements. The criticisms concerned developments that had accompanied the decisions of the Crucial Decade and they carried an insistence that the decisions of the past years, sound as
they were, had to be extended by fresh and bold
policies.

In the language of the dissidents, one phrase was
becoming especially persistent: "national purpose." It
was projected into the discussion as early as Khrushchev's visit to America, when Walter Lippmann wrote
in his potent prose: "The critical weakness of our
society is that for the time being our people do not
have great purposes which they are united in wanting
to achieve. The public mood of the country is defensive, to hold on to and to conserve, not to push forward and to create. We talk about ourselves these days
as if we were a completed society, one which has
achieved its purposes, and has no further business to
transact." Discussion of the point received even
greater impetus a few weeks later when the widely
respected George Kennan went before the Women's
National Democratic Club in Washington, asked a disturbing question, and gave a still more disturbing answer: "If you ask me . . . whether a country in the
state this country is in today: with no highly developed sense of national purpose, with the overwhelm-

ing accent of life on personal comfort and amusement, with a dearth of public services and a surfeit of privately sold gadgetry, with a chaotic transportation system, with its great urban areas being gradually disintegrated by the headlong switch to motor transportation, with an educational system where quality has been extensively sacrificed to quantity, and with insufficient social discipline even to keep its major industries functioning without grievous interruptions—if you ask me whether such a country has, over the long run, good chances of competing with a purposeful, serious, and disciplined society such as that of the Soviet Union, I must say that the answer is 'no.' " The jolting events of mid-1960, during which the basic direction of the United States seemed anything but clear, stimulated talk about the national purpose still further. Soon *Life* and the *New York Times* were joining in running a series of articles on the subject by men ranging from Adlai Stevenson through Professor Clinton Rossiter on to David Sarnoff, chairman of the board of RCA.

Most of the talk about national purpose was more notable for its insistence that we ought to have a clear-cut purpose than for its statement of what the purpose should be. Yet the usual critic did make a connection between the national purpose and the national leadership. As Eisenhower's Administrations closed in 1960, the dissidents were coming to something of an agreement concerning his place in history. Some, usually of a strongly Democratic bent, considered his whole tenure in office a mistake, if not a disaster. A far greater percentage assigned to his first Administration, whatever its demerits, a highly constructive role in bridging deep political divisions within the country and in leading an almost united nation to acceptance of continuing social change at home and coexistence abroad. In this process, the President's vague generalities, his assumption that good will would solve almost anything, even his ability to render the English language nearly incomprehensible, could be deemed assets.

"The first term, yes, I can see its merits," remarked the strongly Democratic Professor Walter Johnson of the University of Chicago, "but the second term—there I draw the line." Most critics felt that the President, his healing mission performed, became a symbol of drift to a nation already far too ready for drift, an exponent of materialism in a country overwhelmed by chrome, a spokesman of the easy solution to an America that had been getting itself into trouble by yearning for easy solutions ever since World War II. Critics were especially sharp in pointing to the Eisenhower of the second term as the glaring example of a new school of leadership in which personality was assumed to be the prime need, public relations the sure method, and the end product was a grinning nothingness—"the bland leading the bland," in the angry phrase of the day.

What positive goals did the critics want, what kind of leadership toward what ends? They were sure that the rampant drive of the individual American for more money and more status was self-defeating. In individual terms, it meant an ever more frantic quest of an ever more evanescent prize. In national terms, it was totally inadequate as a way of life which would attract the uncommitted peoples of the world and give the United States a chance in the decades-long competition with Communism that lay ahead. The situation should be drastically changed by strong leadership, the critics were sure, building on the decisions of the Crucial Decade, sweeping beyond them to a new atmosphere and new decisions.

In foreign policy, the critics insisted that mere acceptance of coexistence was not enough. The United States had to make very clear what it stood for in the world—and in doing this the repetition of snappy phrases about freedom would not be sufficient. It had to give up budget-pinching in appropriating funds for matters connected with foreign policy. Millions more had to be appropriated to make sure that the United States was keeping up with—and getting ahead of—the Soviet Union in the race for scientific knowledge. Millions more had to be appropriated for economic aid abroad.

In domestic policy, the critics went on, the United States must rid itself of the emphasis on the endless increase in consumer goods. What was needed was not the better-equipped American but the American who was a better human being, his life enriched by an altered community atmosphere and by greatly improved facilities for education, medical care, and recreation. Just as the sputniks were going up, the Harvard professor of economics, John Kenneth Galbraith, gave the critical mood tartly effective expression in his widely acclaimed book, *The Affluent Society*. The ideas of a good society on which the United States was operating, Galbraith wrote, were carry-overs from a period when the country had to worry about widespread poverty. They did not fit a society of widespread affluence. Obsolescent thinking was committing us to a senseless pursuit of goods while the human beings floundered. What Galbraith called the "social balance" was wobbling, to a degree where it could take a dangerous plunge.

As the bipartisan hammering went on and the bipartisan counterblasts came, it was clear that the United States was heading into a basic issue. Should the nation continue, in gradually altered form, the mood, the kind of leadership, the basic domestic and foreign policies that it had agreed upon in the Crucial Decade of 1945-55? Or did it need breakaways, genuine breakaways? Was it to be consolidation or innovation— more circumspect consolidation of the decisions of the Crucial Decade or venturesome innovation to a new kind of leadership, basically different ideas, a rethinking if not a redefinition of the whole national purpose?

The answer to the question lay somewhere in the realm of murky imponderables. For those who were certain that the United States would choose and hold to the path of genuine innovation, there was always history's yawning reminder. Fat and satisfied nations like the America of 1960 have rarely been innovating societies. For those who were positive that the answer would be more consolidation, there were circumstances which even 5,000 years of history had never previously produced. The fat and satisfied America of 1960 faced annihilation if its foreign policy did not adequately meet swiftly changing circumstances. Having geared its life to endless upper mobility, it was endlessly subjected to the demands of millions for the better life in a constantly expanding definition of that phrase.

Americans of the Crucial Decade, catching the earlier intimations of these extraordinary situations, had moved—uncertainly, irritably, but with notable speed—to meet the fiat of facts. A nation that had adjusted that fast and that far in ten years could surprise the world, not to speak of itself, by the way it responded to more decades that were certain to have their own crucial qualities.

Note on the Sources
and Acknowledgments

THIS BOOK rests in large part on the mass of printed materials which concern the years 1945-60. In a few instances, where manuscript collections were available and seemed of importance, I turned to them. The sources were also supplemented by interviews and by correspondence with men and women who made the history. Most of the interviews and some of the correspondence were undertaken to gather material for a particular episode and occurred before the writing. In addition, as is indicated in the Preface, I used extensive correspondence (and in a few cases interviews) after the manuscript was prepared, asking people who were participants in the history to check my factual accuracy.

About eighty-five per cent of the men and women to whom I wrote responded and their letters contain a good deal of contemporary history, not all of which is incorporated in this book and some of which is completely confidential. It is my hope that in time these materials may be deposited in the Princeton University Library, where they could be consulted by people with a serious research purpose.

Some of the participants in the history of the period have requested that I make no public acknowledgment of their aid. The others who helped me by letters or interviews are (all titles are omitted): Dean Acheson, John Alsop, Stewart Alsop, Warren R. Austin, Lauren Bacall, Bernard M. Baruch, Ales Bebler, Leslie L. Biffle, Herbert Block, Vannevar Bush, James F. Byrnes, John M. Chang, Winston Churchill, Mark W. Clark,

Clark M. Clifford, J. Lawton Collins, W. Bradley
Connors, Claude B. Cross, Willard Edwards, George
M. Elsey, Morris L. Ernst, Alonzo Fields, Thomas K.
Finletter, Cody Fowler, Karl M. Frost, J. W. Ful-
bright, Walter F. George, Donald J. Gonzales, Wal-
lace H. Graham, Gordon Gray, Ernest A. Gross,
Leslie R. Groves, Rudolph Halley, Friedrich A. von
Hayek, John D. Hickerson, John G. Hill, Paul G.
Hoffman, Cale J. Holder, Lloyd P. Hopwood, Emmet
John Hughes, J. Raymond Jones, H. V. Kaltenborn,
Samuel H. Kaufman, George F. Kennan, Renwick C.
Kennedy, Alfred C. Kinsey, Charles H. Kraus, Trygve
Lie, A. C. McAuliffe, F. L. McCluer, Frank C. Mc-
Connell, Joseph W. Martin, Jr., Stephen A. Mitchell,
Mrs. Blair Moody, John J. Muccio, Karl E. Mundt,
Thomas F. Murphy, Paul A. Myers, W. H. Mylander,
Djura Nincic, Frank Pace, Jr., Norman Vincent Peale,
Mrs. John R. Rice, Branch Rickey, William A. Rob-
erts, Dean Rusk, Mrs. Dorothy Schiff, Louis B. Seltzer,
Merriman Smith, Oliver P. Smith, John R. Steelman,
Adlai E. Stevenson, Herbert Bayard Swope, Strom
Thurmond, Edward J. Thye, Harold C. Urey, Charles
A. Voso, Henry A. Wallace, Mary Jane Ward, and
Frederick Woltman.

In some instances, a relative or associate took care
of my inquiries. These included Louis J. Gallagher,
Murray Glaubach, Victor J. Hammer, Arthur Mann,
and Richard Wallace.

Friends and strangers, who were not mentioned as
part of the history but who have a special knowledge
about some phase of the story, criticized parts of the
manuscript or aided in other ways. In this connection,
I would particularly like to thank Jack Anderson,
Robert J. Butow, Harold W. Chase, Marquis Childs,
Kenneth W. Condit, W. Frank Craven, Benjamin J.
Custer, Frederick S. Dunn, Robert F. Futrell, E. Harris
Harbison, James A. Kritzeck, J. Norman Lodge, Mrs.
Helen Taft Manning, John Miller, Jr., Walter Millis,
Newton N. Minow, Louis Morton, James Rorty,

Roger W. Shugg, Harold Stein, Gordon B. Turner, and John J. Wright.

I am very genuinely indebted to the above men and women and, in thanking them, I would like to repeat with special emphasis the customary statement that any factual errors or inadequacies of interpretation are exclusively my responsibility. Some of the people who were kind enough to aid me disagreed with my interpretation of a particular event or personality or even of the whole decade. Others disagreed not only with respect to interpretation but in the area of factual statements. Their recollection was different, in more or less important degree, from the form which I decided to report after consideration of the total evidence that I was able to discover.

Writing a book inevitably piles up other types of debts, and in the case of this particular volume they are so numerous that I will not try to describe most of them. I can only hope that I was able to express something of my appreciation along the way toward completion of the book. I do want to mention here that in the preparation of the original *Crucial Decade,* Mr. Bennett Hill gave me able assistance for many months, and that at a critical juncture in the work Mr. Fredrick Aandahl's generous readiness to call on his bibliographical skill removed a considerable worry. I would also like to state, with my appreciation, that the Princeton University Research Fund provided financial assistance which expedited the research and that a number of members of the firm of Alfred A. Knopf, Inc., gave unstinted co-operation and encouragement.

Index

THE TEXT of this book was set on the Linotype in *Janson,* an excellent example of the influential and sturdy Dutch types that prevailed in England prior to the development by William Caslon of his own incomparable designs. Composed, printed, and bound by The Colonial Press Inc., Clinton, Mass. Cover design by BEN SHAHN.

A free catalogue of VINTAGE BOOKS will be sent at your request. Write to Vintage Books, 457 Madison Avenue, New York, New York 10022.

VINTAGE HISTORY—EUROPEAN

A free catalogue of VINTAGE BOOKS will be sent at your request. Write to Vintage Books, 457 Madison Avenue, New York, New York 10022.

VINTAGE POLITICAL SCIENCE
AND SOCIAL CRITICISM